JSP
for practical program design

Kay Dudman

Middlesex University

UCL
PRESS

First published in 1996 by UCL Press

UCL Press Limited
University College London
Gower Street
London WC1E 6BT

The name of University College London (UCL) is a registered
trade mark used by UCL Press with the consent of the owner.

British Library Cataloguing-in-Publication Data
A CIP catalogue record for this book is available from the British Library.

ISBN: 1-85728-407-0 PB

Typeset in Sabon and Univers.
Printed and bound by
Biddles Ltd, Guildford & King's Lynn, England.

To JDD

for support and encouragement thoughout the development of this book
(and countless other times . . .)

Contents

Preface

The design of this book is based on teaching the JSP (Jackson Structured Programming) methodology to undergaduates and postgraduates over a period of a number of years. I am grateful for the comments and feedback that have been provided by students who have taken these courses. The aim of the book is to provide readers with an understanding of the concepts behind the JSP methodology in order that they may apply it for themselves; simply using the notation is not sufficient, it must be used appropriately. The answer to the question "Why is this wrong?" can lead to a greater understanding than a simple response to "Is this right?". I have included illegal structures as "understandable mistakes" in the early sections for this reason.

It is not necessary for readers of this text to have experience with any particular programming language; indeed, one of the virtues of JSP is that it is language independent. Examples have been given in Pascal, C and COBOL as these are languages which students of JSP are likely to have met in the course of their studies, or will be meeting while they are learning JSP. The COBOL language is widely used in industry in a JSP development environment.

The book is intended to explain, illustrate and demonstrate the JSP methodology to students of computing science, business computing, information technology, computing and information systems, business systems analysis and related themes at the level of BTEC HND, BSc first and second year, and conversion MSc courses, and also to programmers working in industry.

Reference is given, where appropriate, at the end of each chapter to other texts on the JSP methodology. Readers may like to follow the suggestions for further reading to gain a different perspective on the topic being discussed, and to attempt the exercises presented in this and the other texts in order to gain practical experience and confidence in using JSP.

It has been suggested that structured methods, such as JSP, are "on the way out" with the introduction of object-oriented methods and knowledge engineering approaches. The simplicity and flexibility of the JSP approach is such that it can be adapted to different situations and circumstances. JSP was originally developed when most programs ran in a batch environment; JSP can be used successfully in this context, but also in the area of interactive systems which now prevail. The top-down decomposition approach taken in JSP could lend itself to modelling in a knowledge representation environment, each level down being akin to an "is-a" link. Semantic networks could be modelled using tree structures composed from JSP constructs (networks are not legal in JSP). I am sure JSP has the potential to be used for years ahead, perhaps in different contexts.

Kay Dudman
London, October 1995

Acknowledgements

I should like to thank all the students who have studied JSP with me; their comments, questions, difficulties and feedback have helped me understand where they have had problems with the methodology and which areas they found simple and easy to understand. I hope that seeing things from these different viewpoints has enabled me to provide explanations which will support other students of JSP.

My thanks to Alastair Measures for implementing and testing the C version of the program in Chapter 8.

Thank you to Andrew Carrick of UCL Press for discussing the original proposal and providing support through to completion of the finished manuscript.

PDF and JSP-Tool are software products of LBMS.

COBOL is an industry language and is not the property of any company or group of companies, or of any organization or group of organizations.

No warranty expressed or implied, is made by any contributor or by the CODASYL COBOL Committee as to the accuracy and functioning of the programming system and language. Moreover, no responsibility is assumed by any contributor, or by the committee, in connection therewith.

The authors and copyright holders of the copyrighted material used herein are:
- FLOW-MATIC (trademark of the Sperry-Rand Corporation);
- Programming for Univac(R) I and II, Data Automation Systems copyrighted 1958, 1959 by Sperry-Rand Corporation;
- IBM Commerical Translator, Form No. F28-8013, copyrighted 1959 by IBM;
- FACT DSI 27A5260-2760 copyrighted 1960 by Minneapolis-Honeywell.

Each has specifically authorized the use of this material in whole or in part, in the COBOL specifications. Such authorization extends to the reproduction and use of COBOL specifications in programming manuals or similar publications.

CHAPTER 1

Introduction

Why should a programming methodology be used? Let us consider the purpose of writing programs in this context. The aims and objectives of using a program design methodology (such as Jackson Structured Programming) are to produce correct software to carry out a given task and to achieve user satisfaction with the software that has been designed for that purpose. We must also consider that there may be changes over time: the user requirements, or the task itself, may change; alternatively, the data requiring processing may change. Programs may need to be changed, and not necessarily by the person who wrote them; program maintenance is a major workload. In addition, the provision of *ad hoc* reports may mean that "one-off" queries need to be made. We need a programming methodology to allow us to construct programs to carry out certain tasks, and to permit changes to be made quickly and easily. We will be using Jackson Structured Programming (JSP), a method developed by Michael Jackson and described in his book, *Principles of program design*, in 1975.

Let us examine the nature of instructions and data declarations that are included when we write a program, without considering any particular programming language.

We use instructions, such as those illustrated in Table 1.1, in conjunction with others, to implement an algorithm. Input data is transformed by some process to produce output data, that is, results.

We can see that there are different classes to which instructions belong:

sequence   one instruction after another
selection   choice: one instruction or another
iteration   looping: instruction(s) many times

Instructions can be used as building blocks: we can construct compound instructions, using the structures available to us, such as procedures, subroutines or paragraphs.

Data declarations follow the same classification as that for instructions:

sequence   one data item after another
selection   choice: one data item or another
iteration   looping: many data items of the same type

This is one of the important features of JSP as programs are designed on the

Table 1.1 Classification of instructions and data.

Instructions	Data declarations
Linear constructs	
`pay := payrate * hours;`	`const`
`tax := pay * taxrate;`	`max = 20;`
`net := pay - tax;`	`var`
	`x : integer;`
Constructs involving choice	
`if x > max then`	`type`
`  writeln ('finish')`	`  student = record`
`else`	`    name : string[20];`
`  writeln('x is: ',x);`	`    case sandwich : boolean of`
	`      false : (year: integer) ;`
`case month of`	`      true : employer : string[20];`
`  1, 3, 5, 7, 8, 10, 12 : days := 31;`	`    startdate : date;`
`  4, 6, 9, 11          : days := 30;`	`    enddate : date;`
`  2                    : days := 28;`	`  end;`
`end;`	
Constructs with multiple occurrences	
`while a < b do`	`working-storage section.`
`begin`	`01 tel-table.`
`  writeln(a,' is less than ',b);`	`  02 entries occurs 10 times`
`  a := a + 1;`	`    03 exch pic x(9).`
`end;`	`    03 code pic x(7).`
`for i := 1 to 5 do`	`table : array [1..20] of char;`
`  writeln(i, ' squared is ',i*i);`	

basis of the underlying data structures for input and output.

In considering the design of a specific program, we can look at the overall problem, and how it is made from component parts, which may themselves have component parts. This is the *top-down* approach. Alternatively, we can look at the individual problem components and see how they fit together to give larger problem components, each fitting with others to give still larger components, which make up the problem as a whole. This is the *bottom-up* approach. These approaches echo two important concepts in systems theory: the black box principle and the principle of holism.

1.1 The black box principle

A process has known inputs, known outputs and a known function, but the internal mechanism of that function is unknown (Fig. 1.1). A program can be regarded in the same way, as a process that takes input and produces output. When we look at a program in more detail, we can see that it is made of a

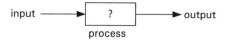

Figure 1.1 Input, process and output of a black box,

hierarchy of "black boxes", identifiable sections of code, e.g. functions and procedures, linking with each other, as the output of one provides the input for another.

1.2 The principle of holism

The principle of holism states that the *whole* is greater than the sum of its parts. For example, a watch is more than a collection of components – assembled correctly it tells the time; using only one eye we can see clearly, but with both eyes we have three-dimensional vision. This can be compared to a jigsaw puzzle – the picture is more easily interpreted when the pieces are joined together.

In the same way, a program can be thought of as having been built from collections of instructions to give functions and procedures; these interact with each other to produce a working system.

1.3 Data and instructions

We can think of two basic categories: instructions and data (Fig. 1.2). The methods of program design can be compared to various other approaches that have been proposed for the development of programs, such as coding and testing, modular programming and structured programming. JSP also employs these components, but in addition matches program structure and data struc-

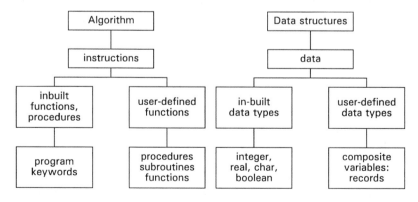

Figure 1.2 Instructions and data structures

3

tures, to ensure that the design of a program meets the requirements.

JSP deals with the design of structured programs and is a programming methodology that meets the requirements of a software design method in that it enables the production of correct programs, supports the control of software projects that may be large, allows systematic methods to be employed throughout the development of a program, uses a method that can be taught and is practical, stresses the importance of the transformation of input to produce output, and provides for the early diagnosis of errors.

When a program has been designed using JSP, it offers the benefits that the program is easy to maintain and modify, the design may be easily followed, and conversion to code is straightforward and automatic. Program design is based on data.

1.4 Principles of JSP

When constructing a program, it is important to ensure that:
- the program has a unique point of entry;
- the program has a unique exit point;
- there must be a path passing through each node in the structure diagram.

Thus all parts of the program must be accessible; there must be no "dead ends" that cannot be reached. JSP allows hierarchical decomposition of the task to be undertaken. A top-down approach is used to develop the structure of the program; a bottom-up approach is employed when identifying the activities that need take place at each stage. It has been found that all programming problems can be solved using only three program component types:
- sequence
- iteration
- selection

JSP provides a method of identifying each component type within data structures, and hence within the process structure that is produced from the data structures.

The design of a program using JSP involves:
- analysis
- task definition
- program creation

1.4.1 Analysis

The problem is analyzed and data structure diagrams are created to represent input and output. These data structures are used as the basis for creating a process structure which is the underlying design of the program itself.

1.4.2 Task definition

The elementary operations that need to be carried out are identified and allocated to appropriate areas of the process structure representing the program.

1.4.3 Program creation

The process structure, including the operations that have been allocated, are transformed into schematic logic (a kind of pseudocode also known as structure text). The schematic logic may be translated into a computer programming language to produce a program to deal with the task required.

The individual steps required in creating a program using JSP are given in Table 1.1, with the relevant chapter(s) identified.

1.4.4 Advanced JSP techniques

The elaboration of a basic design in order to cater for errors that may occur in input data is considered in Chapter 9.

Chapter 10 uses a case study for the design of an interactive customer database system in order to illustrate that techniques originally developed for a batch environment can equally well be used in interactive system design. The case study illustrates the need for backtracking.

Chapter 11 introduces the technique of backtracking, which can be employed when insufficient information is available to decide on the appropriate path for processing to continue; this problem is known as a *recognition difficulty*. In order to deal with this problem, an assumption is made and processing continues until further information becomes available that either confirms or refutes the assumption that was made. If the assumption was incorrect, then *backtracking* takes place to enable the alternative processing path to be followed.

If it is found that input and output data structures cannot be merged because there is a conflict rather than a correspondence between them, this is referred to as a *structure clash*. The JSP approach to dealing with a structure clash is *program inversion*. Chapter 12 discusses the different kinds of structure clash that may occur and examines the technique of program inversion. The technique may also be applied in other contexts as it allows the implementation of co-routines.

When dealing with large programs, it may be inappropriate for the complete program to be loaded; rather, only that section of code that is likely to be executed needs to be loaded. Chapter 13 illustrates the technique of program dismemberment in graphic and tabular form, demonstrating how a program may be divided into manageable smaller sections.

Table 1.2 The individual steps required in creating a program using JSP

1. Draw the input data file structure	**Ch. 2** Data structures
2. Draw the output data file structure	**Ch. 3** Input and output data file structures
3. Identify the correspondences between the input data file structure and the output data file structure	
4. Merge the input data file structure and output data file structure on the points of correspondence to produce a basic process structure diagram	**Ch. 4** Correspondences and process structures **Ch. 5** Creating the final process structure
5. Add "start" and "end" process boxes to sequences on basic program structure to form the final process structure diagram	
6. Allocate conditions to the selections and iterations that exist on the basic process structure diagram	**Ch. 6** Adding conditions and operations
7. List all elementary operations and give each a unique identification number	
8. Allocate the elementary operations to appropriate parts of the final process structure diagram	
9. Generate the schematic logic (pseudocode) from the final process structure diagram	**Ch. 7** Generating schematic logic
10. Translate the schematic logic into the desired computer programming language	**Ch. 8** Producing code

The problem of designing a program where there is more than one source of input data is discussed in Chapter 14.

There are software tools available to assist the program designer in generating code, either generating the schematic logic directly from the process structure diagram or taking a further step by creating a program in a specific language (typically COBOL, C or Pascal) via a program generator. Chapter 15 contains a step-by-step tutorial to getting started with one such tool, JSP-Tool. Another software tool, PDF (Program Development Facility), is demonstrated in Chapter 16.

1.5 Further reading

Jackson (1975).
Holmes (1991), Section 2.1.
King & Pardoe (1992), Chapter 1.
Storer (1991), Chapter 1.
Thompson (1989), Chapters 1 and 2.

CHAPTER 2

Data structures

2.1 JSP structure diagrams

All JSP structure diagrams are constructed from a single basic building block (Fig. 2.1). It is possible to combine such building blocks in a hierarchical manner to represent either data or processes; hence JSP structure diagrams can be used to represent data files for input and output, and from this foundation the structure of a program that will transform input data into output can be obtained (Fig. 2.2). It is important that the data structures are created first, rather than attempting to write code too early in the design of a program. The structure of the program is determined by the structure of the data. The processes will have associated instructions that can be implemented in a programming language.

We need to be able to express the concepts of sequence, selection and iteration using JSP; the building blocks can then be linked together and each component type can be identified.

Figure 2.1   The basic building block.

Figure 2.2   A program as a process with input and output.

2.2 Sequence

A sequence is an ordered series of elements, the first sequence component appearing on the left, with subsequent elements shown one by one to the right. The order in which each component appears within a sequence is important.

Suppose a file containing records of employee details is maintained. Each record might contain information in the following order:

employee number
employee name
date of birth
grade
date joined

Examples of individual records with the above format would be as shown in Table 2.1. We could represent the employee record (not just the record for a particular individual) in JSP terms as a sequence (Fig. 2.3). Note that the order in which items appear in the diagram is the same order as they appear in the record. When describing the diagram, the **employee record** is referred to as a *sequence*, and the **employee number, employee name, date of birth, grade** and **date joined** are *sequence components*. Here the sequence components are elementary components (or leaves, or terminal nodes) because they have not been subdivided into smaller units. The structure of a sequence in general is shown in Figure 2.4.

Table 2.1 Examples of individual records.

01928	07193	10623
Smith E	Duran D	Patton B
11 11 1953	17 05 1960	07 02 1948
Programmer	Architect	Accountant
01 08 1986	10 04 1989	01 06 1976

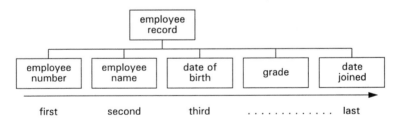

Figure 2.3 The employee record represented as a sequence.

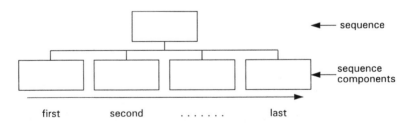

Figure 2.4 General sequence format.

2.2.1 Combining sequence structures

It is possible to identify a sequence within a sequence; for example, name could be subdivided into last name and initial and the dates could be expressed as a sequence of day, month and year.

Figure 2.5 shows that **employee name** is a *sequence* of employee last name and employee initial (in that order). Figure 2.6 illustrates that **date of birth** is a *sequence* of day, month and year (in that order). Figure 2.7 demonstrates that **date joined** is a *sequence* of day, month and year (in that order).

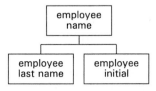

Figure 2.5 Employee name as a sequence.

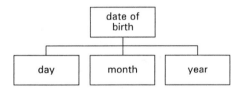

Figure 2.6 Date of birth as a sequence.

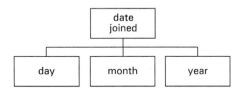

Figure 2.7 Date joined as a sequence.

These sequence structures can be combined with the **employee record** sequence structure (as shown in Figure 2.8), which would be read in the following manner:

- An **employee record** is a *sequence* of employee number, employee name, date of birth, grade and date joined.
- The component **employee name** is a *sequence* of employee last name and employee initial.
- The component **date of birth** is a *sequence* of day, month and year.
- The component **date joined** is a *sequence* of day, month and year.

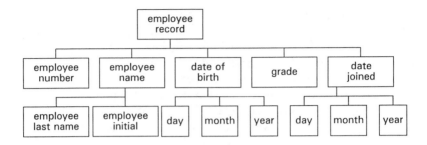

Figure 2.8 The employee record sequence structure.

The structure diagram has a tree structure, with branches dividing from the centre, and the branches themselves then subdividing. The tree structure in Figure 2.8 is rather like an inverted tree, or like the roots of a tree underground. The root is at the top (here, employee record). The root has several branches that end either in a terminal node (e.g. employee number, grade), or in a node that itself has further branches (e.g. employee name, date of birth and date joined).

The sequence structure can be used to represent both data and processes, i.e. instructions.

2.2.2 How not to combine sequences

It can be seen that the **date of birth** and **date joined** components are both *sequences* of day, month and year. It might appear tempting to draw the structure in such a way that day, month and year are shared between **date of birth** and **date joined**, but this would constitute a serious error and result in an illegal structure (Fig. 2.9).

The structure shown in Figure 2.9 is illegal in JSP; it forms a graph (or network) rather than a tree, because the branches under date of birth and date joined have come together. Structures of this nature are never seen in JSP; all JSP diagrams must be trees.

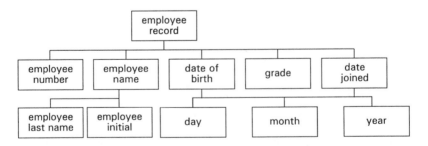

Figure 2.9 An illegal structure for the employee record.

As a structure (but not a JSP structure) Figure 2.9 would imply that date of birth and date joined have the same value, i.e. the date of birth and date joined would be exactly the same date, and this is impossible.

2.3 Exercises

1. Draw a JSP structure diagram of a student record, using only those elements specified in the following description:

   A student record consists of the name of the student, the student registration number, date of birth, course attended, year of course.

2. Draw simple JSP structure diagrams for the following elements of the student record specified in Exercise 1:
   (a) each student name is represented as last name followed by first name;
   (b) student registration number is year of entry combined with a unique application number;
   (c) date of birth is held as year, month and day (to facilitate sorting into age order).

3. Draw the full JSP structure diagram for the student record described in Exercise 1, incorporating the elements from Exercise 2.

4. Draw the JSP structure diagram for which the description is as follows.

   The academic year is a sequence of three terms: term 1, term 2 and term 3. Term 3 is a sequence of revision followed by an examination.

5. Describe in words what the JSP structure diagram shown in Figure 2.10 represents.

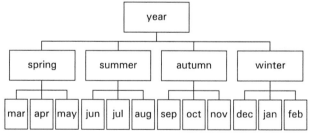

Figure 2.10 A JSP structure diagram.

2.4 Selection

A selection allows a choice of precisely one element from a range of options. Imagine the choice of what to spread on toast at breakfast (Fig. 2.11). The "o" symbol in the top right-hand corner of each of the lower boxes in the figure indicates that *only one* of these elements may be chosen, i.e. "selected". A **spread** is a *selection* with selection components jam, honey and marmalade. The "o"

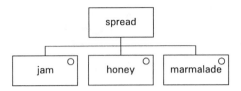

Figure 2.11 The breakfast selection.

symbol must appear in every box that is a selection component. The order in which the options appear is not important as only one choice can be made.

It would be possible to allow for the choice of spreads to be jam, honey, marmalade or nothing at all. The null option (nothing at all) would be represented on the diagram as a selection component with a dash (Fig. 2.12).

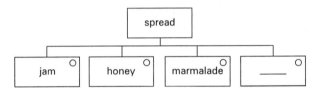

Figure 2.12 The breakfast selection with a null option.

For the rest of this example, it will be assumed that the null option will not be taken, and that one of the available spreads will be chosen. The format of a selection in general is given in Figure 2.13. A selection diagram can be used to represent data or processes, i.e. instructions.

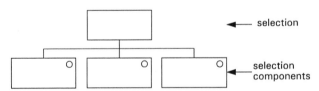

Figure 2.13 General selection format.

2.4.1 Combining selections

There may be a choice between orange or lemon marmalade. If the marmalade component is considered separately, it could be expressed as a selection itself, of either orange or lemon (Fig 2.14). This could then be incorporated into the original structure, giving Figure 2.15.

An alternative approach would be to consider that orange marmalade and lemon marmalade are spreads in their own right and therefore another solution would be to add a further selection component, showing orange marmalade and lemon marmalade as two different spreads (Fig. 2.16).

12

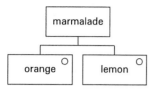

Figure 2.14 Marmalade as a selection.

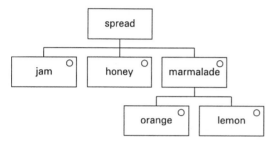

Figure 2.15 Combining selections.

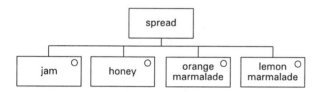

Figure 2.16 An alternative approach to the breakfast selection.

2.4.2 How not to combine selection structures

An individual person working for a company will be either male or female and the JSP structure diagram in Figure 2.17 illustrates this. This person, whether male or female, will also be either married or unmarried (Fig. 2.18).

We need to be able to combine these two possibilities into a single structure to illustrate that a person can be either male or female and also either married or unmarried. The solution attempted in Figure 2.19 is an illegal structure

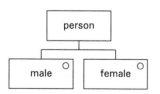

Figure 2.17 The structure diagram showing gender.

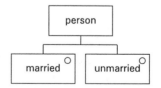

Figure 2.18 The structure diagram showing marital status.

13

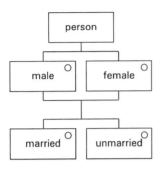

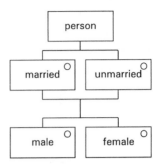

Figure 2.19 An illegal structure combining gender and marital status.

Figure 2.20 A second illegal structure combining gender and marital status.

because it forms a network rather than a tree; it is not legal for the branches to come together again in a JSP structure diagram. The structure in Figure 2.20 is also illegal for the same reason.

There are three possible ways in which we could represent a person in these circumstances.

Option 1 A person is either male or female. A male person may be married or unmarried; a female person may be married or unmarried. Figure 2.21 shows that an individual may be married or unmarried following the initial division of male or female.

Option 2 A person may be married or unmarried. A married person may be male or female; an unmarried person may be male or female. Figure 2.22 illustrates that a person may be male or female following the distinction between whether the individual is married or unmarried.

Option 3 The last possibility is that a person may be categorized as falling into one of four combined categories: female unmarried, male unmarried, female married and male married. In this final representation (Fig. 2.23), there is no subdivision based on an initial choice; the selection components are all at the same level and cater for all the four possibilities that have been described.

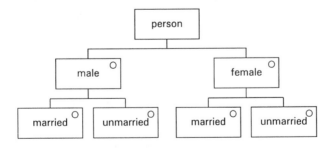

Figure 2.21 A structure combining gender and marital status.

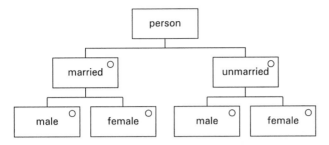

Figure 2.22 A second structure combining gender and marital status.

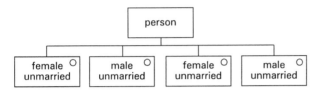

Figure 2.23 A third structure combining gender and marital status.

2.5 Exercises

1. A company employee may be either a technical specialist or an administrator. Express this as a JSP structure diagram.

2. A technical specialist within an organization may be a lawyer, an accountant, a systems analyst, an architect or a chemist. A company employee who is a chemist may work in the field of organic or inorganic chemistry. Express this as a JSP structure diagram.

3. A company administrator could work in one of the following departments: personnel, payroll and pensions, registry and records, sales, marketing or purchasing. Use a JSP structure diagram to describe this.

4. Combine the details described in Exercises 1 to 3 to produce a single JSP diagram.

5. An athlete may be tall (5 feet 10 inches or above) or below this height and each individual will be male or female. Show how this can be expressed in a JSP structure diagram in different ways.

6. When applying to study for a degree, an applicant may receive several offers for a place. The possibilities are:
   - the applicant is offered a place conditional on examination results;
   - the applicant is offered an unconditional place;
   - the applicant is rejected.

   It is also possible that a decision has yet to be made, in which case this is recorded as an outstanding decision. Show how the different decisions relating to an applicant could be described as a JSP structure diagram. Consider other solutions using JSP diagrams.

7. When an applicant has received an offer of a place, the possible responses are:
   - accept a conditional offer as first choice;
   - accept a conditional offer as second choice (insurance);
   - decline a conditional offer;
   - accept an unconditional offer as first choice (no other offers may be held);
   - accept an unconditional offer as second choice;
   - decline an unconditional offer;
   - the applicant withdraws.

   Demonstrate how the different responses to an offer of a place may be represented using a JSP structure diagram. Consider other possible solutions using JSP structure diagrams.

8. A particular course of study runs in three different modes: full time, part time (day release) and part time (evenings only). Show how the different modes can be represented as a JSP structure diagram. Consider other solutions using JSP diagrams.

2.6 Iteration

Sometimes it is necessary to indicate that a number of elements of the same kind may be present. The iteration structure shown in Figure 2.24 allows us to represent this. The symbol "*" indicates the iterated component. Here, the structure diagram shows that an hour is made up of many minutes. The **hour** is the *iteration* and it is made up of the *iterated component*, which is **minute**. It is important to remember that an iteration may occur zero or more times (as opposed to a repetition which may occur one or more times). The format of an iteration in general is shown in Figure 2.25.

Figure 2.24 An hour as an iteration.   **Figure 2.25** General iteration format.

2.6.1 Combining iteration structures

We can combine structure diagrams where common elements exist. For example, we could also say that a **minute** is made up of **seconds** and represent this using a structure diagram (Fig. 2.26). We can combine this structure with the previous one so that we can represent an iteration within an iteration (Fig. 2.27). This allows us to represent the fact that an **hour** is made up of **minutes** and a **minute** is made up of **seconds**.

An iteration can be used to represent data or processes, i.e. instructions.

16

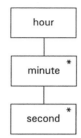

Figure 2.26   A minute as an iteration.

Figure 2.27   An iteration containing an iteration.

2.6.2 How not to combine iteration structures

It will sometimes be necessary to represent one iteration after another; for example, it is possible to have a course that consists of a number of modules in the first year, followed by a number of modules in the second year. The structure shown in Figure 2.28 is not legal in JSP and cannot be used to represent this situation.

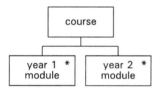

Figure 2.28   An illegal structure for course.

The structure in Figure 2.28 is not legal because there is a conflict of components: the **course** structure is attempting to be an *iteration* (because of the "*" symbol in the lower boxes) and a *sequence* at the same time (because of the order in which the components appear); this is not allowed. In order to represent the structure of the course as described, it is necessary to introduce a further layer, so that the course can be described as a *sequence* of year 1 followed by year 2, and at the next level down **Year 1** is an *iteration* of module (Fig. 2.29), and **Year 2** is an *iteration* of module (Fig. 2.30).

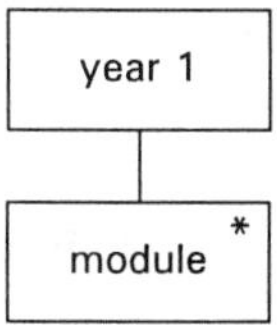

Figure 2.29   Year 1 as an iteration of module.

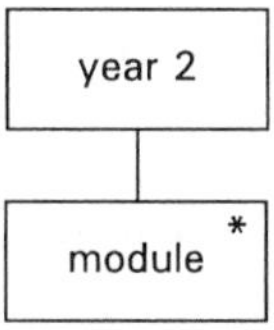

Figure 2.30   Year 2 as an iteration of module.

17

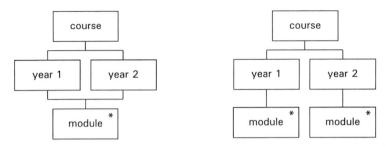

Figure 2.31 Another illegal structure for course.

Figure 2.32 A valid structure for course.

It is important to keep the iterated component **module** separate for year 1 and year 2; to merge them as shown in the structure shown in Figure 2.31 is not allowed in JSP. All JSP structure diagrams must be trees, and Figure 2.31 is a graph as the branches come together again. This in itself, if it were to be allowed, would imply that modules are shared between year 1 and year 2, which is not the case.

Figure 2.32 shows how the course structure can be represented in JSP terms: course is a sequence of year 1 and year 2, year 1 is an iteration of module (as several modules would need to be taken in each year) and year 2 is also an iteration of module.

2.7 Exercises

1. A century consists of 100 years. Each year lasts 365 days (ignoring leap years for this exercise). A century could also be considered to consist of 10 decades. Show different ways in which a century can be represented using JSP structure diagrams.

2. A particular industry, e.g. travel, consists of a number of individual companies (such as travel agents). An individual company may have several branches in different locations. Each branch employs a number of staff. Illustrate the structure of the industry using a JSP diagram.

3. A university has many employees. The university is divided into a number of schools; within each there may be several departments. Each department may be subdivided into groups; within each group there are several members of staff. Show how the university can be represented using a JSP structure diagram.

4. A library contains many books. Each book has many chapters and each chapter has many pages. There are many lines on each page and every line will contain zero or more words, i.e. there will be some blank lines on each page. Show how this could be represented using a JSP diagram.

2.8 Combining different structures

The structures that have been considered up to now have comprised of only one component type. It is possible to mix component types so that a structure contains sequence, selection and iteration. It is important to remember that each box in the diagram may belong to *only one* of the three component types.

2.8.1 Sequence and iteration

A file may contain many records of the same kind, and this can be expressed in JSP terms as file being an *iteration* of record (Fig. 2.33). Another file may contain records of two different types:
- many records of the same type (e.g. one record per student)
- a final record (e.g. total number of students)

Figure 2.34 gives an example of an illegal structure attempting to represent the above. We cannot allow this combination of structures: it would mean that **file** would be attempting to be simultaneously both an *iteration* (because of the "*" symbol) and a *sequence* (because of the left to right order in which the component boxes appear).

Figure 2.33 An iteration.

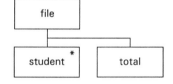

Figure 2.34 An illegal structure.

Another layer in the structure diagram must be introduced in order to create a valid structure to represent the file that has been described. This is achieved by recognizing that the constructs of sequence and iteration are both required. A new box, **file body**, must be introduced to allow the structure of **file** to be a *sequence*; the **file body** box can then be an *iteration* of student record and the

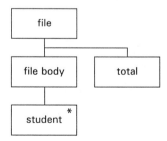

Figure 2.35 A valid structure.

19

integrity of the JSP structure diagram is maintained. Figure 2.35 shows that **file** is a *sequence* of file body followed by a total record, and that **file body** is an *iteration* of student record. This example introduces the term "body" as a collective term for the main part of a component that must be described at a lower level.

2.8.2 Sequence and selection

Suppose we want butter on toast before we put on our choice of spread (Fig. 2.36). We need to identify a *sequence* and then a *selection* (Fig. 2.37). We could choose between butter and low cholesterol margarine before we add our choice of spread (Fig. 2.38).

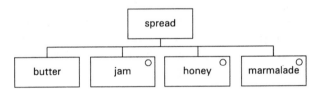

Figure 2.36   An illegal structure for the breakfast selection.

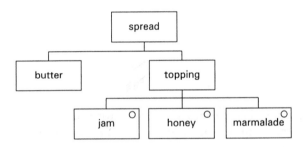

Figure 2.37   A valid structure for the breakfast selection.

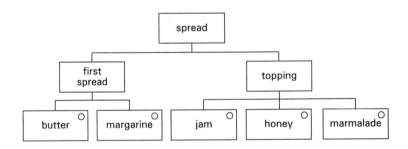

Figure 2.38   A valid structure for the breakfast selection with choice of first spread.

In this structure, **spread** is a *sequence* of first spread and topping. The **first spread** is a *selection* of butter or margarine. The **topping** is a *selection* of jam, honey or marmalade.

2.8.3 Sequence, iteration and selection

A file contains many student records followed by a total. Each student record may represent an undergraduate or a postgraduate. The JSP structure diagram (Fig. 2.39) to represent this file will be constructed from a *sequence* of file body followed by total. The file body will be an *iteration* of student record. The student record component will be a *selection* of undergraduate or postgraduate.

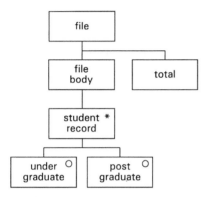

Figure 2.39 An example of a structure diagram showing sequence, iteration and selection.

2.9 Identifying structures and components

A box alone does not tell us which kind of *structure* it is: it is necessary to look at the next level down in order to identify the type of the level above. It is possible to identify which type of *component* a box is, as a mark (or absence of a mark) will distinguish between sequence, selection and iteration components.

A JSP construct consists of a heading and component parts. The leaves, or terminal nodes, are elementary components; the non-terminal nodes are composite components.

In the next example (Fig. 2.40) a structure involving sequence, selection and iteration structures is analyzed, identifying the construct and component type of each individual box.

Each box in Figure 2.40 will now be described in terms of sequence, selection and iteration, indicating whether the box is a construct or a component.

21

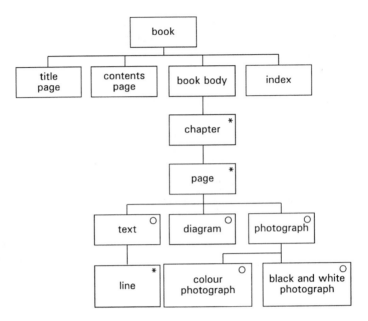

Figure 2.40 A structure diagram for a book showing sequence, iteration and selection.

Box 1: **book**

What is **book** (Fig. 2.41)?

Figure 2.41 Book, a root node.

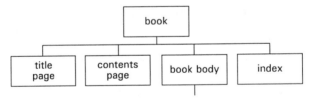

Figure 2.42 Book, a sequence.

Book is a root node. To identify the construct, we need to look at the next level down (Fig. 2.42). **Book** is a *sequence* of **title page**, **contents page**, **book body** and **index**.

Box 2: **title page**

What is **title page** (Fig. 2.43)?

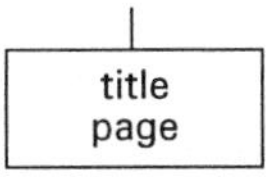

Figure 2.43 `Title page`, a sequence component.

Title page is a sequence component. It is an elementary component. There will be a single title page at the beginning of the book.

Box 3: **contents page**

What is **contents page** (Fig. 2.44)?

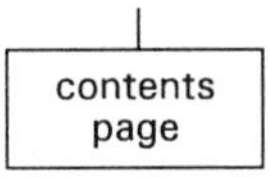

Figure 2.44 `Contents`, a sequence component.

Contents page is a sequence component. It is an elementary component. The book contains a contents page, which appears after the title page.

Box 4: **book body**

What is **book body** (Fig. 2.45)?

Figure 2.45 `Book body`, a sequence component.

Figure 2.46 `Book body` as an iteration of `chapter`.

Book body is a sequence component. It is not an elementary component. To identify the construct, inspect the next level down (Fig 2.46). The book body follows the contents page but precedes the index. **Book body** is an *iteration* of **chapter**.

Box 5: **chapter**

What is **chapter** (Fig. 2.47)?

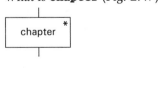

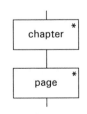

Figure 2.47 `Chapter`, an iterated component.

Figure 2.48 `Chapter` as an iteration of `page`.

23

Chapter forms an iterated component. It is not an elementary component. To identify the construct, examine the next level down (Fig. 2.48). The book contains several chapters. **Chapter** consists of an *iteration* of **page**.

Box 6: **page**

What is **page** (Fig 2.49)?

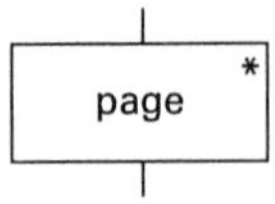

Figure 2.49 **Page**, an iterated component.

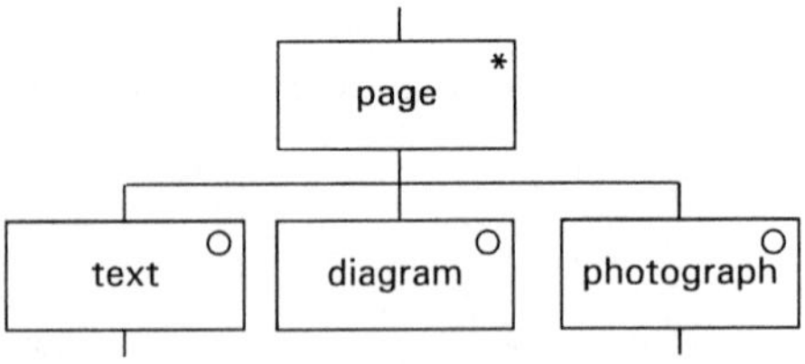

Figure 2.50 **Page** as a selection.

Page is an iterated component. It is not an elementary component. To identify the construct, look at the next level down (Fig. 2.50). Each chapter within the book contains a number of pages. **Page** is a *selection* of **text, diagram** or **photograph**; each page may therefore contain written narrative, a diagram or a photograph. This definition does not permit a page to contain a combination, such as a diagram with text.

Box 7: **text**

What is **text** (Fig. 2.51)?

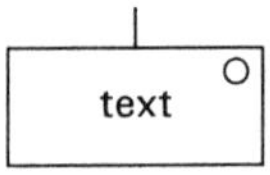

Figure 2.51 **Text**, a selection component.

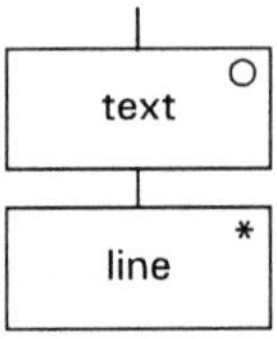

Figure 2.52 **Text** as an iteration of **line**.

Text is a selection component. It is not an elementary component. To identify the construct, examine the next level down (Fig. 2.52). **Text** is an *iteration* of **line**. Each page of text in the book will consist of many lines.

Box 8: **line**

What is **line** (Fig. 2.53)?

Figure 2.53 **Line**, an iterated component.

Line forms an iterated component, which is an elementary component. These lines constitute a page of text.

Box 9: **diagram**
What is **diagram** (Fig 2.54)?

Figure 2.54 Diagram, a selection component.

Diagram is a selection component. It is an elementary component. A page within the book may hold a diagram if it does not have lines of text or a photograph.

Box 10: **photograph**
What is **photograph** (Fig. 2.55)?

Figure 2.55 Photograph, a selection component.   **Figure 2.56** Photograph as a selection.

Photograph is a selection component. It is not an elementary component. To identify the construct, inspect the next level down (Fig. 2.56). **Photograph** is a *selection* of **colour photograph** or **black and white photograph**. A page within the book may have a single photograph, which may be either colour or black and white.

Box 11: **colour photograph**
What is **colour photograph** (Fig. 2.57)?

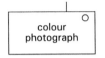

Figure 2.57 Colour photograph, an elementary selection component.

Colour photograph is an elementary selection component. If the page holds a colour photograph, it must not contain anything else (such as text, a diagram or another photograph).

Box 12: **black and white photograph**
   What is **black and white photograph** (Fig. 2.58)?

Figure 2.58 Black and white photograph, an elementary selection component.

Black and white photograph is a selection component. It is an elementary component. A page holding a black and white photograph may not contain anything else.

Box 13: **index**
   What is **index** (Fig. 2.59)?

Figure 2.58 Index, an elementary sequence component.

   Index is an elementary sequence component. It is the last part of the book.
It can be seen from the above examples that constructs can be identified by examining the mark in the lower level box, which is the construct component:

   sequence   no mark in lower box(es)
   selection   "o" symbol in lower boxes
   iteration   " * " symbol in lower box

A box that contains a "o" symbol is not a selection, it is a selection component; the box above is the selection.
   A box that contains a " * " symbol is not an iteration, it is an iterated component; the box above is the iteration.

2.10 Identifying constructs from narrative

In the description of a problem, there are certain key words or phrases that can provide a clue as to the JSP construct that would be appropriate. Some of these phrases are given below.

2.10.1 Phrases implying sequence

The key phrases that imply a sequence construct are characterized by hinting at some order in which the elements appear, e.g. by specifying the starting element or the final element, by naming a particular sequence (such as alphabetical or numeric order) or by indicating the relative position in which elements appear.

... first there is ... , then ...	... this and ...
... the initial value is	... this comes first ...
followed by ...	... this comes before ...
... at the beginning ...	... this comes after ...
... starting with ...	... this comes last ...
... these appear in order ...	... finally there is ...
... ending with ...	... terminating with ...
... finishing with ...	

2.10.2 Phrases implying selection

Phrases that are used when a selection is the appropriate structure are identified by the inclusion of the concept of choice or by indicating that some variation or an alternative option is available and acceptable.

... it is possible that ...	... can be selected ...
... perhaps ...	... one of these ...
... one of the options is ...	... sometimes ...
... this is voluntary ...	... occasionally ...
... it can be either ... or ...	... usually ... , but ...
... either of these ...	... often ...
... there is a choice ...	... frequently ...
... they may elect to ...	... maybe ... or maybe not ...

2.10.3 Phrases implying iteration

Phrases that indicate that an iteration should be employed exhibit the idea of a repeated occurrence, whether it occurs a large or small number of times. The use of a plural in itself often means that an iteration construct is required.

... there are many ...	... in a group ...
... there are several ...	... in a batch ...
... once or more ...	... each and every ...
... again and again ...	... to all of ...
... there are a few ...	... more than ...
... a number of ...	... plurals: people, records, pages,
... there are some ...	lines, etc.
... there are lots ...	

2.11 Exercises

1. A vending machine dispenses a bar of chocolate when the correct money is inserted (there is only one type of chocolate bar available in the machine). Use a structure diagram to illustrate the activity of inserting money and taking a bar of chocolate. *Hint*: *sequence* – the order of activities is important.

2. A more sophisticated vending machine dispenses a variety of bars of chocolate: plain chocolate, milk chocolate, fruit and nut, white chocolate (all at the same price). Draw a structure diagram to illustrate the action of choosing which bar of chocolate is to be dispensed (ignoring all other activities, such as inserting money, for the present). *Hint*: *selection* – a bar of chocolate can only be *one* of those available, so the order is not important.

3. Consider the purchase of several chocolate bars from the machine described in Exercise 2. Draw the structure diagram. *Hints*: *selection* – a bar of chocolate can only be *one* of those available, so the order is unimportant; *iteration* – there may be many purchases.

4. A book consists of a number of pages. On each page there are many lines, and on each line there are many words. Draw the structure diagram. *Hint*: *iteration* – a book has many pages, etc.

5. A report consists of several pages. At the top of each page is a header showing the title on one line, followed by a number of lines of information. Totals appear at the foot of each page on one line. Use a structure diagram to describe the report.

6. A book has a title page, contents list, several chapters and an index. Each chapter has a title and several pages of text, and may or may not have suggestions for further reading. Express the structure of the book using a JSP diagram.

7. An art gallery maintains a catalogue of all its exhibits, whether they are on show to the public or not. The catalogue is arranged in alphabetical order of artist and chronological order of the completion of the work. There is an indicator as to whether the work is currently on display or in store. Draw a JSP structure diagram to represent the art gallery catalogue.

2.12 Further reading

Holmes (1991), Sections 2.2–2.5.
King & Pardoe (1992), Chapters 2 and 3.
Storer (1991), Chapter 2.
Thompson (1989), Section 5.3.

CHAPTER 3

Input and output
data file structures

One of the main principles behind JSP is that computer programs are to process data. It is therefore essential that the structure of the input data and the structure of the required output are considered and represented in such a way that it is possible to convert the input into the output.

Data files will hold data elements related to the problem to be solved: the information required by the end-user can be extracted from data stores. Jackson suggests that process logic should be based on data logic in order to produce a robust program that may be easily changed for the majority of amendments.

3.1 Data file structures

We want data to be stored in such a way that it can be retrieved for processing in a variety of ways. This implies data independence.

We do not need to draw the absolute data structure of a file or database for every program – we select a representation that is true and that satisfies the requirements of the task.

Data files are normally only described down to the level of records: a record is the smallest unit of information that can be obtained by the program from a data file (depending on language, implementation and system).

When deciding on the data structures to be used we must know *what* the program is required to do.

Example
Suppose we wish to count the number of male and female students on a course. The student file could be represented in many ways. We need to draw a data structure diagram for the input file that will suit our purposes and is an accurate representation of the data in the file.

Draw a data structure that you think might be suitable *before* looking at Figure 3.1.

Figure 3.1 is a true representation of the input data file: the input file contains a number of student records, i.e. **student file** is an *iteration* of **student record**. Although this is a true representation of the input file, it does not provide sufficient detail to deal with the problem. The requirement is to count the number of male and the number of female students; it is therefore necessary to be able to distinguish between records for male students and those for female students. The construct required to give this additional level of detail is the *selection*; the iterated component **student record** needs to be shown as a *selection* of **male** or **female** student (Fig. 3.2).

Figure 3.1 **Student file** as an iteration of **student record**.

Figure 3.2 A more detailed diagram of the **student file**.

This structure shows:

- **Student file** is an *iteration* of **student record**.
- **Student record** is a *selection* of **male** or **female**.

We can also consider the appearance of the output: we require a line to be printed containing details of the total of each type of student, male and female. This is represented by the output data structure diagram in Figure 3.3, where it can be seen that the output file consists of a total line. The output file is a *sequence* with **total line** as the only component.

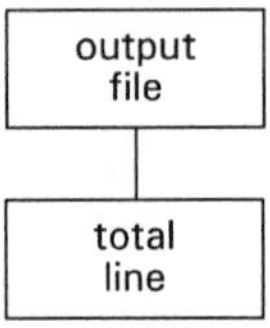

Figure 3.3 The output file consisting of **total line**.

3.2 File structures and record patterns

We can examine a file structure to determine if it reflects a particular pattern of records. It is possible for a file structure to represent more than one pattern of records. Similarly, it can be established whether a particular file structure is incompatible with a given pattern of records.

Example

Figure 3.4 is an input data file structure diagram, which shows that the input file is a sequence of record type A, followed by zero or more records of type B, then a record either of type C or type D (but not both), and finally a record of type E. Therefore a file containing the record sequence A B B B C E would be represented by the file structure diagram, but a file containing A C D E would not (as it is not possible to have both C and D type records within this file).

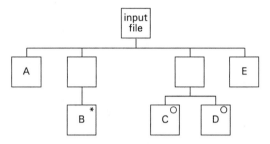

Figure 3.4 An input data file structure diagram.

Consider whether the following record sequences are compatible with the file structure diagram:

A B C D E	No – cannot have both C and D type records.
A C E	Yes – iteration of B means zero or more B records.
A D E	Yes – iteration of B means zero or more B records.
A B C E	Yes – a single B record and C is chosen rather than D.
B D E	No – a type A record is missing at the beginning.
A B C	No – a type E record is missing at the end.
A B D D D E	No – only one record of type D is permitted.
A C D D E	No – cannot have both C and D; only one record of type D is permitted.
A B B B D E	Yes – iteration allows for zero or more B records.
A B B B C E	Yes – iteration allows for zero or more B records.

3.3 Exercises

Draw the input and output data file structures for the following:

1. From a file of student records, you wish to list all students who are taking a course in history.

2. From the same student file you wish to list all the female students who are taking a mathematics module.

3. From the same student file you wish to list all the chemistry students who are male.

4. From the same student file you wish to list all the environmental science students who are female, and print the total number of these students and the grand total of all students on the file.

5. From the same student file you wish to find the total number of all philosophy students who are over 25 years old.

6. From an employee file you wish to list all the employees earning over £30,000 who speak Italian.

7. From the same employee file you wish to print out details of all employees who are not qualified in accountancy.

8. From the same employee file you wish to print out details of all employees who speak Russian and Greek.

9. From the same employee file you wish to print out details of all employees who have a degree in mathematics but work outside the London area.

10. From the same employee file you wish to print out details of all employees who speak either French or German (or both), and print the total number of staff in each of these categories.

11. From the same employee file you wish to calculate the number of staff working in the UK, and those abroad, and the grand total of all staff.

12. The data structure shown in Figure 3.5 represents a file that may contain records A, B, C, D and E. These are the leaves of the tree.

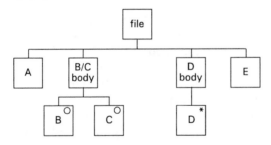

Figure 3.5 The data structure of Exercise 12.

Is the file structure compatible with each of the following record sequences?

(a) A B C D E	(e) A B E E	(i) A B D D D E
(b) A C E	(f) A B E	(j) A C D D E
(c) A D E	(g) B D E	(k) A C B E
(d) A B C E	(h) A B C	(l) A C C D E

13. This structure of another file is given in Figure 3.6. Is the file structure compatible with each of the following record sequences?

(a) P Q S	(e) Q S Q S R S	(i) P P R S P P R S
(b) P P R S P Q S	(f) R S P P P R S	(j) R S P R S
(c) Q S Q S	(g) Q R S	(k) P S
(d) P R S	(h) R S	(l) S P Q R

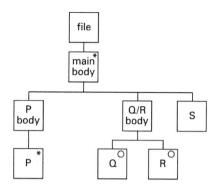

Figure 3.6 The data structure of Exercise 13.

3.4 Further reading

King & Pardoe (1992), Chapters 2 and 3.

CHAPTER 4

Correspondences
and process structures

We need to create input file structures and output file structures so that our program can transform input to produce output. Most programs make use of at least two files: input and output. By merging the input data file structure and the output data file structure we are able to create a basic process structure for our program.

4.1 Definition of correspondence

For a correspondence to exist, an element must occur in the input data structure and the output data structure:
- the same number of times
- in the same order
- in the same context

Elements are considered to occur in the same context if they occur under the same criteria, and if input directly generates output. If there is no correspondence between an input data file structure and an output data file structure, this implies that it is not possible to generate the output required from the input data. The correspondence of items between the input data file structure and the output data file structure must be one to one; a one to many correspondence is not allowed.

4.2 Merging on the points of correspondence

When merging data structures, we look for correspondences in the structures. We are looking for points at which processing one file will correspond to the processing of another file. Where there are points of correspondence on the input and output data file structures, these boxes will merge to produce a single process box on the process structure diagram. Consider the simple example given in Figure 4.1.

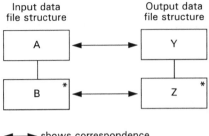

→← shows correspondence

Figure 4.1 Correspondences between data file structures for input and output.

The input data file A is processed to produce the output data file Y, and therefore A and Y correspond. The basic process structure will contain a box AY produced from merging A from the input structure and Y from the output structure.

In the input data file structure, it can be seen that A is an iteration of B. In the output data file structure, Y is an iteration of Z. Every record represented by the iterated component B in the input structure has an equivalent record Z in the output structure; these elements occur the same number of times, in the same order and in the same context. There is therefore a correspondence between B and Z. The two boxes B and Z can be merged to form a single process box BZ on the basic process structure diagram (Fig. 4.2).

Figure 4.2 Data structures merged on points of correspondence to form basic process structure: A and Y merge to form box AY; B and Z merge to form box BZ.

This example illustrates the basic principle of establishing the points of correspondence and merging the input and output data structures in order to produce a basic process structure. The following examples demonstrate how points of correspondence can be established when considering input and output data file structures created for simple tasks, such as printing reports based on data in an input file.

4.3 A lack of correspondence

When an attempt is made to merge the input and output data file structures, it will often be found that a box exists on one of the diagrams that has no box to which it corresponds on the other diagram. For example, if it is required to calculate a total, a box to represent the total will appear on the output structure but not on the input structure diagram. This does not present a problem; what has occurred is that there is a *lack of correspondence*. It is important to recognize the difference between a lack of correspondence and a structure clash. The former is caused by the presence of a box on one of the data file structure diagrams that is not present in the other. A structure clash is a more serious problem, and demonstrates that there is conflict between the two structures, in that the rules of correspondence are broken. The technique of program inversion can be used to deal with a structure clash; this situation is considered in Chapter 12.

4.4 Structure clashes

A structure clash between the input and output data file structures occurs if the rules of correspondence are broken. One possibility is that the order in which the elements appear on the input file is different from that required on the output file. This situation is referred to as an ordering clash. Another typical cause of a structure clash is the requirement for the output to be grouped into sections that are not the same size as the pages of the report. This is known as a boundary clash, because the boundaries of the pages do not coincide with the boundaries of the groups in which the data occur. Chapter 12 discusses structure clashes in detail, and illustrates how such problems are handled.

4.5 Merging data structures – demonstrations

Demonstration 1: List employees

Input file 1
An input file contains employee records in alphabetical order (Fig. 4.3).

Output file 1
An output report file is printed listing employee records in alphabetical order (Fig. 4.4).

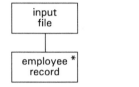

Figure 4.3 The input data file structure for Demonstration 1.

Figure 4.4 The output data file structure for Demonstration 1.

Identify the points of correspondence

The processing of the input file will lead to the generation of output: there is a correspondence at the top level. These two boxes will merge to produce a single box on the basic process structure diagram.

For each employee record in the input file there will be a single line printed on the output report. The records in the input file are in the same order as those on the output file and they occur in the same context. There is therefore a correspondence between employee record on the input data file structure and employee report line on the output data file structure: these two boxes will merge to produce a single box on the basic process structure diagram (Fig. 4.5).

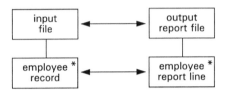

Figure 4.5   Correspondence between input and output data file structures for Demonstration 1.

The data from the input data file is manipulated via the program to produce the output report. There is, therefore, a correspondence at the top level between the input data structure and the output data structure.

Each employee record occurs once, in alphabetical order, on the input data file. On each line of the report an employee record is printed, in alphabetical order. The employee records on the input data file occur in the same order, the same number of times and in the same context as the lines on the report. There is therefore a correspondence between **employee record** in the input data structure and **employee record line** in the output data structure.

Merge to form basic process structure 1

Figure 4.6 shows the basic process structure diagram for Demonstration 1.

Figure 4.6   Basic process structure diagram for Demonstration 1.

Demonstration 2: List employees and calculate total

Input file 2

An input file contains employee records in alphabetical order (Fig. 4.7).

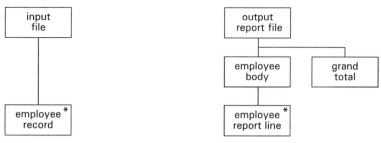

Figure 4.7 The input data file structure for Demonstration 2.

Figure 4.8 The output data file structure for Demonstration 2.

Output file 2

An output report file is printed, listing employee records in alphabetical order followed by a grand total of all employees (Fig. 4.8).

Identify correspondences

The input file box corresponds to the output report box as the input data file generates the output report: these boxes will merge to form a single process box on the process structure diagram.

The report body box on the output data structure is a body box to maintain the integrity of the structure diagram, allowing the sequence and iteration constructs to be represented. There is no correspondence between this and any box on the input data structure diagram and therefore this box must appear in the final process structure without merging with a box from the input structure.

The grand total box on the output data structure does not correspond to a box on the input data structure because the total is only calculated after all the records have been processed; it does not exist in the input data structure. This is a lack of correspondence and not a structure clash. There is no conflict between the input data structure and the output data structure, simply a box in one structure that has no equivalent in the other structure. The total box must appear in the process structure diagram, although there is no input structure box with which it is able to merge.

The employee records box on the input data structure corresponds to the employee report line box on the output data structure; the records occur in

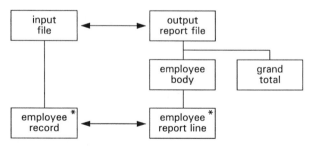

Figure 4.9 Correspondence between input and output data file structures for Demonstration 2.

39

the same order and the same number of times, and input generates output. These boxes will merge to form a single process box on the process structure diagram (Fig. 4.9).

Merge to form basic process structure 2

Figure 4.10 shows the basic process structure diagram for Demonstration 2.

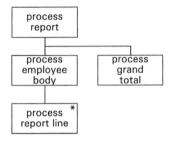

Figure 4.10   Basic process structure diagram for Demonstration 2.

Demonstration 3: List employees and calculate total with report title

Input file 3

An input file contains employee records in alphabetical order (Fig.4.11).

Output file 3

An output report file is printed with a title, followed by a list of employee records in alphabetical order and finally a grand total of all employees (Fig. 4.12).

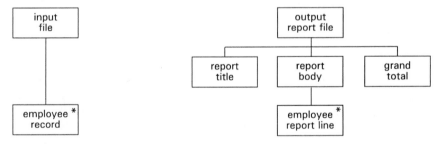

Figure 4.11   The input data file structure for Demonstration 3.

Figure 4.12   The output data file structure for Demonstration 3.

Identify correspondences

The input file box on the input data structure corresponds to the output re-port box on the output data structure, as the input file is processed to generate the output report.

The report title box on the output data structure does not correspond to any box on the input data structure, because the input data file does not con-tain the title of the report. This is a lack of correspondence and not a structure

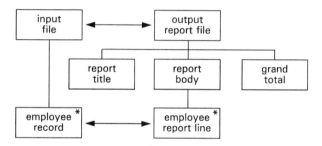

Figure 4.13 Correspondence between input and output data file structures for Demonstration 3.

clash, as there is no conflict between the two data structures. It is clear that the report title must appear before the lines on the report containing employee records and therefore the report title box must appear before the processing of employee records in the main body of the report on the process structure diagram (Fig. 4.13).

The report body box on the output data structure is a body box to maintain the integrity of the output data structure, so that the concepts of sequence and iteration can be represented. This box does not correspond to any box on the input data structure, but neither does it conflict with the input data structure. The report body box must be represented on the process structure diagram, after the production of the title, but before printing the total.

The employee report line box on the output data structure corresponds to the employee record box on the input data structure: input generates output and each report line occurs the same number of times and in the same order as each employee record. These two boxes will merge to form a single box on the process structure diagram.

The grand total box does not correspond to any box on the input data structure as the input file does not contain the grand total; it must be calculated as each record is processed and then printed at the end of the report. This is a lack of correspondence and not a structure clash. It is clear that the grand total must appear as the last item in the report, and will be represented by a box on the process structure diagram.

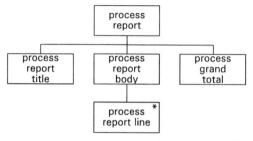

Figure 4.14 Basic process structure diagram for Demonstration 3.

Merge to form basic process structure 3
Figure 4.14 shows the basic process structure diagram for Demonstration 3.

Demonstration 4: Calculate total number of employees

Input file 4
An input file contains employee records in alphabetical order (Fig. 4.15).

Output file 4
An output report file is printed giving the total number of employees (Fig. 4.16). Individual employee records are not printed.

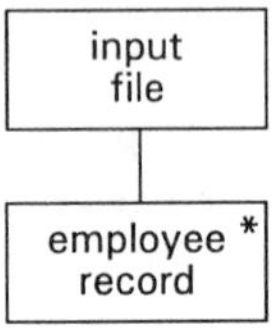

Figure 4.15 The input data file structure for Demonstration 4.

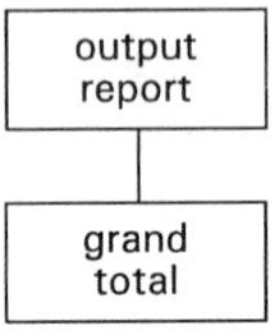

Figure 4.16 The output data file structure for Demonstration 4.

Identify correspondences
The input file is processed to produce the output file: there is therefore a correspondence at the top level.

Individual employee records are not printed, and therefore they do not appear in the output data structure (Fig. 4.17). There is a lack of correspondence between the employee records box on the input data structure and the output data structure. A box to represent the employee records must appear in the process structure diagram in order that each employee record may be processed to calculate the grand total. The logical position for the employee records component is before the grand total component in the process structure diagram (Fig. 4.18).

The grand total does not correspond to any component on the input data structure: there is a lack of correspondence. The grand total must be repre-

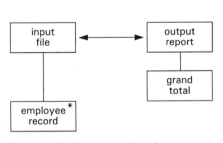

Figure 4.17 Correspondence between input and output data file structures for Demonstration 4.

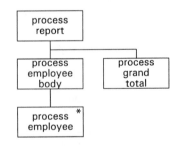

Figure 4.18 Basic process structure diagram for Demonstration 4.

sented by a box on the process structure diagram in order to process the grand total once it has been calculated. The logical position for the grand total is after all the employee records have been processed.

Merge to form basic process structure 4
Figure 4.18 shows the basic process structure diagram for Demonstration 4.

Demonstration 5: List female employees

Input file 5a
An input file contains employee records in alphabetical order (Fig. 4.19).

Output file 5
An output report is required listing only the female employees in alphabetical order (Fig. 4.20).

Figure 4.19   The input data file structure for Demonstration 5.

Figure 4.20   The output data file structure for Demonstration 5.

Identify correspondences
The input file is processed to produce the output report: there is a correspondence at the top level.

The employee records component on the input data structure diagram does not correspond to the female employee report line component in the output data structure diagram as, although the records will be in the same order, not all the records in the input file will be printed in the output report, i.e. the records for male staff will not appear on the output report although they are present on the input file. There is no correspondence between these components and it is not possible to merge the two structures because of this (Fig. 4.21). It will be necessary to redesign the input data file structure in order to find a representation that reflects the nature of the problem.

Input File 5b
The input data file structure (Fig. 4.22) now distinguishes between male and female employees and this enables the problem to be solved.

Identify correspondences
The input file is processed in order to generate the output report file: there is a correspondence at the top level.

There is no correspondence between the employee record box on the input data structure and any box on the output data structure, as only the records for

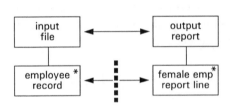

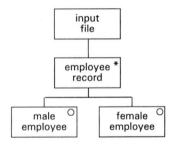

Figure 4.21 Rules of correspondence not satisfied between input and output data file structures for Demonstration 5.

Figure 4.22 Redesigned input data file structure for Demonstration 5.

female employees appear on the output report. The employee record box must appear in the process structure diagram, as all records need to be read and processed.

The male employee box on the input data structure diagram shows a lack of correspondence with the output structure diagram. It will be necessary for a box to appear in the process structure diagram as it will be necessary to process male employee records in a different way from female employee records.

The female employee box on the input data structure diagram corresponds with the female employee report line box on the output data structure diagram: the records appear in the same order, the same number of times and in the same context (the records on the input file generate the records on the

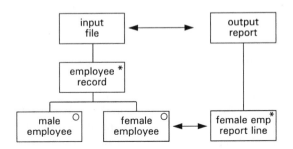

Figure 4.23 Correspondence between modified input data file structure and output data file structure for Demonstration 5.

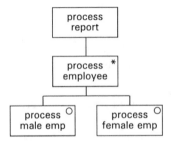

Figure 4.24 Basic process structure diagram for Demonstration 5.

44

output report); these two boxes will merge to form a single box on the process structure diagram (Figs 4.23 & 4.24).

Merge to form basic process structure diagram
Figure 4.24 shows the basic process structure for Demonstration 5.

Demonstration 6: List employees, 50 records per page

Input file 6
An input file contains employee records in alphabetical order (Fig. 4.25).

Output file 6
An output report file is produced listing employee records in alphabetical order, one employee record is printed per line and there are 50 lines per page (Fig. 4.26).

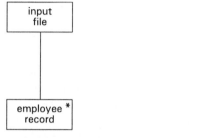

Figure 4.25 The input data file structure for Demonstration 6.

Figure 4.26 The output data file structure for Demonstration 6.

Identify correspondences
The input file is processed to generate the output file: there is a correspondence at the top level.

There is a lack of correspondence between the page box on the output report structure and the input structure: the input file structure has no concept of a page boundary, but there is no clash as the records are not grouped in a way that would conflict with the number of lines per page. A box must appear in the process structure diagram to deal with the grouping of lines on the output report into pages.

The employee records box on the input data structure diagram corresponds to the employee report line box on the output data structure diagram: input records occur the same number of times and in the same order as output lines on the report page, and input generates output. These two boxes will merge to form a single box on the process structure diagram (Figs 4.27 & 4.28).

Merge to form basic process structure 6
Figure 4.28 shows the basic process structure diagram for Demonstration 6.

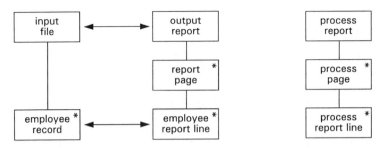

Figure 4.27 Correspondence between input and output data file structures for Demonstration 6.

Figure 4.28 Basic process structure diagram for Demonstration 6.

Demonstration 7: List employees by department with titles, totals and paging

Input file 7
An input file contains employee records grouped by department (Fig. 4.29).

Output file 7
An output report file is produced listing employee records, grouped by department. Some departments are small and more than one will fit onto a single page; other departments are large and will need several pages in order to list all members of staff within each one. One record is printed per line and there are 50 lines per page. A department title is printed before the employee records for that department and the total number of staff within each department is printed when all staff records for that department have been printed. The total number of employees in each department has to be calculated: this information is not stored explicitly on the input file (Fig. 4.30).

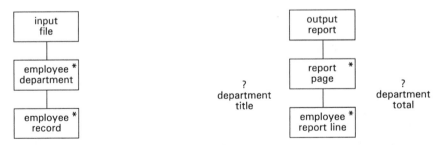

Figure 4.29 The input data file structure for Demonstration 7.

Figure 4.30 An attempt to construct the output data file structure for Demonstration 7.

It can be seen that there will be difficulties with this problem. As the number of departments appearing on a page may vary, it is not possible to identify where the department titles and totals will appear in relation to the pages. It will be necessary to show that any line on the report could be an employee record, a department total or a department title (Fig. 4.31).

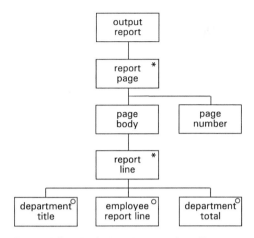

Figure 4.31 Redesigned output data file structure for Demonstration 7.

Identify correspondences

The input file is processed to generate the output file: there is a correspondence at the top level.

There is a structure clash between the employee department on the input data structure and the page box on the output report structure: there is no relationship between page and department. It is not possible to merge the two data structures to form a single program to solve the problem in its present form.

One approach would be to change the problem so that the grouping into departments is ignored, and employee records are printed one per line, 50 lines per page (this is illustrated in Demonstration 6 above), but this will ignore the titles and totals associated with each department.

Another approach would be to set aside the same number of pages for each department; this would mean that a page group would correspond to the concept of department. The problem here is that all page groups must be as large as the number of pages required for the department with the highest number of staff. This will lead to many other departments having blank pages in the report, simply to maintain the relationship between page group and department.

The solution to the problem in its present form is to use one of the more advanced techniques of JSP, program inversion. This requires the design of two programs rather than one.

The employee records box on the input data structure diagram corresponds to the employee report line box on the output data structure diagram: input records occur the same number of times and in the same order as output lines on the report page, and input generates output.

The department title box on the output data file structure shows a lack of correspondence with the input data file structure as the department title is not stored in the input file except as a field within each employee record.

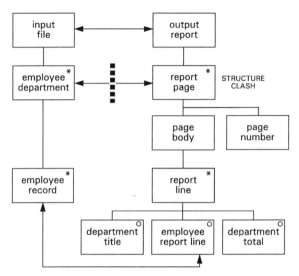

Figure 4.32 Lack of correspondence between input and output data file structures for Demonstration 7.

The department total box on the output data file structure exhibits a lack of correspondence with the input data file structure; the department total can only be calculated by processing each employee record for that department (Fig. 4.32).

It is not possible to merge these two structures in order to form a basic process structure because of the structure clash between employee department on the input data structure and report page on the output data structure. The solution is to develop two programs. One program will process the original input file and produce an intermediate data file. This intermediate file will contain the department titles, department employee records and department totals. The intermediate file will then be used as the input data file to the second program, which will produce the output in paged format.

4.6 More on correspondences

It must be possible to reconstruct each of the original data structures from the combined structure by removing all boxes that do not correspond to the particular data structure.

The final structure must have an elementary box for every elementary box on each file. A box that occurs in one structure but not in the other may simply show a lack of correspondence and it must therefore appear in the process structure diagram. This is a lack of correspondence which should not be confused with a structure clash.

An elementary box will be shared by two files when there is a correspondence between elementary components of the original data structures.

There are problems that can prevent the merging of data structures. For example, it may be impossible to insert a box logically in the correct position because of certain conditions, or it may be impossible to establish a correspondence: input may be in a different order from that required for output. These are structure clashes, for which there is a standard approach to solution. This will be discussed in a later section.

It is important that a structure clash is not confused with a lack of correspondence. A structure clash means that there is conflict between the input and output data structures, whereas a lack of correspondence means that an item may occur in the output data structure with no direct equivalent in the input data structure (for example, the heading on a report).

4.7 Exercises

Consider the following problems, draw the input and output data file structures, identify the points of correspondence and merge to form the basic process structure in each case. (Note that some of these problems are continued from exercises in the previous chapter, whereas others are variations on similar exercises.)

1. From a file of student records, you wish to list all students who are taking a course in history.

2. From the same student file you wish to list all the female students who are taking a mathematics module.

3. From the same student file you wish to list all the chemistry students, subdivided into organic and inorganic chemistry, and give the total number of organic and inorganic chemistry students, as well as the combined total of all chemistry students.

4. From an employee file you wish to list all the employees earning over £30,000 who speak Italian.

5. From the same employee file you wish to produce a report with a title, then print out details of all employees who are not qualified in accountancy. The final part of the report gives the total number of staff qualified in accountancy, the total number not so qualified, and the total number of employees.

6. From the same employee file you wish to produce a report with a title, then print out details of all employees who speak Russian and Greek, then give the following totals: total number of staff who speak Russian only, total number of staff who speak Greek only and the grand total of all staff.

7. From the same employee file you wish to calculate the total number of employees who have a degree in mathematics but work outside the London area. Only the total number is required, not a printed listing of the individuals.

4.8 Further reading

Holmes (1991), Sections 2.6, 9.2 and 9.5.
King & Pardoe (1992), Chapter 4.
Storer (1991), Chapter 5.
Thompson (1989), Chapter 11.

Creating the final process structure

In order to generate a program from the basic process structure, it will be necessary to allocate conditions and operations to the process structure. This is discussed in detail in Chapter 6. Although operations could be added to process boxes in the example process structure diagrams developed in Chapter 4, it can be seen that there is no clear location for placing operations that deal with the "housekeeping" activities that are required in most programs. It is at this stage that a basic process structure diagram needs to be inspected with a view to making provision for such activities to be included in the program.

5.1 Preparing for "housekeeping" activities

The basic process structure may not contain process boxes for certain "housekeeping" activities, such as opening and closing files, initializing page number etc. It is possible to add operations such as these directly to the structure, but there is a danger that when an attempt is made to do so the process structure may be invalidated. For example, if we take demonstration example 1 from the previous section, it is clear that we would want to open the input and output files before processing can commence and close the files again when processing has concluded. If we were to add operations to open and close the files on the basic process structure as it stands, the structure would be invalidated (Fig. 5.1).

Figure 5.1 An illegal structure in which **process data file** is attempting to be both an iteration and a sequence.

The structure in Figure 5.1 is illegal because **process data file** is attempting to be both an *iteration* (because of the "*" symbol in the process employee component) and a *sequence* (because of the left-to-right arrangement of opening the files, process employee and closing the files).

5.2 Adding body boxes

The solution is to employ a body box; this enables a valid process structure to include the opening and closing of data files. A valid version of the process structure diagram would now appear as shown in Figure 5.2, with the inclusion of a body box to maintain the integrity of the design. This process structure diagram is valid, but the activities of opening and closing files do not belong to a named process other than **process data file**.

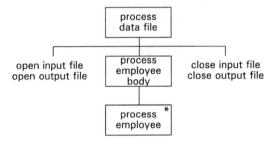

Figure 5.2   A valid process structure diagram including "housekeeping" activities.

5.3 Adding start and finish boxes

A development of employing a body box is to insert not just a body box, but a complete sequence, as shown in Figure 5.3. This has the advantage that the operations to open and close files are now allocated to a named process box. Another benefit is that it is less likely that the basic process structure will be invalidated by adding operations, as all operations can now be added to terminal nodes, i.e. to elementary components.

Now that the sequence layer has been added, the basic process structure has been transformed into the final process structure. Conditions and operations can now be added to this structure to complete the design of the program.

Each of the basic process structure diagrams from Section 4.5 of Chapter 4 will require the addition of sequence components in order to carry out similar "housekeeping" activities.

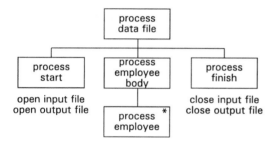

Figure 5.3 A process structure with a sequence layer to accommodate "housekeeping" activities.

Process structure 1: list employees

The basic process structure is shown in Figure 5.4. Files will need to be opened before any records are processed, and closed when processing is complete. The final process structure is shown in Figure 5.5.

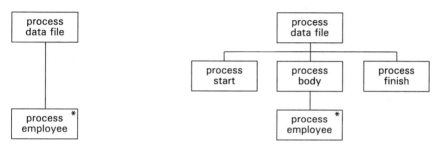

Figure 5.4 Basic process structure diagram for demonstration 1.

Figure 5.5 Final process structure diagram for demonstration 1.

Process structure 2: list employees and calculate total

The basic process structure is shown in Figure 5.6. Files will need to be opened, and the value of the grand total must be initialized to zero, before any records are processed. It will also be necessary to close the files after the grand total has been printed. The final process structure is shown in Figure 5.7.

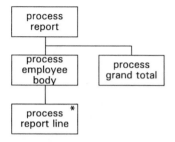

Figure 5.6 Basic process structure diagram for demonstration 2.

53

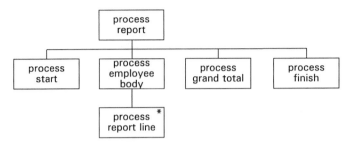

Figure 5.7   Final process structure diagram for demonstration 2.

Process structure 3: list employees and calculate total with report title
The basic process structure is shown in Figure 5.8. Files will need to be opened and the grand total initialized to zero before the report title is printed and any records are processed. It will also be necessary to close the files after the grand total has been printed. The final process structure is shown in Figure 5.9.

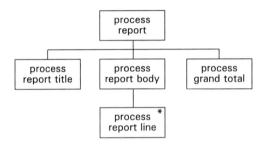

Figure 5.8   Basic process structure diagram for demonstration 3.

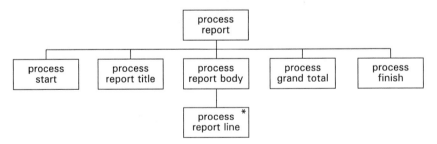

Figure 5.9   Final process structure diagram for demonstration 3.

Process structure 4: calculate total number of employees
The basic process structure is shown in Figure 5.10. The input and output files will need to be opened, and the grand total initialized to zero, before any records are processed. The files must also be closed after the grand total has been printed. The final process structure is shown in Figure 5.11.

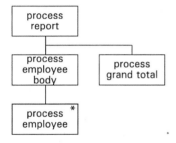

Figure 5.10 Basic process structure diagram for demonstration 4.

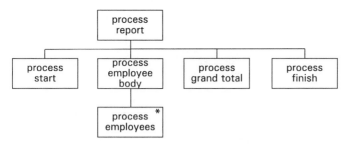

Figure 5.11 Final process structure diagram for demonstration 4.

Process structure 5: list female employees

The basic process structure is shown in Figure 5.12. The files must be opened before records can be read and processed. When all records have been processed, the files must be closed before the program finishes running. The final process structure is shown in Figure 5.13.

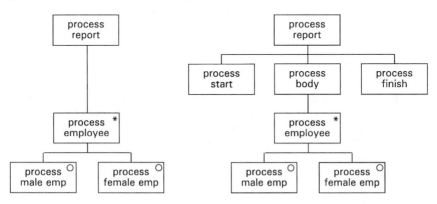

Figure 5.12 Basic process structure diagram for demonstration 5.

Figure 5.13 Final process structure diagram for demonstration 5.

Process structure 6: list employees, 50 records per page
The basic process structure is shown in Figure 5.14. The input and output data files must be opened before processing can begin. When all records have been processed, it will be necessary to close the input and output data files. The pages in the output report must contain 50 lines each; it is therefore necessary to initialize a line counter at the beginning of each page to count the number of lines as each record is printed. When all 50 lines have been printed on a page, it is necessary to print the page number at the bottom of the current page before jumping to the next page to be printed. The final process structure is shown in Figure 5.15.

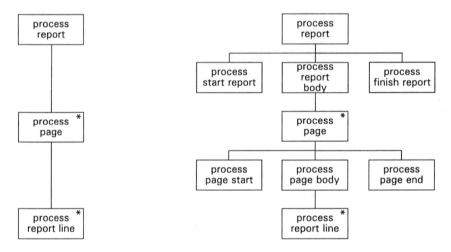

Figure 5.14 Basic process structure diagram for demonstration 6.

Figure 5.15 Final process structure diagram for demonstration 6.

5.4 Exercises

From the input and output file structures for the exercises below, identify the "housekeeping" activities that need to be performed and add process boxes to the process structure diagram to allow these actions to be made.

1. From a file of student records you wish to list all students who are taking a course in history.

2. From the same student file you wish to list all the female students who are taking a mathematics module.

3. From the same student file you wish to list all the chemistry students, subdivided into organic and inorganic chemistry, and give the total number of organic and inorganic chemistry students, as well as the combined total of all chemistry students.

4. From an employee file you wish to list all the employees earning over £30,000 who speak Italian.

5. From the same employee file you wish to produce a report with a title, then print out details of all employees who are not qualified in accountancy. The final part of the report gives the total number of staff qualified in accountancy, the total number not so qualified, and the total number of employees.

6. From the same employee file you wish to produce a report with a title, then print out details of all employees who speak Russian and Greek, then give the following totals: total number of staff who speak Russian only, total number of staff who speak Greek only, and the grand total of all staff.

7. From the same employee file you wish to calculate the total number of employees who have a degree in mathematics but work outside the London area. Only the total number is required, not a printed listing of the individuals.

5.5 Further reading

Holmes (1991), Section 2.6.
King & Pardoe (1992), Chapters 3 and 4.
Storer (1991), Sections 3.1–3.2.
Thompson (1989), Sections 2.1–2.3.

CHAPTER 6

Adding conditions and operations

Merging the input file structure and the output file structure produces the process structure. This is a static logical representation of the processes required for transforming input via a process to output.

To transform the process structure into a program we need to supply more information:

conditions   on iteration(s) and selection(s)
operations   tasks to be performed.

Conditions are associated with process structures, *not* data structures. We need to define conditions when a selection is made to distinguish between one choice and another, and when an iteration is used to determine when the loop terminates.

Example
We wish to count the number of male and the number of female students. The input and output file structures are shown in Figure 6.1. There is a correspondence at the top level only; there is only a single total line, not one for each student record, so there is a lack of correspondence between each of the other boxes.

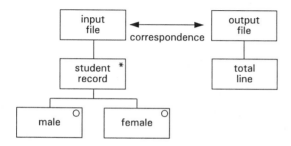

Figure 6.1   Input and output data file structures showing correspondence.

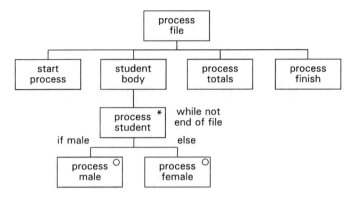

Figure 6.2 Process structure.

We merge the input and output file structures to produce a basic process structure and add boxes to deal with "housekeeping" activities, this gives us the final process structure (Fig. 6.2), to which we can add conditions and operations. We need to add conditions to the iteration and the selection, and operations to the terminal nodes.

6.1 Conditions in programming languages

An expression will take the form of a test, and will result in a Boolean value of "true" or "false" being returned depending on whether the test succeeded. The following are examples that could be tested:
- test for end of file
- compare two values
- test value against limit
- test value between two limits
- logical AND of two tests
- logical OR of two tests
- test if value is equal to zero
- test if value is greater than another
- test if value is not equal to another
- test if value is less than or equal to another

What are conditions like in the Pascal language?

```
not EOF
not EOLN
(temp > 100) and (weight <10)
(ans = 'y') or (ans = 'Y')
count > 12
size <> max
```

What are conditions like in the C language?

```
!= EOF
!done
number <= 100
value == 25
num * num > 500
(number < 1) || (number > 5)
(a == 2) && (c == 3)
```

What are conditions like in the COBOL language?

```
EOF = "Y"
EOF = "Y" OR COUNT > 12
DEPT NOT = S-DEPT OR EOF = "Y"
RECORD-TYPE = "A"
HOURS > 40
AMOUNT NUMERIC AND > 400
AMOUNT + 1 LESS THAN 6
```

Conditions may be added to the structure diagram, or given as a list to which reference is made, e.g. c1, c2, etc.

6.2 Allocating conditions to selections

It is not necessary to give a condition for the final part of a selection; the final part will only be taken if the initial condition is false. The final part of a selection is condition-less, like **else** within an **if ... then ... else ...** statement, so that all selection possibilities are met.

6.3 Allocating conditions to iterations

It is important to recognize the difference between an *iteration* and a *repetition* when allocating conditions to iterations. An iteration can occur *zero or more times*, whereas a repetition will take place *at least once*. This distinction is particularly important when it comes to processing input files. Imagine that the first read statement finds that the input file is empty; attempting to process a non-existent record would cause a run-time error. In this situation it can be seen that an iteration is required (so that no records are processed), whereas a repetition would allow processing to proceed as if a record had been successfully read from the input file.

This problem also has implications for the allocation of operations to read the input file, resulting in the employment of the read ahead-read next convention. This approach is discussed in Section 6.4.1.

6.4 Allocating operations

The steps we have covered so far include:
- input data file structure
- output data file structure
- data structures merged to give process structure
- conditions added on selections and iterations

In order to create a program from the process structure we need to specify the elementary operations. There are two types of operation:

    internal data   calculations, copy data between variables

    external data   open and close files, read and write

The operations are listed *in any order* and each is given a unique number. Examples of typical operations are:

1. Stop run
2. Open input student-file
3. Close print-file
4. Write one-line from data-line
5. Add 1 to counter
6. Subtract tax from gross
7. Move spaces to data-line
8. Move 0 to total

It is sometimes useful to consult a checklist to ensure that all operations have been considered. A checklist of typical operations is shown in Figure 6.3.

Done	Operations checklist
	finish processing
	open all files
	close all files
	get input data
	initialize variables for calculations
	initialize variables for conditions
	store data for later use
	calculate output data
	print output results

Figure 6.3 A checklist of typical operations.

In the student record example the operations required are:
1. `stop processing`
2. `open student file`
3. `open report file`
4. `close student file`
5. `close report file`
6. `read a student record from the input student file`
7. `print final totals on output report file`

8. **add 1 to male total**
9. **add 1 to female total**
10. **set female total to zero**
11. **set male total to zero**
12. **initialize end of file flag on input student file to false**

Note that we do *not* have **if student = male** in the operations list because this selection forms part of the structure of the program and is not an operation. It would be a serious error to include it in the operations list.

We now allocate the operations to the terminal nodes of the process structure (Fig. 6.4). Note that we have allocated operation 6 (**read a student record**) three times; we do not need more than one definition of this operation and we may refer to it as many times as we require by allocating the operation number to the structure as and when required.

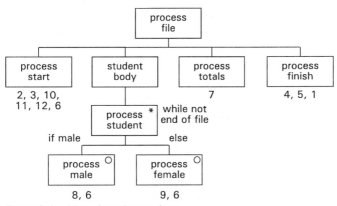

Figure 6.4 Allocation of operations.

It is possible to combine activities into a single operation; for example, operations 2 and 3 to open the input and output files could be grouped into a single operation to perform both these actions. At this stage, it is suggested that each action is represented by a single operation; this makes debugging the design easier and producing the code simpler.

If more than one operation is allocated to a box, we must ensure that the operations appear in the correct sequence.

6.4.1 Allocating read statements

The position in which read statements are allocated to the process structure is crucial to the design of the program. As can be seen from Figure 6.4, the read statement (operation 6) has been allocated three times; once in the read ahead position (**start process**), and again in the read next position for each selection component (**process male** and **process female**). This means that there will be one more read executed than there are records on the file (including the case of an empty data file).

The allocation of a read statement in the read ahead position is important as it will determine whether the iteration will be entered. Thus, if the input file is empty, the end of file flag will be set to true and therefore no records will be processed.

The allocation of a read statement in the read next position governs the continuation of the iteration after the previous record has been processed. This read statement must be placed after all operations processing the previous record; if that record was the last record on the file, the read next statement will trigger the end-of-file condition, which will terminate the iteration.

If the *read ahead–read next convention* were not followed, and a read statement were to be allocated as the first operation within the iteration, run-time errors would result when the end of file is reached as attempts would be made to process a non-existent record by the operations allocated after the read within the iteration.

6.5 Allocating conditions and operations to process structures

The conditions and operations relating to each of the process structures created in the worked examples of Chapters 4 and 5 can now be identified and allocated.

Process structure 1: list employees
The final process structure is shown in Figure 6.5.

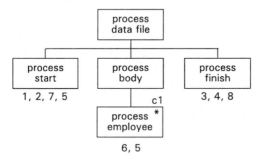

Figure 6.5 Final process structure diagram for demonstration 1.

The condition on the iteration is:
`c1: not end of input file`
The operations list is:
1. `Open input file`
2. `Open output file`
3. `Close input file`

  4. `Close output file`
  5. `Read record from input file`
  6. `Write record to output report`
  7. `Initialize end of input file flag to false`
  8. `Stop processing`

Process structure 2: list employees and calculate total
The final process structure is shown in Figure 6.6. The condition on the iteration is:
`c1: not end of input file`
The operations list is:
  1. `Open input file`
  2. `Open output file`
  3. `Close input file`
  4. `Close output file`
  5. `Read record from input file`
  6. `Write record to output file`
  7. `Initialize end of input file flag to false`
  8. `Initialize total to zero`
  9. `Add 1 to total`
 10. `Write total to output file`
 11. `Stop processing`

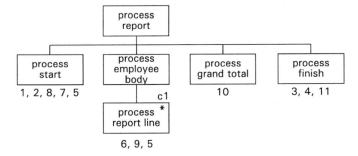

Figure 6.6 Final process structure diagram for demonstration 2.

Process structure 3: list employees and calculate total with report title
The final process structure is shown in Figure 6.7. The condition on the iteration is:
`c1: not end of input file`
The operations list is:
  1. `Open input file`
  2. `Open output file`
  3. `Close input file`

4. Close output file
5. Stop processing
6. Initialize end of input file flag to false
7. Read record from input file
8. Write record to output file
9. Write total to output file
10. Add 1 to total
11. Initialize total to zero
12. Write "Employee Report" to output file

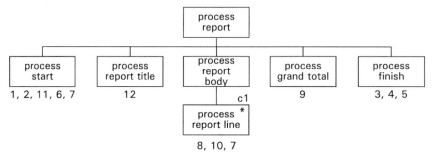

Figure 6.7 Final process structure diagram for demonstration 3.

Process structure 4: calculate total number of employees

The final process structure is shown in Figure 6.8. The condition on the iteration is:

c1: not end of input file

The operations list is:

1. Open input file
2. Open output file
3. Close input file
4. Close output file
5. Read record from input file
6. Initialize total to zero
7. Add 1 to total

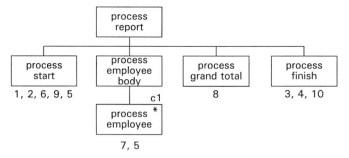

Figure 6.8 Final process structure diagram for demonstration 4.

8. **Write total to output file**
9. **Initialize end of input file flag to false**
10. **Stop processing**

Process structure 5: list female employees

The final process structure is shown in Figure 6.9. The conditions are:

c1: not end of input file
c2: male employee
c3: else

The operations list is:

1. **Open input file**
2. **Open output file**
3. **Close input file**
4. **Close output file**
5. **Read record from input file**
6. **Write record to output file**
7. **Initialize end of input file flag to false**
8. **Stop processing**

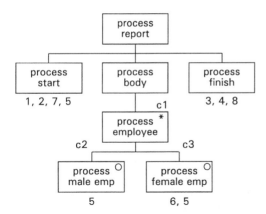

Figure 6.9   Final process structure diagram for demonstration 5.

Process structure 6: list employees, 50 records per page

The final process structure is shown in Figure 6.10. The conditions are:

c1: not end of input file
c2: not end of input file, not end of page

The operations list is:

1. **Open input file**
2. **Open output file**
3. **Close input file**
4. **Close output file**
5. **Read record from input file**

6. **Write record to output file**
7. **Initialize end of input file flag to false**
8. **Initialize line count to zero**
9. **Add 1 to line count**
10. **Stop processing**
11. **Advance to next page**

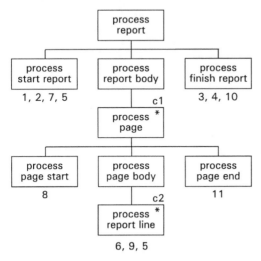

Figure 6.10   Final process structure diagram for demonstration 6.

6.6 Exercises

From the input and output file structures for the exercises below, establish the points of correspondence, merge the data structures to form a process structure, specify the conditions and operations and allocate the operations to the process structure.

1. From a file of student records you wish to list all students who are taking a course in history.

2. From the same student file you wish to list all the female students who are taking a mathematics module and print the total number of female maths students, followed by the total number of *all* students on the file.

3. From the same student file you wish to list all the chemistry students, subdivided into organic and inorganic chemistry, and give the total number of organic and inorganic chemistry students, as well as the combined total of all chemistry students.

4. From an employee file you wish to list all the employees earning over £30,000 who speak Italian.

5. From the same employee file you wish to produce a report with a title, then print out details of all employees who are not qualified in accountancy. The final part

of the report gives the total number of staff qualified in accountancy, the total number not so qualified, and the total number of employees.

6. From the same employee file you wish to produce a report with a title, then print out details of all employees who speak Russian and Greek, then give the following totals: total number of staff who speak Russian only; total number of staff who speak Greek only; and the grand total of all staff.

7. From the same employee file you wish to calculate the total number of employees who have a degree in mathematics, but work outside the London area. Only the total number is required, not a printed listing of the individuals.

6.7 Further reading

Holmes (1991), Sections 2.7–2.10.
King & Pardoe (1992), Chapters 4 and 5.
Storer (1991), Chapter 3.
Thompson (1989), Chapter 5 and Section 6.2.

CHAPTER 7

Generating schematic logic

The process structure, together with the conditions and operations that have been allocated, is converted into schematic logic. Keywords are used to identify each of the constructs.

7.1 Generating the schematic logic

There are schematic logic keywords to correspond with the logical constructs of sequence, selection and iteration. There are also keywords to indicate the end of a component and identify other choices within a selection:

seq   sequence
sel   selection
itr   iteration
 or   other choices within a selection (**alt** is also used)
end   end of structure (e.g. end of sequence, etc.)

We can read the schematic logic from the structure diagrams. Note that the operations appear as a sequence below the process box to which they have been allocated.

7.1.1 Generating the schematic logic for a sequence

A sequence with operations allocated is shown in Figure 7.1. Here, A is a sequence of B, C and D. Each of the terminal nodes has operations allocated to

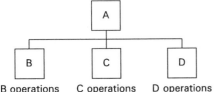

B operations   C operations   D operations
Figure 7.1   A sequence with operations allocated.

71

it. The order of these operations is important and therefore the operations themselves form a sequence. When the schematic logic for this structure is created, each construct is identified by a keyword, including the terminal nodes that are treated as being sequences of the operations that they contain.

The schematic logic for the sequence structure shown in Figure 7.1 is:

```
A seq
    B seq
        do B operations
    B end
    C seq
        do C operations
    C end
    D seq
        do D operations
    D end
A end
```

7.1.2 Generating the schematic logic for an iteration

An iteration with operations allocated is shown in Figure 7.2. In this structure diagram, G is an iteration of H. The elementary component H has been allocated a number of operations; as the order of operations is important, H is regarded as a sequence of these operations.

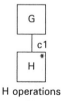

H operations

Figure 7.2   An iteration with operations allocated.

There are two possible formats for describing a condition on an iteration. In the first format, the condition is tested to identify the point at which the value changes so that it becomes true, i.e. the test for exit is for *continuation* of the loop. In this context, the condition is being used to ask the question "should looping continue?". If exit from the loop depended on the detection of the end of the input file, the iteration would finish when the end of file marker was read. The test for end of file would return the value *false* until the end of file is encountered, whereupon the value *true* would be returned. The start of a statement **while not end of input file** is an example of this type of loop.

The schematic logic for the iteration structure shown in Figure 7.2 using the first format is:

```
G itr while not c1
    H seq
        do H operations
    H end
G end
```

In the second version, the condition is tested until the value changes so that it becomes false, i.e. the test for exit is for *termination* of the loop. In this context, the condition is being used to ask the question "should looping cease?". The test for exit from the loop could depend on a value being less than a designated maximum value. As looping continues, the counter is less than the target value and so the test for exit fails as the value *true* is returned. When the maximum value has been reached by the counter, the value *false* is returned as it is no longer true that the counter is less than the target value.

The statement **while i < max** is an example of this type of loop. In this context, the phrasing of the condition on the iteration may lend itself to the following schematic logic. Care must be taken to ensure that the structure is a true iteration (zero or more traversals of the loop) and not a repetition (at least one execution).

The schematic logic for the iteration structure shown in Figure 7.2 using the second format is:

```
G itr until c1
    H seq
        do H operations
    H end
G end
```

7.1.3 Generating the schematic logic for a selection

The selection construct with operations allocated is shown in Figure 7.3. In this structure diagram, I is a selection of J, K or L. Each of the selection components J, K and L has been allocated operations. In order to reflect the order in which the operations appear, components J, K and L are each considered to be sequence constructs, with the operations as sequence components.

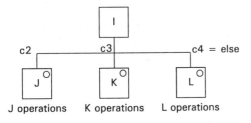

Figure 7.3 A selection with operations allocated.

A schematic logic for selection structure above:

```
I sel if c2
    J seq
        do J operations
    J end
I or c3
    K seq
        do K operations
    K end
I or c4 (else)
    L seq
        do L operations
    L end
I end
```

It is also possible to use the **alt** keyword to identify the different options within a selection. In this case the **alt** keyword would be substituted for **or** in the above schematic logic.

7.2 Converting process structure into schematic logic

At this stage we are now able to draw the input and output data structures, identify points of correspondence and merge to produce the basic process structure. This is then elaborated to cater for "housekeeping" activities, so that the conditions and operations can be allocated to the final process structure.

The next step is to write the schematic logic from the process structure diagrams, which constitutes the program itself, free from the constraints of implementation in any specific programming language. In order to obtain a program that runs in the required environment the schematic logic must be translated into the required programming language. This can be done manually, as described in Chapter 8. Alternatively, code generation may be performed with the aid of a software tool such as JSP-Tool or PDF, the use of which is described in Chapters 15 and 16 respectively.

At the present stage in the development of a program, we are able to convert a JSP process structure into schematic logic by reading the structure diagram. The keywords are used to indicate the beginning and end of each type of construct, and the operations allocated to terminal nodes of the process structure diagram are treated as sequence components. Conditions form part of the structure of the program, and are therefore part of the schematic logic, linked to selections and iterations.

Example

This example gives a process structure diagram (Fig. 7.4), and the schematic logic together with a description of each construct alongside the schematic logic (Table 7.1).

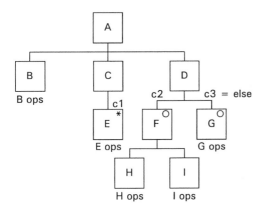

Figure 7.4   The process structure diagram.

Table 7.1   The schematic logic and a description.

Schematic logic	Description
`A seq`	A is a sequence of
`  B seq`	B elementary component
`    do B operations`	with B operations
`  B end`	end of B
`  C itr until c1`	C is an iteration while not c1
`    E seq`	E elementary component
`      do E operations`	with E operations
`    E end`	end of E
`  C end`	end of iteration C
`  D sel if c2`	D is a selection if c2
`    F seq`	F is a sequence of
`      H seq`	H elementary component
`        do H operations`	with H operations
`      H end`	end of H
`      I seq`	I elementary component
`        do I operations`	with I operations
`      I end`	end of I
`    F end`	end of sequence F
`  D or c3 (else)`	D otherwise
`    G seq`	G elementary component
`      do G operations`	with G operations
`    G end`	end of G
`  D end`	end of selection D
`A end`	end of sequence A

We could also read the structure in the following manner:

A is a **sequence** of B, C and D;
    B is an elementary component;
    C is an **iteration** of E;
        E is an elementary component;
    D is a **selection** of F or G
        F is a **sequence** of H and I
            H is an elementary component
            I is an elementary component
        G is an elementary component

7.3 Converting schematic logic into process structure

We can also reconstruct the structure diagram from the schematic logic, as shown in Table 7.2, and Figure 7.5.
    This could also be expressed as:

A is an **iteration** of B while c1
    B is a **sequence** of C, D and E
        C is an elementary component
        D is an elementary component
        E is a **selection** of F if c2
            F is an elementary component
        E otherwise G
            G is an elementary component

The diagram for this is shown as Figure 7.5.

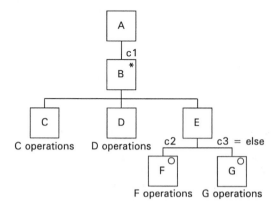

Figure 7.5 The process structure diagram reconstructed from the schematic logic of Table 7.2.

Table 7.2 The schematic logic and a description.

Schematic logic	Description
`A itr until c1`	A is an iteration while not c1
`  B seq`	B is a sequence of
`    C seq`	C elementary component
`      do C operations`	with C operations
`    C end`	end of C
`    D seq`	D elementary component
`      do D operations`	with D operations
`    D end`	end of D
`    E sel if c2`	E is a selection if c2
`      F seq`	F elementary component
`        do F operations`	with F operations
`      F end`	end of F
`    E or else`	E otherwise
`      G seq`	G elementary component
`        do G operations`	with G operations
`      G end`	end of G
`    E end`	end of selection E
`  B end`	end of sequence B
`A end`	end of iteration A

7.4 Generating schematic logic with operations and conditions

We can generate the schematic logic for the program we designed earlier to count the number of male and female students on a student file. Note that the operations that have been added have been described as sequences. The process structure is shown in Figure 7.6.

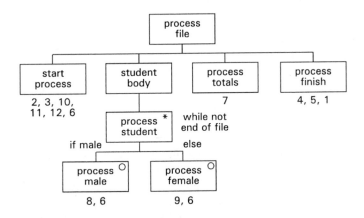

Figure 7.6 The process structure diagram for counting the number of male and female students.

77

The schematic logic from this process structure is as follows.

```
process file seq

    start process seq
        2. open student file
        3. open report file
        10. set female total to zero
        11. male total to zero
        12. initialize EOF student file to false
        6. read a student record
    start process end

    student body itr while not end of file

        process student record sel if male

            process male seq
                8. add 1 to male total
                6. read a student record
            process male end

        process student record or (else)

            process female seq
                9. add 1 to female total
                6. read a student record
            process female end

        process student record end

    student body end

    process totals seq
        7. print final totals on report file
    process totals end

    process finish seq
        4. close student file
        5. close report file
        1. stop processing
    process finish end

process file end
```

When converting the schematic logic into any particular programming language the individual operations must be translated into statements that are correct within the syntax of the chosen language. It is also necessary to convert the structure of the program into the chosen language to retain the components of the design: sequence, iteration and selection. It is the combination of the operations and the program design structure translated into a programming language that give rise to the final program.

It is important to maintain the structure of the schematic logic in the final program; we can do this by using comments to indicate the start and end of each component. The conditions and operations were specified and allocated to the final process structures that have been used as examples. Now that this has been done, the schematic logic for each can be generated.

Process structure 1: list employees
The final process structure is shown in Figure 7.7.

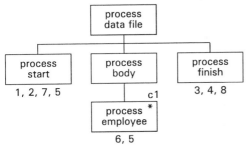

Figure 7.7 Final process structure diagram for demonstration 1.

The condition(s) are:
`c1: not end of input file`
The operations list is:
1. `Open input file`
2. `Open output file`
3. `Close input file`
4. `Close output file`
5. `Read record from input file`
6. `Write record to output report`
7. `Initialize end of input file flag to false`
8. `Stop processing`

The schematic logic is:

```
process data file seq

    process start seq
        do 1. open input file
        do 2. open output file
        do 7. initialize end of input file flag to false
        do 5. read record from input file
    process start end

    process body itr while not end of input file

        process employee seq
            do 6. write record to output report
            do 5. read record from input file
```

79

```
        process employee end
    process body end

    process finish seq
        do 3. close input file
        do 4. close output file
        do 8. stop processing
    process finish end

process data file end
```

Process structure 2: list employees and calculate total
The final process structure is shown in Figure 7.8.

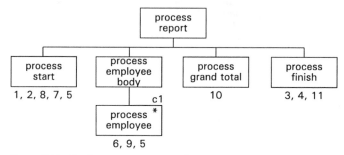

Figure 7.8 Final process structure diagram for demonstration 2.

The condition(s) are:
c1: not end of input file
The operations list is:
1. **Open input file**
2. **Open output file**
3. **Close input file**
4. **Close output file**
5. **Read record from input file**
6. **Write record to output file**
7. **Initialize end of input file flag to false**
8. **Initialize total to zero**
9. **Add 1 to total**
10. **Write total to output file**
11. **Stop processing**

The schematic logic is:

```
process report seq

    process start seq
        do 1. open input file
        do 2. open output file
```

```
      do 8. initialize total to zero
      do 7. initialize end of input file flag to false
      do 5. read record from input file
   process start end

   process body itr while not end of input file

      process employee seq
         do 6. write record to output report
         do 9. add 1 to total
         do 5. read record from input file
      process employee end

   process body end

   process grand total seq
      do 10. write total to output file
   process grand total end

   process finish seq
      do 3. close input file
      do 4. close output file
      do 11. stop processing
   process finish end

process report end
```

Process structure 3: list employees and calculate total with report title
The final process structure is shown in Figure 7.9.

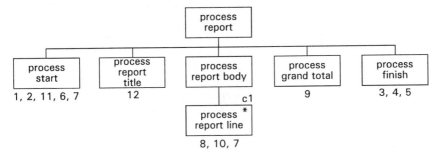

Figure 7.9 Final process structure diagram for demonstration 3.

The condition(s) are:
c1: not end of input file
The operations list is:
1. **Open input file**
2. **Open output file**
3. **Close input file**
4. **Close output file**

81

5. Stop processing
6. Initialize end of input file flag to false
7. Read record from input file
8. Write record to output file
9. Write total to output file
10. Add 1 to total
11. Initialize total to zero
12. Write "Employee Report" to output file

The schematic logic is:

```
process report seq

    process start seq
        do 1. open input file
        do 2. open output file
        do 11. initialize total to zero
        do 6. initialize end of input file flag to false
        do 7. read record from input file
    process start end

    process report title seq
        do 12. write "Employee Report" to output file
    process report title end

    process report body itr while not end of input file

        process report line seq
            do 8. write record to output report
            do 10. add 1 to total
            do 7. read record from input file
        process report line end

    process report body end

    process grand total seq
        do 9. write total to output file
    process grand total end

    process finish seq
        do 3. close input file
        do 4. close output file
        do 5. stop processing
    process finish end

process report end
```

Process structure 4: calculate total number of employees
The final process structure is shown in Figure 7.10.

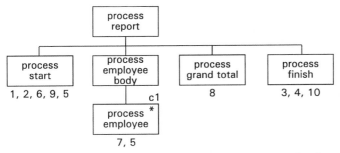

Figure 7.10   Final process structure diagram for demonstration 4.

The condition(s) are:

c1: not end of input file

The operations list is:

1. **Open input file**
2. **Open output file**
3. **Close input file**
4. **Close output file**
5. **Read record from input file**
6. **Initialize total to zero**
7. **Add 1 to total**
8. **Write total to output file**
9. **Initialize end of input file flag to false**
10. **Stop processing**

The schematic logic is:

```
process report seq

    process start seq
        do 1. open input file
        do 2. open output file
        do 6. initialize total to zero
        do 9. initialize end of input file flag to false
        do 5. read record from input file
    process start end

    process employee body itr while not end of input file

        process employee seq
            do 7. add 1 to total
            do 5. read record from input file
        process employee end

    process employee body end

    process grand total seq
        do 8. write total to output file
```

```
process grand total end

process finish seq
    do 3. close input file
    do 4. close output file
    do 10. stop processing
process finish end

process report end
```

Process structure 5: list female employees
The final process structure is shown in Figure 7.11.

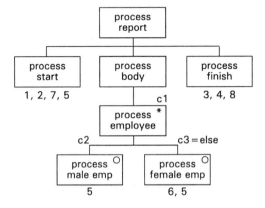

Figure 7.11   Final process structure diagram for demonstration 5.

The conditions are:
c1: not end of input file
c2: male employee
c3: else
The operations list is:
1. **Open input file**
2. **Open output file**
3. **Close input file**
4. **Close output file**
5. **Read record from input file**
6. **Write total to output file**
7. **Initialize end of input file flag to false**
8. **Stop processing**

The schematic logic is:

```
process report seq

    process start seq
        do 1. open input file
```

```
        do 2. open output file
        do 7. initialize end of input file flag to false
        do 5. read record from input file
    process start end

    process body itr while not end of input file

        process employee sel if male

            process male emp seq
                do 5. read record from input file
            process male emp end

        process employee or else

            process female emp seq
                do 6. write record to output report
                do 5. read record from input file
            process female emp end

        process employee end

    process body end

    process finish seq
        do 3. close input file
        do 4. close output file
        do 8. stop processing
    process finish end

process report end
```

Process structure 6: list employees, 50 records per page
The final process structure is shown in Figure 7.12.

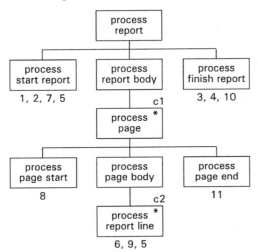

Figure 7.12 Final process structure diagram for demonstration 6.

The conditions are:

```
c1: not end of input file
c2: not end of input file, not end of page (line count < 50)
```

The operations list is:

1. `Open input file`
2. `Open output file`
3. `Close input file`
4. `Close output file`
5. `Read record from input file`
6. `Write record to output file`
7. `Initialize end of input file flag to false`
8. `Initialize line count to zero`
9. `Add 1 to line count`
10. `Stop processing`
11. `Advance to next page`

The schematic logic is:

```
process report seq

    process start report seq
        do 1. open input file
        do 2. open output file
        do 7. initialize end of input file flag to false
        do 5. read record from input file
    process start report end

    process report body itr while not end of input file

        process page seq

            process page start seq
                do 8. initialize line count to zero
            process page start end

            process page body itr while not end of input
            file, not end of page (line count < 50)

                process report line seq
                    do 6. write record to output file
                    do 9. add 1 to line count
                    do 5. read record from input file
                process report line end

            process page body end

            process page end seq
                do 11. advance to next page
            process page end end

        process page end
```

```
process report body end

process finish report seq
    do 3. close input file
    do 4. close output file
    do 10. stop processing
process finish report end

process report end
```

7.5 Exercises

1. Write the schematic logic for the structures shown in (a) Figure 7.13, (b) Figure
   7.14, (c) Figure 7.15 and (d) Figure 7.16.

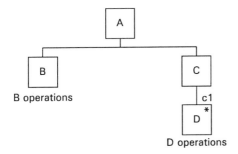

Figure 7.13 Structure for Exercise 1(a).

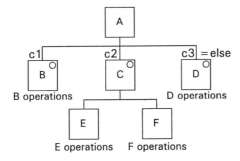

Figure 7.14 Structure for Exercise 1(b).

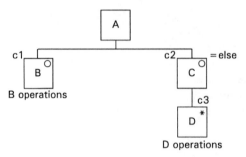

Figure 7.15 Structure for Exercise 1(c).

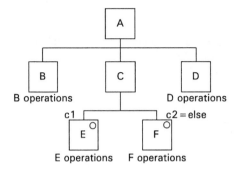

Figure 7.16 Structure for Exercise 1(d).

2. Reconstruct the process structures from the schematic logic:

(a) **A seq**

    B seq

        C seq

            do C operations

        C end

        D seq

            do D operations

        D end

    B end

    E sel if c1

        F seq

            do F operations

        F end

    E or c2 (else)

        G seq

            do G operations

        G end

```
      E  end
      H  itr while c3
         J  seq
              do J operations
         J  end
      H  end
    A  end
```

(b)
```
    A  itr while c1
      B  sel if c2
         C  itr while c5
            D  seq
                do D operations
            D  end
         C  end
      B  or c3
         L  seq
            E  seq
                do E operations
            E  end
            F  sel if c6
               P  seq
                  G  seq
                      do G operations
                  G  end
                  H  seq
                      do H operations
                  H  end
               P  end
            F  or c7 (else)
               J  seq
                  do J operations
               J  end
            F  end
         L  end
      B  or c4 (else)
         K  seq
            do K operations
         K  end
      B  end
    A  end
```

Consider the following problems. Generate the schematic logic for each process structure. (Note that some of these problems are continued from exercises in the previous chapter, whereas others are variations on similar exercises.)

i. From a file of student records, you wish to list all students who are taking a course in history.

ii. From the same student file you wish to list all the female students who are taking a mathematics module, and print the total number of female maths students, followed by the total number of *all* students on the file.

iii. From the same student file you wish to list all the chemistry students, subdivided into organic and inorganic chemistry, and give the total number of organic and inorganic chemistry students, as well as the combined total of all chemistry students.

iv. From an employee file you wish to list all the employees earning over £30,000 who speak Italian.

v. From the same employee file you wish to produce a report with a title, then print out details of all employees who are not qualified in accountancy. The final part of the report gives the total number of staff qualified in accountancy, the total number not so qualified, and the total number of employees.

vi. From the same employee file you wish to produce a report with a title, then print out details of all employees who speak Russian and Greek, then give the following totals: total number of staff who speak Russian only; total number of staff who speak Greek only; and the grand total of all staff.

vii. From the same employee file you wish to calculate the total number of employees who have a degree in mathematics, but work outside the London area. Only the total number is required, not a printed listing of the individuals.

7.6 Further reading

Holmes (1991), Chapters 5, 8 and 9, Sections 13.1–13.2.
King & Pardoe (1992), Chapters 6 and 7.
Storer (1991), Chapter 4.
Thompson (1989), Section 6.

CHAPTER 8

Producing code

The process structure diagram, with its conditions and operations, is converted into schematic logic. The schematic logic can be translated into a programming language, such as Pascal, C or COBOL.

8.1 Coding the operations

The operations in the schematic logic for counting the numbers of male and female students would translate into Pascal, COBOL and C as follows.

Operation 1. Stop processing

```
Pascal    end
C         return;
          };
COBOL  STOP RUN.
```

Operation 2. Open student file

```
Pascal    assign(stufile, 'stufile');
          reset(stufile);
C         studentfile = fopen("stufile.dat", "r");
COBOL  OPEN STUFILE FOR INPUT.
```

Operation 3. Open report file

```
Pascal    assign(report, 'report');
          rewrite(report);
C         studentfile = fopen("file2", "w");
COBOL  OPEN REPORT FOR OUTPUT.
```

Operation 4. Close student file

```
Pascal    close(stufile);
C         fclose(studentfile);
COBOL  CLOSE STUFILE.
```

Operation 5. Close report file

```
Pascal    close(report);
C         fclose(reportfile);
COBOL     CLOSE REPORT.
```

Operation 6. Read a student record

```
Pascal    readln(stufile, name, sex);
C         fscanf(studentfile, "%s %s", name, sex);
COBOL     READ STUFILE AT END MOVE "Y" TO EOF.
```

This assumes that the data is stored in a text file and that there are two string variables **name** and **sex** into which the data is read. In Pascal it is important to use **readln** rather than **read** when testing for the end of the file.

Note that in COBOL an explicit reference is made to updating the end of file flag, **EOF**. It is also necessary to initialize the end of file flag before the first **read** statement is executed; this is done here in operation 12.

Operation 7. Print final totals on report file

```
Pascal    writeln(report, female-total:10, male-total:10);
C         fprintf(reportfile, "\n %10d %10d",female_total,
          male_total);
COBOL     MOVE FEM-TOTAL, MALE-TOTAL TO REPORT-LINE.
          PRINT REPORT-LINE AFTER 1.
```

It is only possible to print one line at a time in COBOL, so it is important to **MOVE** all data that is to be printed on one line into the printing area before generating the output.

Operation 8. Add 1 to male total

```
Pascal    male_total := male_total + 1;
C         male_total++;
COBOL     ADD 1 TO MALE-TOTAL.
```

Operation 9. Add 1 to female total

```
Pascal    female_total := female_total + 1;
C         female_total++;
COBOL     ADD 1 TO FEMALE-TOTAL.
```

Operation 10. Set female total to zero

```
Pascal    female_total := 0;
C         female_total = 0;
COBOL     MOVE ZERO TO FEMALE-TOTAL.
```

Operation 11. Set male total to zero
Pascal   `male_total := 0;`
C   `male_total = 0;`
COBOL   **`MOVE ZERO TO MALE-TOTAL.`**

Operation 12. Initialize **EOF** *student file to false*
Pascal   not required
C   not required
COBOL   **`MOVE "N" TO EOF.`**

In Pascal and C the programmer is not required to initialize the end-of-file flag. The variable **EOF** is set to false until an attempt is made to read past the end of file when **EOF** will automatically be set to true. In COBOL, however, the programmer is required to initialize the end-of-file flag, and supplement the read statement (operation 6) with an instruction to update **EOF** when an attempt has been made to read past the end of file. The end-of-file flag must be initialized before the first read statement is made in a program.

8.2 Coding the control structures

It can be seen that each elementary operation can be translated easily into a programming language. Notice that at this stage only the operations have been translated. It will also be necessary to implement the control structures (selections and iterations) in the chosen language, but these control structures are part of the program design and must not appear in the operations list.

8.2.1 Coding a sequence

It is simple to code a sequence. All operations within a sequence are given in the order that they appear in the schematic logic when they are translated into a programming language.

```
<statement>
<statement>
...
<statement>
```

8.2.2 Coding an iteration

The implementation of an iteration depends on the programming language in use. It will be remembered that an iteration may occur zero or more times, so that it would not be appropriate to use a **repeat** . . . **until** construct as a repetition can occur one or more times; this could mean a loop being executed once when it should not be executed at all.

In Pascal, a typical implementation of an iteration would involve the use of a **while** loop:

```
while not EOF do
    <statement>;
```

If the statement is a compound statement, i.e. there are several statements to be executed within the **while** loop, the statements are grouped together between **begin** and **end**, thus:

```
while not EOF do
    begin
        <compound statement>
    end;
```

It would also be possible to use a **for** loop, for example, if dealing with a fixed number of elements in an array:

```
for i := 1 to max do
    <statement>
```

Note that in Pascal **<statement>** may be a compound statement grouping several simple statements together between **begin** and **end**. In C, a **while** loop is similar to the analogous Pascal construct, with statements being grouped together within braces (i.e. { and }).

Different versions of COBOL have different facilities available for implementing an iteration. It should be possible to use **IF** . . . **THEN** . . . **GO TO** in conjunction with **GO TO** . . . to achieve the iterative construct in all versions of COBOL:

```
BEGIN-LOOP.
IF EOF = "Y" THEN GO TO END-LOOP.
    <STATEMENT . . . STATEMENT>
GO TO BEGIN-LOOP.
END-LOOP.
```

This will mean that the terminating condition is always tested for before entering the loop, ensuring that the iteration will execute zero or more times as required.

Some versions of COBOL provide an in-line **PERFORM** statement, which is similar to the **while** construct in Pascal:

```
PERFORM UNTIL <condition>
    <STATEMENT   . . .   STATEMENT>
END-PERFORM.
```

Note that it is not necessary to use the **PERFORM** verb other than for implementing iterations. Translating the schematic logic into program code in this way gives rise to "flat code", that is, there are no procedures (or subroutines or paragraphs, depending on the terminology).

It is possible to implement schematic logic using nested **PERFORM** statements or procedures, but care must be taken to maintain the structure of the program design by ensuring that the implementation follows the hierarchy of the design. Implementing the program design in other than flat code will give rise to problems when the more advanced techniques of JSP are used (see Chapter 11 on backtracking).

8.2.3 Coding a selection

In order to represent a selection, the **if . . . then . . . else** statement in Pascal can be used:

```
if number > limit then
    <statement>
else
    <statement>
```

If there are more than two choices the programmer may choose to implement these as nested **if . . . then . . . else** statements; alternatively a **case** statement could be employed. Turbo Pascal provides an **else** clause to cover any instances that are not dealt with explicitly in the **case**; standard Pascal does not provide an **else** clause with **case**, so in these circumstances it would be necessary to include the **case** statement within an **if . . . then . . . else** statement in order to ensure that all eventualities have a clearly defined operation. In C, the **if** statement has a similar format to the Pascal version, with the exception that the keyword **then** is not required. Statements within the **if** and **else** parts are grouped together within braces (i.e. { and }).

In COBOL, the **IF . . . ELSE** statement can be used:

```
IF NUMBER < LIMIT GO TO LOW-NUM
    <STATEMENT  . . .   STATEMENT>
GO TO END-OF-IF.
LOW-NUM.
    <STATEMENT  . . .   STATEMENT>
END-OF-IF.
```

Implementing a selection in this way in COBOL means that the code tests for the condition not being true in order to pass control elsewhere. When the condition is not met, the statements immediately after the **IF** are executed; this avoids having to use the **ELSE** part of the **IF** statement, although the disadvantage is that the test has to be expressed in a negative manner.

It is possible to use the **IF . . . ELSE** statement in COBOL in conjunction with **NEXT SENTENCE** to force the transfer of control to implement a selection:

```
PROCESS-NUMBER-SEL.
    IF NUMBER > LIMIT
        NEXT SENTENCE
    ELSE
        GO TO PROCESS-NUMBER-ELSE.
```

```
PROCESS-NUM-GREATER-SEQ.
        <STATEMENT ... STATEMENT>
PROCESS-NUM-GREATER-END.
GO TO PROCESS-NUMBER-END.
PROCESS-NUMBER-ELSE.
     <STATEMENT ... STATEMENT>
PROCESS-NUMBER-END.
```

The disadvantage here is that the "true" part of the IF statement does not appear within the IF statement itself.

Notice that in the COBOL implementation of the iteration and selection structures use has been made of the GO TO construct. The use of GO TO is often frowned upon because it can lead to "spaghetti code", with the threads of control being difficult to follow even by the original programmer. However, the use of GO TO in the context of iterations and selections is a disciplined use of the structure. If the phrase "transfer control" were to be used instead, the stigma attached to GO TO would be avoided altogether.

It is perhaps worth remembering that when a program is written in a high-level language (such as Pascal, C or COBOL) little thought is given to the structure of the executable code that is produced by the compiler. In the same way, the designer of a program using the JSP methodology should concentrate on aspects of design other than the appearance of the eventual code.

If a CASE (computer-aided software engineering) tool (such as PDF or JSP-Tool) is used, the conversion to a programming language can be achieved through the use of a code-generator module, thus avoiding the mechanical conversion of schematic logic into code by hand.

8.3 Converting schematic logic into a programming language

Combining the operations with the structure of the schematic logic enables a set of instructions to be written that will correspond exactly to the schematic logic of the original design. A complete program would also require the programmer to define the names and data types of all constants, variables and data structures (such as arrays) in the appropriate section of the program in order to produce executable code.

The example discussed earlier of counting the number of male and female students from a student file is developed further here. The schematic logic generated from the JSP process structure is converted into Pascal, C and COBOL to illustrate how the translation of elementary operations and control structures can be achieved within the framework of the program design using the JSP methodology.

The schematic logic from this example process structure has been annotated to indicate the way in which each part will be translated into a programming language, whether as a comment, a program construct or a program statement. Note that not all languages will have exactly the same relationship between schematic logic and the program code; for example, COBOL requires that the end-of-file flag is explicitly set within the program, whereas this is not necessary in Pascal. A general rule of thumb is that operations translate into program statements; iteration and selection structures convert into program constructs (e.g. **while** for an iteration and **if** for a selection), and sequence structures are represented by comments in the final program. The end-of-structure indicators in the schematic logic may correspond to end-of-program construct keywords in the program, or may be represented by comments (e.g. the end of a program is designated by **end.** in Pascal; this would reflect **process file end** in the schematic logic).

The outline relationship between the schematic logic and a programming language is as follows:

```
process file seq                              comment
  start process seq                           comment
    2. open student file                      statement
    3. open report file                       statement
    10. set female total to zero              statement
    11. male total to zero                    statement
    12. Initialize EOF student file to false  statement (if req.)
    6. read a student record                  statement
  start process end                           comment
  student body itr while not end of file      CONSTRUCT
    process student record sel if male        CONSTRUCT
      process male seq                         comment
        8. Add 1 to male total                statement
        6. read a student record              statement
      process male end                         comment
    process student record or (else)          CONSTRUCT
      process female seq                       comment
        9. add 1 to female total              statement
        6. read a student record              statement
      process female end                       comment
    process student record end                 comment
  student body end                             comment
  process totals seq                           comment
    7. print final totals on report file      statement
  process totals end                           comment
  process finish seq                           comment
    4. close student file                     statement
    5. close report file                      statement
    1. stop processing                        statement (if req.)
  process finish end                           comment
process file end                               end of program
```

The schematic logic would translate into Pascal as:

```
begin
(* process file seq *)
   (* start process seq *)
   assign(stufile, 'stufile');
   reset(stufile);
   assign(report, 'report');
   rewrite(report);
   female_total := 0;
   male_total := 0;
   readln(stufile, name, sex);
(* start process end *)
(* student body itr *)
   while not eof(stufile) do
      (* process student record sel if male *)
         if sex = 'male' then
         begin
            (* process male seq *)
               male_total := male_total + 1;
               readln(stufile, name, sex);
            (* process male end *)
         end
         else
         begin
      (* process student record or (else) *)
            (* process female seq *)
               female_total := female_total + 1;
               readln(stufile, name, sex);
            (* process female end *)
         end;
      (* process student record end *)
   (* process student body end *)
   (* process totals seq *)
      (writeln(report, female_total:10, male_total:10);
      close(stufile);
      close(report);
      end.
   (* process totals end *)
(* process file end *)
```

CONVERTING SCHEMATIC LOGIC INTO A PROGRAMMING LANGUAGE

The schematic logic would translate into C as:

```c
void main()
{
/* process file seq */
    /* start process seq */
        studentfile = fopen("stufile.dat", "r");
        reportfile = fopen("file2", "w");
        female_total = 0;
        male_total = 0;
        fscanf(studentfile, "%s %s", name, sex);
    /* start process end */
    /* process student itr while not end of file */
        while(!feof(studentfile))
        {
        /* process student record sel if male */
            if(strcmp(sex,"male")==0)
            {
            /* process male seq */
                male_total++;
                fscanf(studentfile, "%s %s", name, sex);
            /* process male end */
            }
            else
            {
        /* process student record or (else) */
            /* process female seq */
                female_total++;
                fscanf(studentfile, "%s %s", name, sex);
            /* process female end */
            };
        /* process student record end */
        };
    /* process student body end */
    /* process student end */
    /* process totals seq */
        fprintf(reportfile, "\n %10d %10d",female_total,
         male_total);
        fclose(studentfile);
        fclose(reportfile);
    /* process totals end */
/* process file end */
return;
};
```

Finally, the same schematic logic would translate into COBOL as:

```
PROCESS-FILE-SEQ.
    START-PROCESS-SEQ.
        OPEN STUFILE FOR INPUT.
        OPEN REPORT FOR OUTPUT.
        MOVE ZERO TO FEMALE_TOTAL.
        MOVE ZERO TO MALE_TOTAL.
        MOVE "N" TO EOF.
        READ STUFILE AT END MOVE "Y" TO EOF.
    START-PROCESS-END.
    STUDENT-BODY-ITR.
    IF EOF = "Y" THEN GO TO STUDENT-BODY-END.
        PROCESS-STUDENT-RECORD-SEL.
        IF STUDENT NOT MALE THEN
            GO TO PROCESS-STUDENT-RECORD-ELSE.
            PROCESS-MALE-SEQ.
                ADD 1 TO MALE_TOTAL.
                READ STUFILE AT END MOVE "Y" TO EOF.
            PROCESS-MALE-END.
        GO TO PROCESS-STUDENT-RECORD-END.
        PROCESS-STUDENT-RECORD-ELSE.
            PROCESS-FEMALE-SEQ.
                ADD 1 TO FEMALE_TOTAL.
                READ STUFILE AT END MOVE "Y" TO EOF.
            PROCESS-FEMALE-END.
        PROCESS-STUDENT-RECORD-END.
    GO TO STUDENT-BODY-ITR.
    STUDENT-BODY-END.
    PROCESS-TOTALS-SEQ.
        MOVE FEMALE-TOTAL, MALE-TOTAL TO REPORT-LINE.
        PRINT REPORT-LINE AFTER 1.
        CLOSE STUFILE.
        CLOSE REPORT.
        STOP RUN.
    PROCESS-TOTALS-END.
PROCESS-FILE-END.
```

Although paragraph headings are normally written in column 8 of a COBOL program, the headings have been indented here in order to stress the similarity to the schematic logic.

8.4 Creating the final program

It is important to remember to add data declarations in producing the final program; the schematic logic will only give the program structure, not the data structures. The data structures will need to be declared in the appropriate manner for the programming language in question in order to produce a complete program that can be compiled and executed.

We are now in a position to make use of a CASE tool, such as PDF (Program Development Facility) or JSP-Tool which will allow us to draw the process structure, add conditions, allocate operations and generate the schematic logic for us. If the operations are extended to include the code of a particular programming language, we can generate code so that the program that we design using JSP can be run.

The initial activities of creating the input and output data structures, finding the correspondences and merging on the points of correspondence to produce the process structure diagram must be carried out manually before the software tool can be employed. The activities that need to be carried out to build the process structure using such a tool are:

1. Create process structure diagram
   - create the process structure by adding boxes
   - give names to the individual process boxes
2. Allocate conditions
   - specify conditions and allocate to iterations and selections
3. Allocate operations
   - enter operations list
   - insert operations box below each terminal node
     for operation numbers
   - allocate operations to the process structure
4. Generate program text
   - generate schematic logic
   - translate schematic logic into a programming language
   - add data declarations to the program

After converting the design into a program, it will be necessary to carry out testing and debugging to ensure that the program does what is expected. If the design principles have been followed, testing and debugging should identify simple errors (syntax errors, run-time errors such as array subscript out of bounds, or a condition not properly specified). A major redesign should not be necessary unless the user requirements have substantially altered.

8.5 Exercises

1. Convert the following schematic logic into the programming language of your choice.

(a) `process total staff seq`
```
        process start seq
            open staff file for input
            open report file for output
            set staff total to zero
            read staff record from input staff file
        process start end
        process staff body itr while not end of staff file
            process record seq
                add 1 to staff total
                read staff record from input staff file
            process record end
        process staff body end
        process total seq
            write company title to output report file
            write staff total to output report file
            write date to output report file
        process total end
        process finish seq
            close staff file
            close report file
            stop processing
        process finish end
    process total staff end
```

(b) `process uk/abroad staff seq`
```
        process begin seq
            open staff file for input
            open report file for output
            set uk-total, abroad-total, grand-total to zero
            write company title to output report file
            read staff record from input staff file
        process begin end
        process main body itr while not end of staff file
            process staff record sel if uk-staff
                write staff record to report file
                add 1 to uk-total
                add 1 to grand-total
                read staff record from input staff file
            process staff record or (else)
```

```
            add 1 to abroad-total
            add 1 to grand-total
            read staff record from input staff file
        process staff record end
    process main body end
    process total seq
        write uk-total to output report file
        write abroad-total to output report file
        write grand-total to output report file
        write date to output report file
    process total end
    process finish seq
        close staff file
        close report file
        stop processing
    process finish end
process uk/abroad staff end
```

Consider the following problems. Produce the code for each process structure, using the programming language of your choice. (Note that some of these problems are continued from exercises in the previous chapter, whereas others are variations on similar exercises.)

2. From a file of student records, you wish to list all students who are taking a course in history.

3. From the same student file you wish to list all the female students who are taking a mathematics module, and print the total number of female maths students, followed by the total number of *all* students on the file.

4. From the same student file you wish to list all the chemistry students, subdivided into organic and inorganic chemistry, and give the total number of organic and inorganic chemistry students, as well as the combined total of all chemistry students.

5. From an employee file you wish to list all the employees earning over £30,000 who speak Italian.

6. From the same employee file you wish to produce a report with a title, then print out details of all employees who are not qualified in accountancy. The final part of the report gives the total number of staff qualified in accountancy, the total number not so qualified, and the total number of employees.

7. From the same employee file you wish to produce a report with a title, then print out details of all employees who speak Russian and Greek, then give the following totals: total number of staff who speak Russian only; total number of staff who speak Greek only; and the grand total of all staff.

8. From the same employee file you wish to calculate the total number of employees who have a degree in mathematics, but work outside the London area. Only the total number is required, not a printed listing of the individuals.

9. From the same employee file you wish to print out details of all employees who speak either French or German (or both) and print the total number of staff in each of these categories.

8.6 Further reading

Delannoy (1989).
Farmer (1989).
Findlay & Watt (1990).
Gottfried (1990).
Haiduk (1990).
Holmes (1991), Chapters 5, 8 and 9 and Sections 13.1–13.2.
King & Pardoe (1992), Chapters 6 and 7.
Konvalina & Wileman (1987).
Perry (1993).
Robson (1990).
Storer (1991), Chapter 4.
Thompson (1989), Section 6.

CHAPTER 9

Error handling

9.1 Classifying input data

Input data can be classified in different ways, depending on whether it is what was required, what was anticipated or otherwise.

- *Good data* can be defined as input to the system as intended. This contrasts with *error data*, which can be described as data input to the system which differs from that intended.
- *Valid data* can be defined as input data for which a program operation is specified, as opposed to *invalid data*, which categorizes data for which no program operation is specified.

Programs check for *error data*, not invalid data. When a program checks for error data, an operation is specified for that error; such an error is therefore not invalid data. In circumstances where no operation has been defined because an error has not been anticipated, then that is *invalid data* as the program has no action defined.

We have only considered error-free examples in the programs that have been designed so far. We need to extend the design of our programs so that errors may be trapped and dealt with accordingly, rather than cause the program to fail when unexpected data values are encountered.

Errors may be of different kinds:

- **Insertion** something *in addition* to the correct data has been entered; all the right data will be there, but with errors also present;
- **Substitution** something *instead of* the correct data has been entered; the right number of records will be present, but some records will be incorrect;
- **Omission** one or more elements of the correct data are *missing*; the records that are present are correct, but some are not present.

In making allowances for the possibility of error, we elaborate the basic structure, so that good data are correctly processed and error data are dealt with appropriately. For each example, the basic structure will be elaborated for errors of one particular type and then further elaborated to trap errors of the other two types.

Example

A session at the terminal takes the following form:

> start the terminal session with command statement S1; several S2 command statements may follow, followed by command statement S3; the session is terminated by the command statement S4.

We can draw the process structure that represents this interaction directly as each input is immediately followed by output, i.e. the structure is already "merged" as input and ouput follow each other so closely that the data structures would be the identical and hence the process structure (Figure 9.1) would be the same.

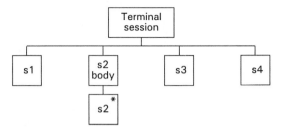

Figure 9.1 Process structure for a terminal session.

If we are dealing with a terminal session it is reasonable to consider that an operator might well make typing errors, and therefore it is necessary to define operations for the case in which error data have been entered.

9.2 Errors of insertion

In dealing with errors of insertion, all the correct data items will be encountered, but additional data (errors) may also be found. In trapping errors of insertion it is important to recognize the good data, and treat such data accordingly, and also to take appropriate action when error data are discovered.

9.2.1 Elaborating for errors of insertion

In order to elaborate for errors of insertion, the first step is to identify iterations in the structure; the iterated component is converted into a selection so that there is a choice of an item of data being either good data or error data. If the iterated component is already a selection, a selection component for errors is added in order to cater for error data as well as the other possibilities.

Iterations to trap errors (known as "garbage groups" or "garbage collectors") are then added to sequences to catch other errors. A "garbage group" will continue to deal with error data until an item of good data is encountered. A "garbage group" has the structure shown in Figure 9.2.

Figure 9.2   The structure of a "garbage group".

The operations allocated to the iterated component would include a read statement so that the condition on the iteration (to determine whether a valid item had been entered) can be tested until such time as a valid entry is made.

The terminal session, elaborated for errors of insertion, would now appear as shown in Figure 9.3. It can be seen, by reading through the structure, that the elaboration for errors of insertion will enable the correct data to be processed, and also allow any error data to be dealt with in an appropriate manner.

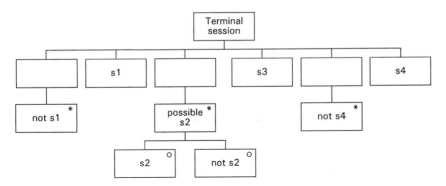

Figure 9.3   The terminal session, elaborated for errors of insertion.

Any initial errors, i.e. anything that is not a command statement S1, are trapped by the garbage collector until a command statement S1 is entered; there would therefore need to be an initial read operation to test the first item entered. This implies that for "housekeeping" purposes, another sequence component needs to be added to the process structure diagram in order to hold this initial read operation.

The process structure elaborated for errors of insertion would now have the appearance of Figure 9.4.

The schematic logic for the initial read and the garbage collector would contain the following operations:

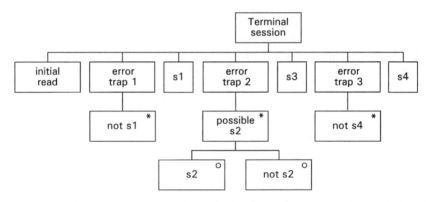

Figure 9.4 The terminal session, elaborated for errors of insertion, with an initial read.

```
initial-read seq
    operation: read data item
initial-read end
error-trap-1 itr while not S1
    not-S1 seq
        operation: print error message
        operation: read data item
    not-S1 end
error-trap-1 end
```

If there are no errors the garbage collector, being an iteration, executes zero times and control is passed directly to the S1 component.

Following the S1, zero, one or more S2s are expected and will be handled by the S2 selection component within the iteration. If there are any errors before the first S2, between several S2s or after the last S2, these will be processed by the error selection component within the iteration. As the error selection component within the iteration will pick up any errors between an S2 and an S3, a garbage collector is not required before the S3 component.

The schematic logic for this error trap would contain the following:

```
error-trap-2 itr while not S3
    possible-S2 sel if S2
        s2 seq
            operation: process S2
            operation: read data item
        S2 end
    possible-S2 or (else)
        not-S2 seq
            operation: print error message
            operation: read data item
        not-S2 end
    possible-S2 end
error-trap-2 end
```

After an S3, there may be zero, one or more errors before the S4, and a garbage collector will detect and handle these. The schematic logic for this garbage collector would contain the following:

```
error-trap-3 itr while not S4
    not-S4 seq
        operation: print error message
        operation: read data item
    not-S4 end
error-trap-3 end
```

S4 is the last item of good data; it would also be possible to have a garbage collector after the S4 component in order to pick up any errors after the S4, as any subsequent data is not required and could therefore be regarded as an error. This would introduce a fourth error trap, and the schematic logic for this garbage collector would be:

```
error-trap-4 itr while not end of file
    end-trap seq
        operation: print error message
        operation: read data item
    end-trap end
error-trap-4 end
```

The above structure will be able to trap errors of insertion (**x**), such as:

(a) `S1 S2 S2 S3 S4`
(b) `x x S1 S2 S3 S4`
(c) `x S1 x S2 x S3 x S4`
(d) `S1 x x S2 x S3 x S4`
(e) `x S1 S2 S3 x S4`
(f) `S1 S2 x S2 x S3 x S4`
(g) `S1 x S2 x x S2 x x S2 x x S3 S4`

If the data contain errors of other types, the above structure will not be able to deal with these successfully. It will be necessary to elaborate the structure further to cater for errors of substitution and omission in addition to errors of insertion.

9.2.2 Elaborating for errors of insertion and further errors

When the original structure has been elaborated for one kind of error (here, errors of insertion) it is then possible to elaborate the structure further so that other errors are also trapped. The above structure is now elaborated (Fig. 9.5) for errors of insertion and further errors (i.e. substitution and omission), and will be able to detect any error it meets when processing.

The structure in Figure 9.5 will deal with any errors in the data, whether they are errors of insertion, substitution or omission. Any errors will be trapped by the initial garbage group until a valid item of data is encountered.

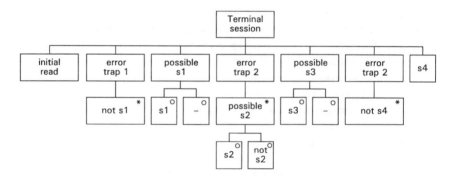

Figure 9.5 The terminal session, elaborated for errors of insertion and further errors.

As the structure has been elaborated for all three kinds of error, it is possible that S1 may be present or absent. If S1 is present, the S1 selection component will be activated. If S1 is absent either something else has been entered, in which case the garbage collector before S1 will deal with this error of substitution, or S1 has been omitted, in which case the null branch of the selection component (designated by "-" in the box) will be taken.

On entering the iteration of possible S2 components, a good S2 will activate the S2 selection component, whereas an error will take the other selection component. It is not necessary to have a null component as an iteration already caters for zero or more occurrences of an element. As before, the error selection component within the S2 iteration will trap any errors between S2 and S3. It is possible that there will be no S3, in which case the null component of the S3 selection would be taken. The garbage collector will trap any errors between an S3 and an S4 component, as before. This structure assumes that an S4 item at least will be present (i.e. it is possible to have S4 only in this structure, with no other data present).

The schematic logic for the fully elaborated process structure diagram would be as follows:

```
Terminal-Session seq
    initial-read seq
        operation: read data item
    initial-read end
    error-trap-1 itr while not S1, S2, S3, S4
        not-S1 seq
            operation: print error message
            operation: read data item
        not-S1 end
    error-trap-1 end
    possible-S1 sel if S1
```

```
         S1 seq
            operation: process command statement S1
            operation: read data item
         S1 end
      possible-S1 or (else)
         null-S1 seq
            operation: process missing S1 (do nothing)
         null-S1 end
      possible-S1 end
      error-trap-2 itr while not S3, S4
         possible-S2 sel if S2
            S2 seq
               operation: process command statement S2
               operation: read data item
            S2 end
         possible-S2 or (else)
            not-S2 seq
               operation: print error message
               operation: read data item
            not-S2 end
         possible-S2 end
      error-trap-2 end
      possible-S3 sel if S3
         S3 seq
            operation: process command statement S3
            operation: read data item
         S3 end
      possible-S3 or (else)
         null-S3 seq
            operation: process missing S3 (do nothing)
         null-S3 end
      possible-S3 end
      error-trap-3 itr while not S4
         not-S4 seq
            operation: print error message
            operation: read data item
         not-S4 end
      error-trap-3 end
      S4 seq
         operation: process command statement S4
      S4 end
Terminal-Session end
```

The fully elaborated structure will deal with the following as valid data, containing both good and error data items. Error data are represented by **x**:

(a) **s1 s2 s2 s3 s4**

(b) **x x s1 s2 x s4**

(c) **x x x x s4**

(d) **s1 x x s2 x s3 x s4**

(e) **x s1 x s3 x s4**

(f) **s2 x s2 x x s4**

(g) **s4**

9.3 Errors of substitution

9.3.1 Elaboration for errors of substitution

When we elaborate for errors of substitution we are trying to trap errors where one entry has been made (i.e. substituted) in place of another. We therefore need to introduce a selection to cater for each data element being correct or in substitution for a correct item. The structure in Figure 9.6 will be able to process correct data or an error that has appeared instead of an expected data item.

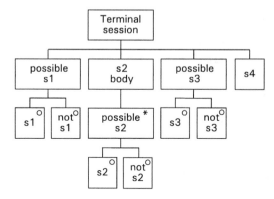

Figure 9.6 The terminal session, elaborated for errors of substitution.

Here, too, we will also need to add a "housekeeping" box to hold the initial read statement that will accept the first entry made by the user. The addition of this activity at the start of the program will enable the first entry to be tested to establish whether it is a command statement S1 or an error.

Where errors of substitution are expected, the correct number of data items will be present, but some of these elements will be in error, i.e. they have been substituted for the correct items.

The process structure diagram with the initial read added will be as in Figure 9.7.

112

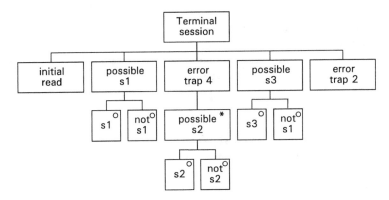

Figure 9.7 The terminal session, elaborated for errors of substitution, with an initial read.

The test on each selection will differentiate between correct data and errors. The schematic logic for the process structure elaborated for errors of substitution will be:

```
Terminal-Session seq
    initial-read seq
        operation: read data item
    initial-read end
    possible-S1 sel if S1
        S1 seq
            operation: process command statement S1
            operation: read data item
        S1 end
    possible-S1 or (else)
        not-S1 seq
            operation: process error
            operation: read data item
        not-S1 end
    possible-S1 end
    error-trap-A itr while not S3, S4
        possible-S2 sel if S2
            S2 seq
                operation: process command statement S2
                operation: read data item
            S2 end
        possible-S2 or (else)
            not-S2 seq
                operation: process error
                operation: read data item
            not-S2 end
        possible-S2 end
    error-trap-A end
```

113

```
        possible-S3 sel if S3
           S3 seq
              operation: process command statement S3
              operation: read data item
           S3 end
        possible-S3 or (else)
           not-S3 seq
              operation: process error
              operation: read data item
           not-S3 end
        possible-S3 end
        S4 seq
           operation: process command statement S4
        S4 end
     Terminal-Session end
```

The following input would be successfully handled by this structure.

(a) S1 S2 S2 S3 S4

(b) S1 X S3 S4

(c) S1 X S2 X S3 S4

(d) S1 X X S2 X S3 S4

(e) S1 S2 X S4

(f) X S2 X S2 X S3 S4

(g) S1 X S2 X X S2 X X S2 X X S3 S4

In order for the structure to deal with errors of insertion and omission in addition to errors of substitution, the structure must be further elaborated.

9.3.2 Elaboration for errors of substitution and further errors

We can further elaborate the structure to trap other errors that may occur in addition to errors of substitution, as shown in Figure 9.8.

The structure in Figure 9.8 is able to detect and handle errors belonging to any of the three error types. The schematic logic for the process structure elaborated for errors of substitution and further errors becomes:

```
Terminal-Session seq
   initial-read seq
      operation: read data item
   initial-read end
   possible-S1 sel if S1
      S1 seq
         operation: process command statement S1
         operation: read data item
      S1 end
```

```
possible-S1 or if not S1
   not-S1 seq
      operation: process error
      operation: read data item
   not-S1 end
possible-S1 or (else)
   null-S1 seq
      operation: process missing S1 (do nothing)
   null-S1 end
possible-S1 end
error-trap-A itr while not S3, S4
   possible-S2 sel if S2
      S2 seq
         operation: process command statement S2
         operation: read data item
      S2 end
   possible-S2 or (else)
      not-S2 seq
         operation: process error
         operation: read data item
      not-S2 end
   possible-S2 end
error-trap-A end
possible-S3 sel if S3
   S3 seq
      operation: process command statement S3
      operation: read data item
   S3 end
possible-S3 or if not S3 and not S4
   not-S3 seq
      operation: process error
      operation: read data item
   not-S3 end
possible-S3 or (else)
   null-S3 seq
      operation: process missing S3 (do nothing)
   null-S3 end
possible-S3 end
error-trap-B itr while not S4
   not-S4 seq
      operation: process error
      operation: read data item
   not-S4 end
error-trap-B end
```

```
S4 seq
    operation: process command statement S4
S4 end
Terminal-Session end
```

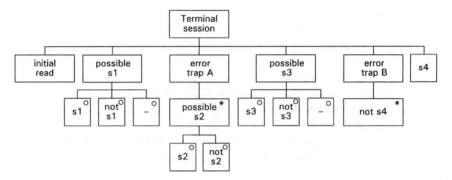

Figure 9.8   The terminal session, elaborated for errors of substitution and further errors.

The following input would be treated correctly by the above structure.

(a) **S1 S2 S2 S3 S4**

(b) **X X S1 S2 X S4**

(c) **X X X X S4**

(d) **S1 X X S2 X S3 X S4**

(e) **X S1 X S3 X S4**

(f) **S2 X S2 X X S4**

(g) **S4**

Note that the interpretation of the way in which the structure handles errors will depend on the conditions that are associated with each iteration and selection. It would be possible to amend the fully elaborated structure by removing the error selection component **not S3** under **possible S3** (giving Figure 9.9); this would require that the error component under **possible S2** would trap errors of substitution for both S2 and S3, and that exit from the **error trap A** iteration would be allowed when either an S3 or an S4 is encountered. If S4 is encountered, it would then be assumed that an S3 was missing.

In Figure 9.9, any error that occurred between S2 and S4 would be handled by the possible S2 selection; exit from the iteration S2 body would be on encountering an S3 or S4 input item. Any errors between S3 and S4 would be picked up by the garbage collector after S3. The schematic logic for the process structure elaborated for errors of substitution and further errors will be:

```
Terminal-Session seq
    initial-read seq
        operation: read data item
    initial-read end
```

```
possible-S1 sel if S1
    S1 seq
        operation: process command statement S1
        operation: read data item
    S1 end
possible-S1 sel if not S1
    not-S1 seq
        operation: process error
        operation: read data item
    not-S1 end
possible-S1 or (else)
    null-S1 seq
        operation: process missing S1 (do nothing)
    null-S1 end
possible-S1 end
error-trap-A itr while not S3, S4
    possible-S2 sel if S2
        S2 seq
            operation: process command statement S2
            operation: read data item
        S2 end
    possible-S2 or (else)
        not-S2 seq
            operation: process error
            operation: read data item
        not-S2 end
    possible-S2 end
error-trap-A end
possible-S3 sel if S3
    S3 seq
        operation: process command statement S2
        operation: read data item
    S3 end
possible-S3 or (else)
    null-S3 seq
        operation: process missing S3 (do nothing)
    null-S3 end
possible-S3 end
error-trap-B itr while not S4
    not-S4 seq
        operation: process error
        operation: read data item
    not-S4 end
error-trap-B end
```

```
S4 seq
    operation: process command statement S4
S4 end
Terminal-Session end
```

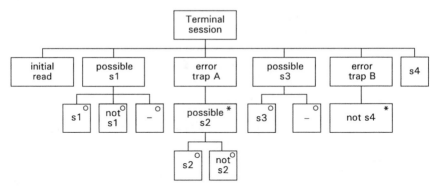

Figure 9.9 An alternative representation of the terminal session to handle errors of substitution and further errors.

9.4 Errors of omission

9.4.1 Elaboration for errors of omission

In elaborating for errors of omission, we are testing for missing items. Selections are needed to indicate that an element may be present or absent (but not replaced by something else). In Figure 9.10 the box with the hyphen indicates the null option; S1 is either present or absent. It is possible that we may want to do nothing if it is found that a particular input item is missing; alternatively, we may want to print a message to state that the expected input was not found. It will be not be necessary to read the next data item if it is established that the item we were expecting is missing; the item we have just read will be one of the following command statements (this is how we would be able to tell

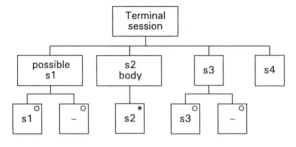

Figure 9.10 The terminal session, elaborated for errors of omission.

118

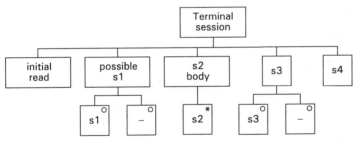

Figure 9.11 The terminal session, elaborated for errors of omission, with an initial read added.

that an input item is missing). The null option is not needed for the iteration, which deals with zero or more occurrences by definition.

In order to test whether the first entry is a command statement S1, it will be necessary to add a process box to hold the initial read operation (Fig. 9.11). Part of processing each subsequent element that is read will be to read the following item so that it can be tested.

The schematic logic is:

```
Terminal-Session seq
    initial-read seq
        operation: read data item
    initial-read end
    possible-S1 sel if S1
        S1 seq
            operation: process command statement S1
            operation: read data item
        S1 end
    possible-S1 or (else)
        null-S1 seq
            operation: process missing S1 (do nothing)
        null-S1 end
    possible-S1 end
    S2-body itr while S2
        S2 seq
            operation: process command statement S2
            operation: read data item
        S2 end
    S2-body end
    possible-S3 sel if S3
        S3 seq
            operation: process command statement S3
            operation: read data item
        S3 end
```

119

```
possible-S3 or (else)
    null-S3 seq
        operation: process missing S3 (do nothing)
    null-S3 end
possible-S3 end
S4 seq
    operation: process command statement S4
S4 end
Terminal-Session end
```

This structure would be able to process input data, even if some of the elements are not present. It is assumed that S4 at least must be present. The following input could be handled by this structure.

(a) **S1 S2 S2 S3 S4**
(b) **S1 S2 S4**
(c) **S2 S4**
(d) **S1 S2 S2 S2 S4**
(e) **S1 S3 S4**
(f) **S3 S4**
(g) **S4**

In order for the structure to be able to cater for data that contains the other two types of error, it is necessary to elaborate the structure to cover this possibility.

9.4.2 Elaboration for errors of omission and further errors

We can further elaborate the structure to trap other errors that may occur in addition to errors of omission (Fig. 9.12).

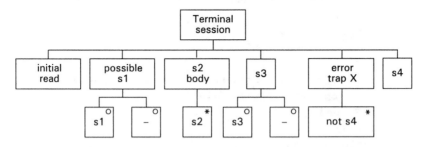

Figure 9.12 The terminal session, elaborated all three types of error.

The structure in Figure 9.12 is able to detect and handle errors belonging to any of the three error types. The schematic logic for the process structure elaborated for errors of omission and further errors will be:

```
Terminal-Session seq
    initial-read seq
        operation: read data item
    initial-read end
    possible-S1 sel if S1
        S1 seq
            operation: process command statement S1
            operation: read data item
        S1 end
    possible-S1 or (else)
        null-S1 seq
            operation: process missing S1 (do nothing)
        null-S1 end
    possible-S1 end
    S2-body itr while S2
        S2 seq
            operation: process command statement S2
            operation: read data item
        S2 end
    S2-body end
    possible-S3 sel if S3
        S3 seq
            operation: process command statement S3
            operation: read data item
        S3 end
    possible-S3 or (else)
        null-S3 seq
            operation: process missing S3 (do nothing)
        null-S3 end
    possible-S3 end
    error-trap-X itr while not S4
        not-S4 seq
            operation: read data item
        not-S4 end
    error-trap-X end
    S4 seq
        operation: process command statement S4
    S4 end
Terminal-Session end
```

The following input would be treated correctly by the above structure:

(a) S1 S2 S2 S3 S4

(b) X X S1 S2 X S4

(c) X X X X S4

(d) **S1 X X S2 X S3 X S4**

(e) **X S1 X S3 X S4**

(f) **S2 X S2 X X S4**

(g) **S4**

In this chapter, we have taken a basic process structure and elaborated the structure for all three kinds of errors, starting with a specific error type for the initial elaboration. The three final structures, fully elaborated for errors, have a different appearance which is determined by the choice of error type for initial elaboration. Process structures designed to expect user input will most commonly be elaborated for errors of insertion in the first instance.

9.5 Exercises

The following structures represent files; valid record types are A, B, C, D and E. Records in error are of type **x**, and may be inserted at any point and in any number. The original records retain their order.

Elaborate the structures below for errors of

(a) insertion

(b) substitution, and

(c) omission

and then elaborate for further errors in each case.

1. A simple input file, contains only two records, A followed by B (Fig. 9.13).

2. An input file contains an initial record A, followed by several B records (Fig. 9.14).

3. An input file contains an initial A record, followed by several B records, and then a single terminating record that may be of type C, D or E (Fig. 9.15).

4. An input file has an initial record of type A, followed by several record pairs, i.e. records B and C together, and a final record that may be of type D or type E (Fig. 9.16).

5. An input file commences with an initial A record, followed by a single record of type B, then several records of type C, and finally a type D terminating record (Fig. 9.17).

6. An input file consists of an initial record of type A, then the main body of the file, containing records B, C and D in that order, and then finally a terminating record of type E (Fig. 9.18).

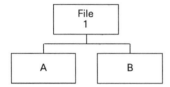

Figure 9.13 The input file structure of Exercise 1.

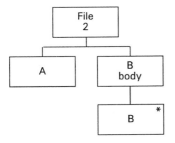

Figure 9.14 The input file structure of Exercise 2.

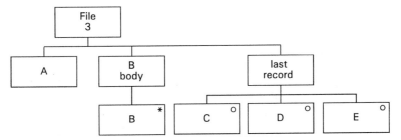

Figure 9.15 The input file structure of Exercise 3.

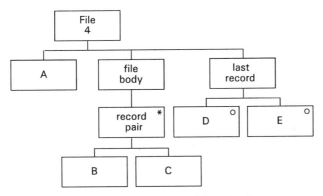

Figure 9.16 The input file structure of Exercise 4.

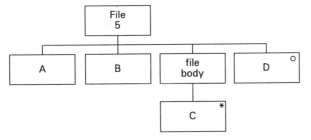

Figure 9.17 The input file structure of Exercise 5.

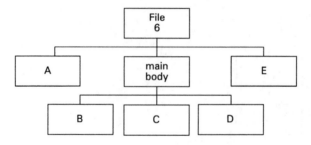

Figure 9.18 The input file structure of Exercise 6.

CHAPTER 10

Case study in program design for interactive systems

The basic methods used in JSP lend themselves to the design of programs in both batch and interactive environments. Designing programs for batch processing requires the identification of suitable input and output data file structures. In the context of interactive systems design, the input and output are often so closely matched that the data structure diagrams are the same, as output "shadows" input.

We will consider the design of a interactive customer database enquiry system, drawing on the techniques that have been met in the earlier sections. The same basic structures of sequence, selection and iteration are used. As the system will be for interactive use, dealing with errors will be particularly important. When a user makes an error in input, it is likely that a correction will be made; the program design therefore will need to be elaborated to cater for errors of insertion (assuming that correct entries will be submitted, but other erroneous input may also be made).

10.1 Design of a program to maintain a customer database

A program is required that will allow changes to be made to a customer database which is interrogated via a terminal. The program will be menu driven and will allow three basic functions to update the records held on the database, plus the option to exit from the customer database system.

10.1.1 Main menu

There will be two screen displays: Main Menu and Customer Information. The main menu screen allows the user to indicate which function is required, together with the customer key to identify the customer record. There is a message area on the lower part of the screen so that operator error and confirmation of action can be drawn to the user's attention. The options at main

125

menu level will be:

    I – insert a new customer into the database
    A – amend details for an existing customer
    D – delete a customer from the database
    X – exit from database

The second screen display for the customer details shows the customer key, the customer name, address and telephone number, and details of the contact person. A response code indicates the guaranteed response time depending on the type of maintenance contract. The contract codes are 1 for basic maintenance (response within one week), 2 for a response the following working day, and 3 for same day response.

There is also an area at the lower part of the screen for messages to be displayed to warn the user of erroneous input or to confirm that a function has been successfully completed.

The customer database system will be developed to allow the user a change of mind, and cancel one of the functions in order to return to the main menu and make another choice.

10.1.2 Input screen displays

The main menu screen will appear as shown in Figure 10.1. When a function has been chosen, the program then displays the Customer Information Screen with details of the customer. The effect of each function is summarized as follows:

- **Insert**   An empty customer information screen is displayed, awaiting details from the user.
- **Amend**   The existing customer information is displayed for amendment by the user.
- **Delete**   The existing customer information screen is displayed but cannot be amended; the user is required to confirm deletion.
- **Exit**   The data files are closed and the user is returned to the system level from which the customer database system was invoked.

The customer information details screen has the layout shown in Figure 10.2.

10.2 Customer database system process structure

The basic process design for the user interacting with the customer database program is described by the process structure diagram in Figure 10.3 (p. 128). This diagram shows that the user may choose Insert, Amend or Delete any number of times and that the session is terminated when the user enters the

```
C U S T O M E R    D A T A B A S E
_____

        M A I N    M E N U



                                   I for insert
                                   A for amend
Function:  [              ]        D for delete
                                   X for exit



Customer:  [                    ]   key number



Messages:  [                          ]
```

Figure 10.1 The main menu screen.

```
C U S T O M E R    I N F O R M A T I O N    D E T A I L S

  Customer key:      [              ]


                                  1 basic maintenance
  Maintenance Code:  [        ]    2 next day response
                                  3 same day response

  Customer Name:     [              ]

  Customer Address:  [                      ]
                     [                      ]
                     [                      ]


  Telephone number:  [              ]

  Contact Name:      [              ]

  Messages:          [                      ]
```

Figure 10.2 The customer information details screen.

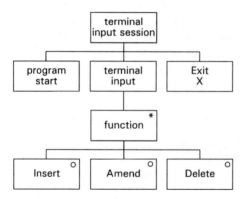

Figure 10.3 The process structure diagram for the customer database program.

Exit command. The database files will be opened under the program start box, and closed on exit.

Since the program will be accepting direct input from a user, we will need to allow for the possibility of errors in input data being made. Once the user has realized that an error has occurred, it is likely that another attempt will be made. This implies that any errors that may occur will be in addition to correct entries and, for this reason, the program structure will be elaborated for errors of insertion. In designing the program, we will initially develop the structure assuming that the input is free from errors; elaboration for errors of insertion will be introduced at a later stage.

A prototype process structure diagram has been created in this example, rather than an input data structure and an output data structure. The reason for this is that the input and output data structure diagrams are so closely interlinked that the structure diagrams would effectively be the same, and hence a single process structure diagram can be created on the basis of the dialogue between the user and the system.

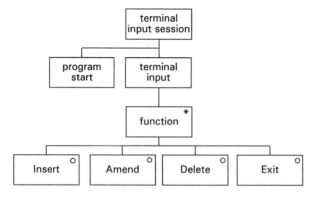

Figure 10.4 A less effective process structure diagram for the customer database program.

The choice presented to the user at the menu is between Insert, Amend, Delete and Exit. The process structure diagram shown in Figure 10.4 illustrates this, but does not represent the terminal session as well as Figure 10.3 because the user will only select Exit once at the end of each session; the condition for exit on the iteration will be "while not X" or "until X".

10.3 Basic dialogue activities

We can identify the basic dialog facilities available at each point in the program:

Insert   Menu: I + customer key + \<enter\>
             Detail: new customer details + \<enter\>

Amend   Menu: A + customer key + \<enter\>
             Detail: amended customer details + \<enter\>

Delete   Menu: D + customer key + \<enter\>
             Detail: \<enter\> – to confirm deletion

Exit   Menu: X to finish the session

We can subdivide the activities of adding, updating and removing records into a request for that activity to be performed (by choosing a particular function) and the entering of the data associated with the function selected.

Insert request   made at: menu
                 produces: blank customer information detail screen

Insert record   made at: blank customer information detail screen
                 produces: menu screen plus customer inserted message

Amend request   made at: menu
                 produces: existing customer information detail screen

Amend record   made at: existing customer information detail screen
                 produces: menu screen plus customer amended message

Delete request   made at: menu
                 produces: existing customer information detail screen

Delete record   made at: existing customer information detail screen
                 produces: menu screen plus customer removed message

10.4 Classifying input errors

Errors can be described as different values entered from those expected; for example, X to Exit from the program is not a valid entry during Insert record

129

as customer information details are expected. To leave the customer database program, X for exit can only be entered at the main menu.

10.4.1 Elaborating for errors of insertion

As in Section 10.2.1, we can assume that the user will enter the correct data, even if errors are also made. We need, therefore, to deal with errors of insertion, and it will be necessary to trap errors at the earliest possible stage. Initially we will design the program assuming error-free input, then we will elaborate for errors. Finally we will simplify the program structure to remove unnecessary repetition of error trapping components.

The approach to elaborating a structure for errors of insertion is to place a garbage group before every sequence component, and to add an error option to selection and iterated components. The basic structure of a garbage group is given in Figure 10.5.

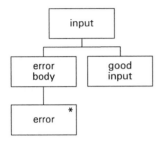

Figure 10.5 The basic structure of a garbage group.

In the process structure we have created we will need to add "garbage groups" (such as that shown above) in order to trap any insertion errors that may be made.

Garbage groups will need to be placed in the structure after every read statement. In addition, the garbage group itself will contain a read statement in order that the next item of data can be read and dealt with in an appropriate manner.

If the data element read in is an error, the garbage group is activated and another data item must be input. If the data element entered is good data the garbage group is not activated and processing continues until the next read statement is encountered where a similar error trap will be in place.

In the context of the system to maintain a customer database the inputs will be abbreviated for ease of reference as activities A1 to A8:

A1 – Program identification
A2 – Insert request
A3 – Insert customer record
A4 – Amend request

A5 – Amend customer record
A6 – Delete request
A7 – Delete customer record
A8 – Exit

What will the structure look like for functions Insert, Amend and Delete? The process structure, without elaboration for errors of insertion, is given in Figure 10.6, and the allocation of component names is shown, together with their abbreviated form, as given above. We can elaborate this structure to deal with errors of insertion. This will involve identifying the positions in the process structure diagram where read operations will be allocated, and placing suitable error traps after the read operations in order to handle any errors, and processing good data in an appropriate manner (Fig. 10.7).

Note that the error traps are placed in the process structure after the read statements, in particular after the read ahead and read next operations (Fig. 10.7). It is only after a read statement has been executed that data will be present for a test to be performed for good or error data.

A similar structure to that which appears under the Insert function will also appear under the Amend and Delete functions.

We can inspect the error trapping functions for each function individually. Error trapping for Insert is shown in Figure 10.8, that for Amend in Figure 10.9 and that for Delete in Figure 10.10.

The error trapping structures are repetitive. This indicates that it may be possible to simplify the structure. We can see from Figures 10.8, 10.9 and 10.10 that a pattern appears: the same kind of iteration is used at the end of every selection part. This would be equivalent to having an error trap at the end of the iteration, rather than repeating the error trapping code within each

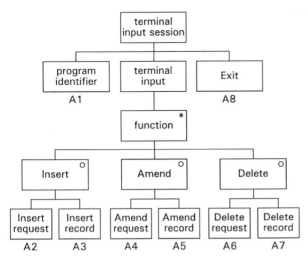

Figure 10.6 A more detailed process structure diagram for the customer database program.

131

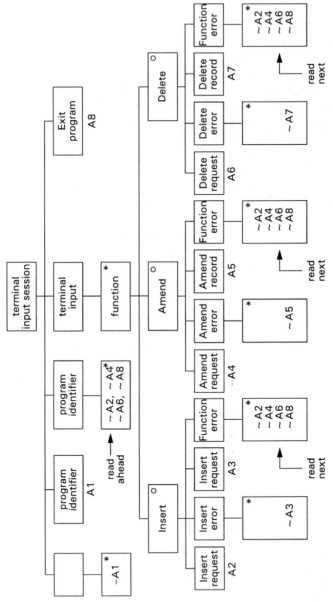

Figure 10.7 The customer database program elaborated for errors of insertion.

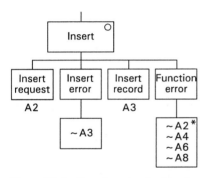

Figure 10.8 Error trapping for Insert.

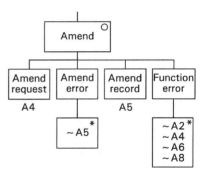

Figure 10.9 Error trapping for Amend.

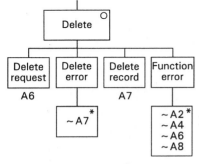

Figure 10.10 Error trapping for Delete.

selection part within the iteration. The process structure shown in Figure 10.11 has been amended to allow for this modification.

It can also be seen from Figure 10.11 (p. 134) that the same error trapping iteration also occurs in the read ahead position (that is, before the iteration has been entered). This multiple use of the same error trap enables the process structure to be simplified, but still retain the ability to trap errors in the data. Simplifying the structure for error detection does not involve changing the overall design of the program which caters for error-free input, rather there are modifications to the elaborations that were made in order to deal with errors.

There are two options available for simplifying the process structure as it currently stands; we can remove both iterations and replace these by a selection and then either introduce a selection or add another component to the existing selection. In undertaking such a simplification we have assumed that different error messages are not required if the error trap is activated at different places within the structure.

Simplification 1. Introducing a selection
The modified process structure is shown in Figure 10.12 (p. 135).

Simplification 2. Adding to an existing selection
The modified process structure is shown in Figure 10.13 (p. 136).

133

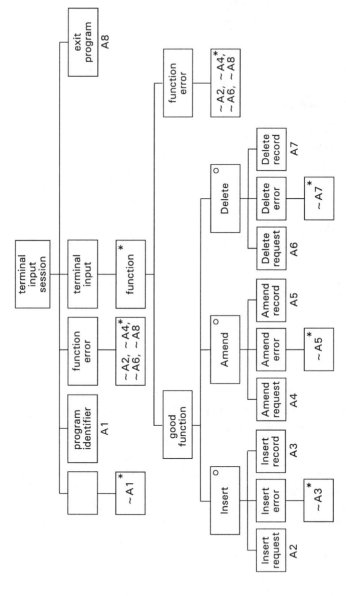

Figure 10.11 The customer database program with simplified error trapping.

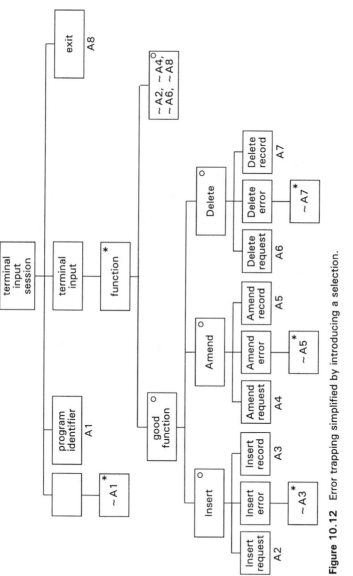

Figure 10.12 Error trapping simplified by introducing a selection.

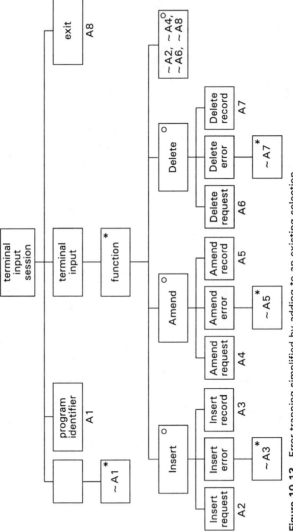

Figure 10.13 Error trapping simplified by adding to an existing selection.

In carrying out both these simplifications it was assumed that there was no requirement to differentiate between different types of error occurring at different points in the structure.

10.5 Implementing the cancel option

We may now consider the effect of adding the Cancel option. In a sense, this is also dealing with errors, as the operator would only want to terminate the execution of a function if an error had occurred, for example updating a record that had already been updated.

We can identify different circumstances in which the choice of the Cancel option would be appropriate.

    I request   – enter data for new customer record

                   – cancel insert function

Cancel makes it possible to terminate following erroneous data entry, e.g. an invalid maintenance code.

    A request   – enter data for existing customer record

                   – cancel amend function

Cancel makes it possible to terminate during the Amend function if the record has already been updated, or the new maintenance code to be entered is not a valid code, or the wrong record has been selected for updating.

    D request   – confirmation deletion of existing customer record

                   – cancel delete function

Cancel makes it possible to terminate during the Delete function if it is found that this is not the record that should be erased, or if deletion of the record is no longer required.

The position in the process structure diagram gives the context of a key press. The Cancel function is only valid at the customer information detail screen. If the Cancel function were to be entered at the main menu, it would constitute an error.

In order to cater for the Cancel option, it will be necessary to expand the structure below each function so that either valid data for that function is entered or the Cancel option is entered. This will require a selection to be added to the process structure.

Expanding the process structure to cater for Cancel within the Insert function, the Amend function and the Delete function is shown in Figures 10.14, 10.15 and 10.16 respectively.

We could, if required, distinguish between different errors and therefore generate a more helpful error message to the user. In the case of adding a customer to the database, two kinds of error are possible in entering data: the wrong key may be pressed (e.g. selecting a function when Insert has already been chosen) or an invalid maintenance code may be entered.

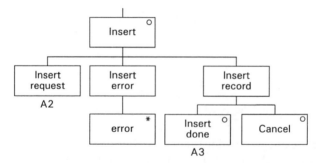

Figure 10.14   Expanding the process structure to cater for Cancel within the Insert function.

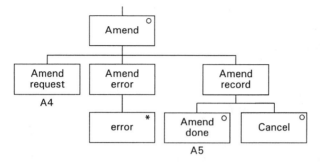

Figure 10.15   Expanding the process structure to cater for Cancel within the Amend function.

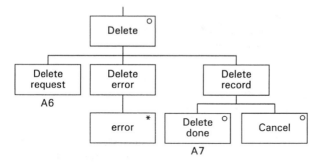

Figure 10.16   Expanding the process structure to cater for Cancel within the Delete function.

The structure shown in Figure 10.17 would distinguish between such errors in the Insert function. A similar amendment could be made to the Amend function. It would not be meaningful to make such a change to the Delete function as the only choice is <enter> to confirm deletion or Cancel; any other entry would constitute an invalid key press.

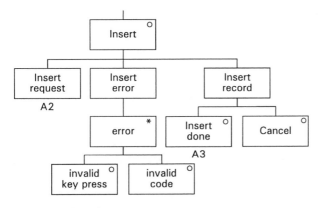

Figure 10.17 Distinguishing between errors in the Insert function.

10.6 Identifying and allocating operations

We can determine what constitutes good data and error data for each function and cater for input in an appropriate manner. It will now be necessary to consider allocating operations to maintain the database.

The operations available to handle database manipulation are:

1. Retrieve customer record
2. Insert new customer record
3. Replace existing customer record
4. Delete existing customer record

These operations can be allocated to the process structure:

A3 = Insert record	operation 2
A4 = Amend request	operation 1
A5 = Amend record	operation 3
A6 = Delete request	operation 1
A7 = Delete record	operation 4

We can now determine the input and output activities relating to the process structure. The full list of operations would be as follows:

1. `Retrieve existing customer record from database file`
2. `Insert new customer record on database file`
3. `Replace existing customer record on database file`
4. `Delete existing customer record from database file`
5. `Write main menu to screen`
6. `Read function from main menu`
7. `Write customer detail screen`
8. `Write "insert new customer record?" in message box`
9. `Write "amend customer record?" in message box`
10. `Write "delete customer record: confirm?" in message box`
11. `Write "record <customer key> inserted" in message box`

12. Write "record <customer key> amended" in message box
13. Write "record <customer key> deleted" in message box
14. Write "insert function cancelled" in message box
15. Write "amend function cancelled" in message box
16. Write "delete function cancelled" in message box
17. Write "error in maintenance code - please try again" in message box
18. Write "error in input - please try again" in message box
19. Read customer record data from customer detail screen
20. Read confirmation/cancel from customer detail screen
21. Write exit message
22. Write "invalid function" in message box
23. Open database file for input/output
24. Close database file
25. Stop processing
26. Write "invalid command" to screen

The operations are now allocated to the customer database process structure diagram, as shown in Figure 10.18.

The initial read takes processing to A1; the database file is then opened. The input and output activities at each component, including database actions, are as given below.

Initial terminal session error

    ~A1   Write "invalid command" to screen

Commence customer database terminal session

    A1   Open database file for input/output
          Write main menu to screen
          Read function from main menu

Insert a new record to the customer database

    A2   Write customer detail screen
          Write "insert new customer record" in message box
          Read customer record data from customer detail screen

I Errors   Write customer detail screen
          Write "error in maintenance code – please try again" in message box
          Read customer record data from customer detail screen

    A3   Insert new customer record on database file
          Write main menu to screen
          Write "record <customer key> inserted" in message box
          Read function from main menu

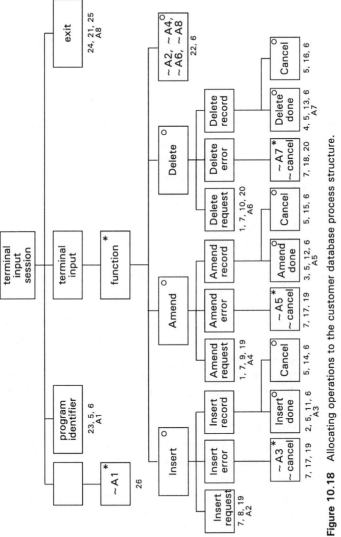

Figure 10.18 Allocating operations to the customer database process structure.

Cancel Write main menu to screen
Write "insert function cancelled" in message box
Read function from main menu

Amend a record on the customer database

A4 Retrieve existing customer record from database file
Write customer detail screen
Write "amend customer record" in message box
Read customer record data from customer detail screen

A Errors Write customer detail screen
Write "error in maintenance code – please try again" in message
box
Read customer record data from customer detail screen

A5 Replace existing customer record on database file
Write main menu to screen
Write "record <customer key> amended" in message box
Read function from main menu

Cancel Write main menu to screen
Write "amend function cancelled" in message box
Read function from main menu

Delete a record from the customer database

A6 Retrieve existing customer record from database file
Write customer detail screen
Write "delete customer record: confirm?" in message box
Read confirmation/cancel from customer detail screen

D Errors Write customer detail screen
Write "error in input – please try again" in message box
Read confirmation/cancel from customer detail screen

A7 Delete existing customer record from database file
Write main menu to screen
Write "record <customer key> deleted" in message box
Read function from main menu

Cancel Write main menu to screen
Write "delete function cancelled" in message box
Read function from main menu

Invalid function

~A2, ~A4, ⎫ Write "invalid function" in message box
 ~A6, ~A8 ⎭ Read function from main menu

Exit from customer database program

    A8 Close database file

         Write exit message

         Stop processing (return to system display)

These operations can now be added to the process structure diagram, together with the database manipulation operations. The next stage in producing the program will be to specify and allocate the conditions.

10.7 Exercises

1. How could the process structure diagram for the case study be developed to allow for additional functions? Such functions could be, for example, to inspect a customer record without changing it, or to print a customer record.
2. Do you consider that elaborating for errors of insertion would be the best choice if the customer database system were to run in batch rather than interactive mode? Explain your reasoning.

10.8 Further reading

King & Pardoe (1992), Chapter 12.
Thompson (1989), Chapter 21.

CHAPTER 11

Backtracking

It is sometimes the case in everyday situations that insufficient information is available in order for us to make a choice between different possibilities. For example, when buying a raffle ticket, it is impossible to know in advance what the winning ticket number will be (unless only one ticket has been sold!). When the draw is made, the holder of the winning ticket number collects the prize and it is not possible to change the ticket you hold for a winning ticket. Let us consider another context, that of solving a crossword puzzle. When a clue has several different candidate solutions, it is not possible to decide which is the correct choice until several other intersecting solutions have been found. We could make an assumption about which is the mostly likely solution; if we later find that we have made the wrong choice, it is possible to amend our entry and replace it with the alternative solution.

No explanation of backtracking would be complete without a story to illustrate the major features; this will be no exception to that unwritten rule.

> Imagine that you had arranged to meet a friend for afternoon tea, and that your friend had given you directions to reach the appointed place. You set out to meet your friend, taking with you a card to post, a library book that a colleague has asked you to return on your way, and enough money to pay for tea (and perhaps a slice of gateau!) and buy a stamp for the card.
>
> You follow the directions that your friend has given you and you come upon a crossroads. The directions tell you to turn, but you are unable to read whether you should take the left or the right turning because it has started to rain and the ink has smudged. What do you do? It is too late to turn back and telephone your friend for further directions – your friend will have departed in order to meet you. The only option appears to be to make a guess and carry on; either you will meet your friend, or you will discover that you made the wrong choice. You decide to take the left turn and continue with your journey.
>
> Happy that you have made a decision and that you are now on your way, you meet a stranger with a fine dog. You speak to the stranger for

a few minutes, and pat the dog. Happy from that chance encounter, you continue on your journey, purchase a stamp and then post the card. As you carry on down the road you see a library, and take in the book that your colleague requested you to return, leaving the book on the library counter.

You believe that your journey must be nearly at an end as your friend assured you that it would take no longer than 15 minutes to walk, and the meeting place was near the library. At this point you begin to realize that you must have made the wrong choice at the crossroads earlier on, and that you will now have to retrace your steps in order to take the other path which must have been the correct one.

Not only must you make your way back to the crossroads (you do not know the area well enough to try to take a shortcut) you must also retrieve the library book that you left in the library. The librarian is pleased that you have come in to collect the book, as you had handed it in to the wrong branch. It does not matter where you bought the stamp or posted the card; you wanted to do that anyway. You make your way back to the crossroads and take the other turning, remembering to return the library book to the correct branch of the library, and arrive just in time to meet your friend as arranged. Your trip has made you work up quite an appetite, so you and your friend enjoy a meal together.

This story illustrates the major features of backtracking; the concept of a choice is present, without sufficient information on which to make a decision with the certainty of being correct. The approach is to make an arbitrary choice. If the choice made was correct, there is no problem as appropriate action has been taken. However, if it becomes clear that the choice was incorrect we must retrace our steps (literally, in the example above) to the point at which the choice was made: this is *backtracking*. It is important during backtracking to return to the previous condition, reversing any changes that would not have been made had the correct choice been selected in the first instance. Any such changes are known as *side effects*. The side effects in the story were:

- meeting the stranger and patting the dog
- returning the library book to the wrong branch
- buying a stamp and posting the card

The first side effect, meeting the stranger and patting the dog, had no effect on the outcome of your journey; it is therefore a *neutral* or *tolerable* side effect.

The second side effect, returning the book to the wrong library, was an error. It was necessary to retrieve the book in order to return it to the correct library; this is an *intolerable* side effect, and must be reversed if it cannot be avoided.

The last two actions, buying a stamp and posting the card, were part of the original plan. As these tasks had to be performed it did not matter which shop or which pillar box was used; these are therefore *beneficial* side effects.

11.1 Recognition difficulties

If we consider the case study introduced in Chapter 10, the development of a program to maintain a customer database system, we have developed a process structure diagram and have identified and added the basic operations, including error handling. The next stage is to add the conditions to the selections and iterations. The condition on the main iteration (for the terminal input function) will control whether the loop is entered by choosing a function or terminated by entering the Exit command X. The condition c1 is therefore `while input is not X` or `until input is X`.

The condition to govern the selection of Insert a new customer record will be governed by the "I" function being entered and by ensuring that the customer record does not already exist on the database. This presents a problem. We cannot know whether the customer record exists on the database at this stage as we have not retrieved a record from the database. This is known as a *recognition difficulty* as the data that is required in order for the test to be made is not present in memory to enable the test to be performed.

One possible solution might be to add operation 1 (get customer) before a function has been chosen. The disadvantage of this approach is that it would be inefficient as the database would be accessed even if an invalid function had been entered.

In circumstances such as these, the JSP approach to the problem is *backtracking*.

11.2 Posit, admit and quit

When faced with a situation where it is not certain which is the correct choice, it is necessary to make a decision in order to proceed further, but allow for the possibility that the choice may be the wrong one. This arbitrary choice in JSP is known as the `posit`; it is the equivalent of a selection, but is used when there is not enough information available to know whether the condition associated with the selection can be satisfied. We therefore make an assumption and continue on this basis until it is successfully completed or proved wrong.

If the choice made at the `posit` was correct, there is no problem. Having made the right choice, processing continues according to plan. It is only when information comes to light that indicates that the wrong choice has been made that corrective action needs to be taken. In JSP terminology, we `quit` from the branch that was taken as it is now known to be in error. `Quit` jumps back to the point at which the choice was originally made so that the alternative branch can be taken. It is essential to consider the nature of any side effects so that remedial action can be taken if necessary. Beneficial and tolerable side effects can be ignored, but intolerable side effects must be identified and reversed if they cannot be avoided.

When it is necessary to **quit** from the wrong branch after it has been discovered that the original **posit** was in error, it is essential to return things to their original state. If we fail to do this we may suffer from side effects. For example, in our story, we must retrieve the library book that was returned to the wrong branch. In JSP terms this represents an intolerable side effect that must either be avoided (by checking the library address inside the front cover first) or reversed (by retrieving the book once returned). The activities of buying a stamp and posting the letter had been planned, and were successfully completed (a beneficial side effect in JSP). Talking to the stranger and patting the dog did not have a significant effect on the final outcome of the journey (seen in JSP terms as a neutral or tolerable side effect). When it is known that we must **quit**, this entails transferring control to the **admit** part. This is equivalent to the **else** part of a selection.

In order to introduce backtracking to the customer database maintenance process structure, we need to break the structure down into two selection parts. This returns the structure to a previous simplification (Fig. 11.1; compare with Fig. 10.12).

We cannot specify a condition for the new selection because it is not possible to tell at this stage whether the **posit** (good function) or **admit** (error) branch is the correct choice. We can therefore assume that the **posit** branch is the correct choice, until it can be proved otherwise.

posit   that the function is good;

quit   jump to the beginning of the admit part if it is found that taking the posit part was an error;

admit   we are in error, therefore backtrack from the **posit** branch to the **admit** part in order to process appropriately.

Thus **posit** assumes that the condition that would be on the selection is true. The **quit** is used to transfer control to the **admit** part if it is found that this assumption is in error. The else part of the selection from the **posit** branch is designated by **admit**.

The following criteria will decide in each function when it is necessary to leave the **posit** branch and transfer control to the **admit** branch:

I (insert)   **quit** if the customer record *is* on the database already

A (amend)   **quit** if the customer record *is not* on the database

D (delete)   **quit** if the customer record *is not* on the database

11.3 Side effects

Backtracking is one method of solving recognition difficulties, but there may be side effects (as illustrated in the story on the introduction to this section).

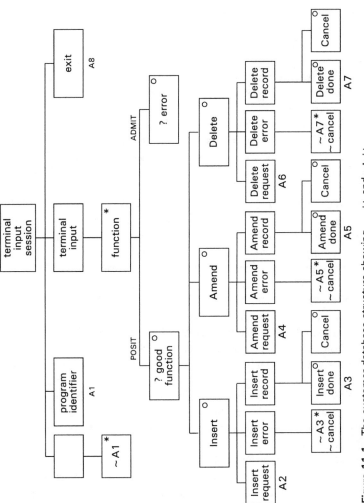

Figure 11.1 The customer database structure showing posit and admit.

- **Beneficial**   Something we had to do anyway, for example, read the next record.
- **Neutral**   Neither good nor bad results, for example, copying a value to a temporary variable.
- **Intolerable**   Something we cannot allow, for example, printing the wrong record.

We must **avoid** or **reverse** intolerable side effects; they cannot be permitted.

The example from the customer database program demonstrates the problem of recognition difficulties, where insufficient information is available in order to make a decision, i.e. it is not possible to determine which selection branch to take. The backtracking solution is to assume that one path will always be taken (the **posit** branch) and only transfer control to the other path (the **admit** branch) when it can be demonstrated that the **posit** branch was the wrong path to take.

If the **posit** branch is the correct path, processing proceeds as intended with no need to transfer control as the right path has been chosen.

If the **posit** branch is later proved to be wrong, any activities that have been performed which would adversely affect the outcome of the program must be reversed; such activities are the side effects discussed above. Actions that would constitute intolerable side effects should be deferred until it is certain that the correct branch has been taken; this may mean retaining values in temporary storage areas before executing an irrevocable action such as printing or changing a record. Control will then be resumed at the **admit** part, which is the equivalent of the **else** part in a selection.

There is no hard and fast rule concerning the allocation of **posit** and **admit** to the **if** and **else** branches of a selection. When the possibility of a recognition difficulty occurring is discovered and it has been decided to implement backtracking, one approach would be to make the assumption that the first choice is good, i.e. **posit** that the function is good. If it is later proved that this assumption was incorrect, the action would be to **quit** from the **posit** branch and transfer control to the **admit** branch, and reverse any unwanted actions that have been taken in the **posit** branch. Processing would then be resumed on the **admit** branch.

As a guideline in the choice of allocating **posit** and **admit**, it may be useful to consider the following:

1. **Posit** that the specific holds true; **admit** in the general case.
2. **Posit** that the processing is error free; **admit** that an error exists
3. If there are problems, try reversing the allocation of **posit** and **admit**.

We would choose the allocation that left us with beneficial or neutral side effects rather than intolerable side effects.

In certain circumstances, alternative approaches may prove attractive, such as the use of a multiple read ahead (continue to read records until there is sufficient data to make the decision), or a redesign of the program (a different approach to the problem may resolve recognition difficulties).

150

11.4 Coding backtracking

The selection within the program structure would normally have a condition; this would be tested to establish whether this branch or an alternative would be entered. As we can see, with a recognition difficulty, it is not possible to decide which branch to take because insufficient information is available in order to make the decision. This means that when code is generated it will not be possible to test a condition; this has the effect of allowing entry to the **posit** branch without a condition being specified. The condition effectively needs to be relocated to a point in the program where sufficient information will be available, and a delayed test is then performed. We should note that this has caused a very unusual state of affairs to arise: a condition appears within the operations allocated to the process structure diagram. The presence of the test, with the accompanying **quit** statement to transfer control to the **admit** part of the structure (i.e. the implied **else**) is sometimes shown in the process structure diagram by an exclamation mark (!) in the box where the **quit** has been allocated. The **posit/admit** is designated by a question mark (?) in what would otherwise be straightforward selection components.

Consider the portion of a process structure diagram shown in Figure 11.2. The schematic logic for the diagram is given, assuming first a simple selection and second elementary backtracking, to illustrate the amendments that need to be introduced in order to replace the schematic logic for a selection with

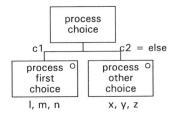

Figure 11.2 Part of a process structure showing selection.

the **posit, quit** and **admit** keywords in order to implement backtracking.

The schematic logic for a selection would appear as follows (without identifying the action of particular operations):

```
process-choice sel if c1
    process-first-choice seq
        operation l
        operation m
        operation n
    process-first-choice end
```

```
process-choice or if c2=else
    process-other-choice seq
        operation x
        operation y
        operation z
    process-other-choice end
process-choice end
```

The schematic logic would need to be amended as shown below in order to implement simple backtracking. Note that the initial selection is replaced by **posit**, and the **else** part of the selection is replaced by **admit**. The **quit** statement indicates that if condition c1 is false, i.e. we have taken the wrong path, control must be transferred to the other branch.

```
process-choice posit c1
    process-first-choice seq
        operation l
        operation m
        quit (process-choice posit c1) if c2
        operation n
    process-first-choice end
process-choice admit c2 (else)
    process-other-choice seq
        operation x
        operation y
        operation z
    process-other-choice end
process-choice end
```

The **quit** statement would be implemented by a programming language statement **if not c1 then goto process-choice admit** or similar, depending on the language used for implementation.

If there are any intolerable side effects that are anticipated in backtracking, additional operations would be required in order to deal with this issue. This might involve storing data in a temporary location rather than writing directly to an output file, storing initial values prior to calculations, or recalculating original values when arithmetic operations have been performed in order to restore the state prior to taking the **posit** branch.

11.5 Exercises

1. Describe the role of **posit**, **admit** and **quit** in backtracking.
2. Include the amendments for backtracking in order to produce the schematic logic for the customer database maintenance system.

3. A program is required to read records from an input file containing details of mechanical components and produce a report identifying incomplete units. The input file records should occur in groups of four (relating to a single unit when the components have been assembled), but sometimes a record may be missing. In these circumstances, the remaining records in the group must be flagged as an incomplete unit and appear on the rejected components report file. Construct the input and output data file structures, identify the points of correspondence and merge to form the basic program structure. Identify and allocate the operations and conditions. Identify any problems (such as recognition difficulties) and propose possible solutions that could be implemented. Consider the nature of any side effects that might be present.

4. An enhanced program is required to read records from an input file containing details of mechanical components and produce a report identifying incomplete or damaged units. The input file records should occur in groups of four (relating to a single unit when the components have been assembled), but sometimes a record might be missing. It is also possible that any one record within a group of four contains a flag that indicates a faulty component. In these circumstances, the remaining records in the group must be flagged as either an incomplete unit or a damaged unit and appear on the rejected components report file. Construct the input and output data file structures, identify the points of correspondence and merge to form the basic program structure. Identify and allocate the operations and conditions. Identify any problems (such as recognition difficulties) and propose possible solutions that could be implemented. Consider the nature of any side effects that might be present.

11.6 Further reading

Holmes (1991), Section 13.8.
King & Pardoe (1992), Chapters 10 and 12.
Storer (1991), Chapter 7.
Thompson (1989), Chapter 20.

CHAPTER 12

Structure clashes
and program inversion

If the input data structure and the output data structure have elements that do not correspond but are in conflict with one another a **structure clash** is said to exist. This means that the input and output data structures cannot be merged to form a single process structure, and therefore another approach has to be found in order to solve the problem.

There are three different types of structure clash caused by incompatibility between input and output data structures:

- ordering
- boundary
- interleaving

12.1 Ordering clash

An ordering clash can be identified if the elements of input data occur in a different sequence from that required for output. This is not the same as, for example, printing out all the female students from a student file; in this case the order is maintained, but only selected records (those relating to female students) are printed.

12.1.1 Ordering clash: simple payroll processing

Imagine that there are two clerks: one calculates the weekly pay for each member of staff, but only if the records are presented in alphabetical order; the second clerk has the task of sorting the payroll records, initially in staff number order, so that they are in alphabetical order for the other clerk to calculate the payroll.

Clearly the payroll clerk will not be able to calculate the pay for each member of staff until the second clerk has sorted the records into alphabetical order. We would therefore have a situation where the payroll clerk would be

Figure 12.1 Sorting staff records.

waiting for the sorting clerk to arrange *all* the payroll records, during which time the payroll clerk would be idle (Fig. 12.1).

The sorting clerk arranges the staff records, producing alphabetically sorted staff records as output. These same records now form the input required by the payroll clerk. The first clerk would process each record in turn, starting from the first; the sorting clerk would be idle while the pay for each member of staff was being calculated (Fig 12.2).

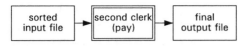

Figure 12.2 Calculating staff payroll.

An important point to note is that the *output* produced by sorting is the same as the *input* required by calculating the pay (Fig. 12.3).

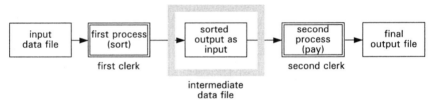

Figure 12.3 The intermediate data file: output from sorting and input to payroll processing.

Rather than have the payroll clerk wait for the other to finish sorting *all* the records before calculating the payroll can begin, we could exploit the fact that the sorting clerk will produce output payroll records in exactly the order that the payroll clerk requires them for processing. This means that the clerk responsible for sorting the records can start by finding the first staff record. At this point, instead of continuing to sort the records, the first staff record can be passed to the payroll clerk so that the pay can be calculated. When this has been done, the sorting clerk can find the second staff record and pass that in turn to the payroll clerk, continuing in this way until each record has been found and the pay calculated. What is happening here is that there are two processes taking place: sorting and the calculation of pay. It is possible for the first to be carried out followed by the second, as would be expected. It is also possible to alternate between the two, as described, each clerk informing the other when a record is ready or a record is required (Fig. 12.4).

This illustrates the major aspects of a structure clash and the JSP approach

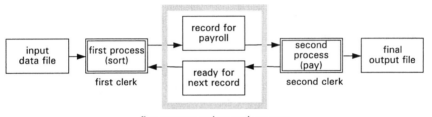

first process and second process
communicate record by record
replaces the need for an intermediate data file

Figure 12.4 Sorting and payroll processing without an intermediate data file.

of program inversion. When it is not possible to merge the input and output data structures because of a structure clash, the next stage in solving the problem is to identify the two processing activities that must take place (here, sorting and payroll calculation). The two processing activities are connected by an intermediate data file; the first stage produces the intermediate data file as output, the second stage takes the intermediate data file as input. At this stage, a solution to the problem has been found; two separate programs are required rather than one.

The JSP approach of program inversion removes the need for the creation of an intermediate file. The first program produces an output file with the records in the order required by the second program (i.e. the records have been sorted into alphabetical order). There is therefore no need for the second program to wait until all the records have been sorted, as the pay for the first record can be calculated as soon as the first record has been found, the pay for the second record calculated when the second record has been identified and so on, until all records have been processed. In practice, with an ordering clash, the solution would be to sort the input file into the required order before proceeding further, but the problem illustrates the principles of program inversion.

12.1.2 Ordering clash: examination results processing

An input data file contains the final degree results for students on various courses. The results are sorted into alphabetical order of student name within course. The input file could have the physical appearance of Table 12.1.

The contents of the input file could be described as an iteration of record; this would be a valid description, but it would ignore the underlying organization of the records in alphabetical order. A better description of the file would be that the input data file contains results for many courses (an iteration of course), and each course may have zero or more students (an iteration of student). The input data structure, that is the logical representation of the file, could be drawn as shown in Figure 12.5.

157

Table 12.1 The input data file for final degree results.

Lucas	James	Business	1
Moore	Vanessa	Business	1
Norris	Neville	Business	3
Williams	Sarah	Business	2i
Brown	Rachel	Computing	2ii
Dawes	Graham	Computing	2ii
Garrett	Brian	Computing	3
Martin	Sheila	Computing	2i
Strong	Malcolm	Computing	1
Adams	Michael	Engineering	2ii
Chisel	Laura	Engineering	2i
Durrant	Petra	Engineering	1
Evans	Robert	Engineering	2ii
Arling	John	Mathematics	2i
Cartier	Eileen	Mathematics	1
Laurent	Lisa	Mathematics	2i
Billings	Mary	Sociology	2i
Craven	Gerald	Sociology	2i

Table 12.2 The output data file for final degree results.

Cartier	Mathematics	1
Duran	Engineering	1
Lucas	Business	1
Moore	Business	1
Strong	Computing	1
Arling	Mathematics	2i
Billings	Sociology	2i
Chisel	Engineering	2i
Craven	Sociology	2i
Laurent	Mathematics	2i
Martin	Computing	2i
Williams	Business	2i
Adams	Engineering	2ii
Brown	Computing	2ii
Dawes	Computing	2ii
Evans	Engineering	2ii
Garrett	Computing	3
Norris	Business	3

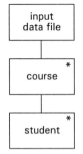

Figure 12.5 Input report file structure diagram.

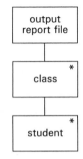

Figure 12.6 Output report file structure diagram.

The output report file holds details of student results; the students are arranged in alphabetical order within degree classification, regardless of the course of study. The output file could have the appearance of Table 12.2.

It would also be true to state that the output file consisted of an iteration of record; this description does not take account of the inherent order of the records within the file. A more detailed description of the output file would be that the report identifies results in several classes of degree (an iteration of class), and that there may be zero or more graduates within each degree classification (an iteration of student).

It should be noticed that the order of records in the input data file is different from the order of the records in the output report file; this violates one of the rules for establishing a correspondence, so a structure clash exists as the data structures are in conflict.

The data structure diagram for this output report file could be drawn as shown in Figure 12.6. The structure of the input is different from the structure of the output, even though they relate to the same items of data. The input data is sorted into a different order from that required for the output results.

When an attempt is made to establish correspondences between the two data structures problems arise (Fig. 12.7). These problems are more than a lack of correspondence; they demonstrate the conflict that exists between the two data structures. This is an example of an **ordering clash** because the order of data in the input file is not mirrored by the order of data in the output file.

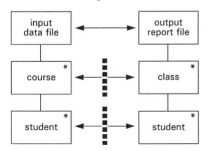

Figure 12.7 Structure clash between input and output data structures.

An ordering clash can be resolved by sorting the input file and then processing the sorted (intermediate) file by a second program in order to produce the required report (Fig. 12.8). When an attempt is made to establish correspondences between the *sorted* input data structure and the final output data structure, no problems now arise (Fig. 12.9).

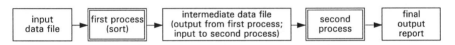

Figure 12.8 Sorting the input data to produce an intermediate data file as input to the second process.

159

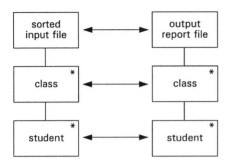

Figure 12.9 Correspondence between input and output data structures after the input has been sorted.

12.2 Boundary clash

In order to identify when a boundary clash has occurred, a variety of different problems are examined. In some circumstances, a relationship between input and output may not appear to be one-to-one, but if some elements are regarded as being part of a group, the one-to-one relationship can still hold, thus avoiding a structure clash.

Note that in the following examples, all the input files are sorted in the order required for the output report; therefore there is no ordering clash.

12.2.1 Report on one page: not a boundary clash

The "Little Kiosk" newsagents only sells the evening paper from 3.30 p.m. each afternoon until 7.00 p.m. each evening. The owner of the kiosk has a home computer and has decided to write a program that will print a report indicating the number of sales made each day for a month. The report will be printed on a single page; as the longest month has 31 days, a report for any one month will not exceed the length of the page. The input data file will simply have the number of papers sold as an entry for each day of the month in question; the input data file is therefore an iteration of the daily sale record.

The input data structure would be as shown in Figure 12.10, while the report would have the appearance of Figure 12.11. The report has the structure of a title at the top of the page, followed by the rest of the report (sequence). The main body of the report is followed by the total number of sales for that month (sequence). There are several lines (iteration) giving the number of sales each day for that month. These make up the main body of the report. This description of the report file assists in constructing the output data structure diagram, which would be as shown in Figure 12.12.

The correspondences between the input and output data structures are as follows (Fig. 12.13). The input data file box corresponds to the output report

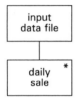

Figure 12.10 Input data structure for the "Little Kiosk" sales report.

```
      = Little Kiosk Sales =

Day in July    Number Sold
       1            24
       2            22
       3            27
       4            29
       5            32
       :            :
      25            22
      26            19
      27            20
      28            22
      29            19
      30            17
      31            18

Total Number Sold: 573
```

Figure 12.11 The "Little Kiosk" sales report.

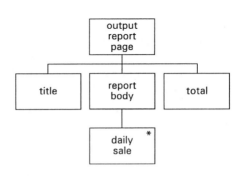

Figure 12.12 The output data structure diagram for the "Little Kiosk" sales report.

page box as the input file produces the output file. The title only exists in the output report as there is no title on the input file; this is a lack of correspondence. Similarly, the total is present only in the output report and not in the input file. For each daily sale record in the input file, there exists a daily sale line on the output report. These lines occur in the same order and the same number of times; therefore there is a correspondence between the daily sale box on the input file and the daily sale box on the output report.

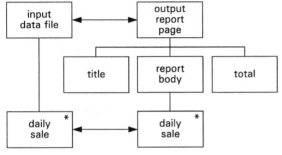

Figure 12.13 Points of correspondence between the input and output data structures for the "Little Kiosk" sales report.

161

This problem does not suffer from a boundary clash; the input and output data structures can therefore be merged on the points of correspondence to form a basic process structure diagram that can be developed into a working program.

12.2.2 Report on one page with many sections: not a boundary clash

A small shop, the "Bonus Bar", sells a variety of goods in each of its sections: stationery, magazines, cards and confectionery. The input file is sorted in date order within section. A report is required at the end of each week showing the individual sales and the total value of sales made in each section on a single page. The report will have a title at the top, and the grand total of sales in all sections at the end of the page.

The input data structure would be as shown in Figure 12.14 and the report would have the appearance of Figure 12.15.

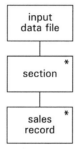

Figure 12.14 Input data structure for the "Bonus Bar" sales report.

The structure of the report page can be described in terms of the JSP constructs sequence and iteration. Reading from the top to the bottom of the page, the report starts with a title, followed by the main part of the report, after which there is the grand total of all sales for the week (sequence). The main part of the report is divided into several sections (iteration). The output data structure would be as shown in Figure 12.16.

The correspondences between the input and output data structures are as follows (Fig. 12.17). The input data file box corresponds to the output report page box as the input file produces the output file. The title only exists in the output report as there is no title on the input file; this is a lack of correspondence. Similarly, the grand total and the section totals are present only in the output report and not in the input file. For each daily sale record in the input file, there exists a daily sale line on the output report; these lines occur in the same order and the same number of times, therefore there is a correspondence between the sales record box on the input file and the sales line box on the output report.

```
        ***Bonus Bar Sales***

Sections              Sales £
--------              -------

All Square              1.75
  :                      :
Farewell!               2.50
Magazines Total        28.90

Birthday Card           1.25
  :                      :
Get Well Soon Card      1.05
Cards Total            12.99

Chunky Bar               .35
  :                      :
All Gold Box            5.99
Confectionary Total    35.24

TOTAL SALES:          238.76
```

Figure 12.15 The "Bonus Bar" sales report.

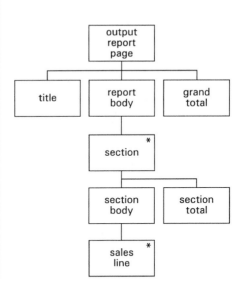

Figure 12.16 The output data structure diagram for the "Bonus Bar" sales report.

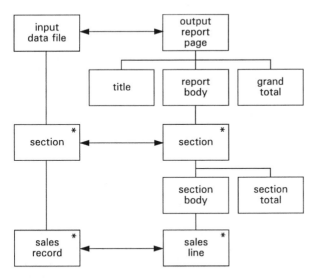

Figure 12.17 Correspondence between the input and output data structures for the "Bonus Bar" sales report.

This problem does not suffer from a boundary clash; the input and output data structures can be merged in the normal way to produce the process structure diagram, and development of the program continues from that point.

163

12.2.3 One department per page: not a boundary clash

The "Sellfast" store sells a variety of goods in each of its sections, for example, gardening, kitchen equipment, luggage and clothing. A report is required at the end of each month showing the sales made in each department on a single page. The input file is sorted in date order within department. The number of transactions per department will not be more than 45 per week. Each department will have a total for the value of the sales made that week. Each page will have a heading (including the month in which the sales were made) and be numbered at the bottom of the page.

The input data file is sorted in date order within section. The input data structure would be as in Figure 12.18 and the report would have the appearance shown in Figure 12.19.

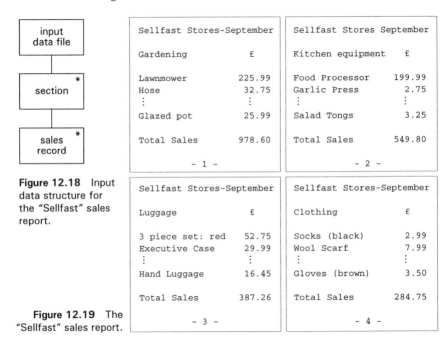

Figure 12.18 Input data structure for the "Sellfast" sales report.

Figure 12.19 The "Sellfast" sales report.

The output report can be translated into its JSP representation. The report has a number of pages (iteration). Each page on the report has a heading, followed by the page body, followed by the total sales and then the page number (sequence). The page body consists of sales records for each item sold within the section during the month (iteration). The output data structure would be as shown in Figure 12.20.

The following correspondences exist between the input and output data structures (Fig. 12.21). The input data file corresponds to the output report file (input generates output). The output report consists of a number of pages;

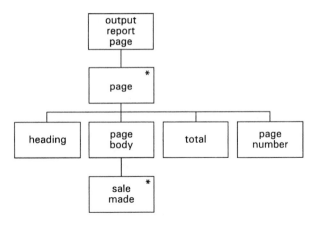

Figure 12.20 The output data structure diagram for the "Sellfast" sales report.

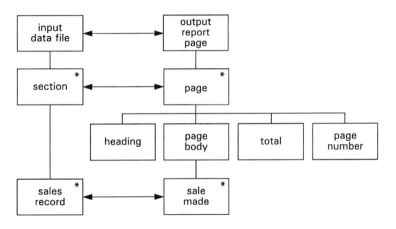

Figure 12.21 Points of correspondence between the input and output data structures for the "Sellfast" sales report.

each page corresponds to a single section on the input data file (the records are sorted in department order). Every sales record on the input data file corresponds to a line printed in the page body of the report showing the sales made for that month within the department.

This problem does not suffer from a boundary clash. Program development can continue by merging the input and output data structures in the normal way to produce the process structure diagram.

12.2.4 Three departments per page: not a boundary clash

The "All-for-One" store requires a weekly report of sales in each of its departments. The input file is sorted in date order within department. Each department is expected to sell no more than 15 items a week and therefore the sales details for three departments may be shown on a single page. Each department will have a total for the value of the sales made that week. Every page will have a heading and be numbered at the bottom of the page.

The records in the input file are sorted in date order within department. This gives us an input data file structure as an iteration of department (there are many departments), and department as an iteration of sale (there may be zero or more sales in each department).

The input data structure would be as as shown in Figure 12.22 and the report would have the following appearance of Figure 12.23.

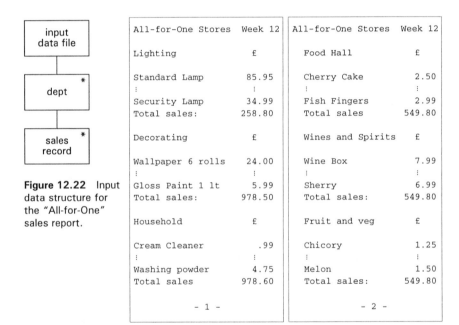

Figure 12.22 Input data structure for the "All-for-One" sales report.

Figure 12.23 The "All-for-One" sales report.

It can be seen from the sample output pages shown above that the output report file has several pages (iteration). Each page contains a heading, then the main body of the page followed by a page number (sequence). The main body of each page is known as a department group. The department group holds details of several departments (iteration); we happen to know in this case that there are three departments on each page. Each department has department sales details, described as a sales body, followed by a department sales total

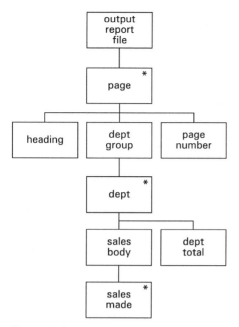

Figure 12.24 The output data structure diagram for the "All-for-One" sales report.

(sequence). The sales body is made up of a line on the report for each sales record within the department; there may be zero or more such lines printed (iteration).

The output data structure would be as shown in Figure 12.24, given the above description.

The following correspondences exist between the input and output data structures (Fig. 12.25). The input data file is processed to generate the output report file: there is a correspondence at the top level. Each department on the input file is represented on the output file, the relationship is one-to-one and the departments appear in the same order, so there is a correspondence at these points. The departments are grouped together in threes to fit onto each page in the output report, but this does not affect the correspondence between each department on the input file and each department on the report. Every sales record in the input data file is represented the same number of times, and in the same order, by a printed line giving details of each sale made on the output report; a correspondence exists between sales record on the input file and sale made on the output file.

This problem does not suffer from a boundary clash because there is a fixed relationship between the number of departments on a page. Note that the relationship is still one-to-one; one department group to one page. There are as many departments in the input file as on the output report, and they appear in the same order.

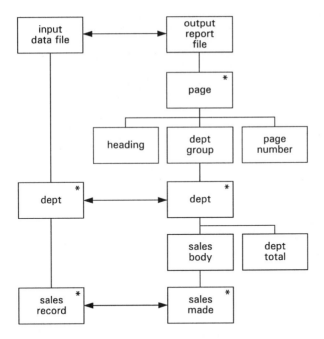

Figure 12.25 Points of correspondence between the input and output data structures for the "All-for-One" sales report.

12.2.5 Two pages per department: not a boundary clash

Another department store, "As Good As Sold", requires a monthly report of sales performance. The input file is sorted in date order in each department. It will not be possible for each department to have all its transactions recorded on a single page. The sales for each department will be represented on the output report file by a group of two pages (to be known as a "page pair"). Each department will have a total for the value of the sales made that week. Each page pair will have a heading.

The input data structure would be as shown in Figure 12.26 and the report would have the appearance of Figure 12.27.

The output data structure could be described in a number of ways. This is one interpretation, with the department sales total as the final item of a page pair (each page pair corresponding to a single department on the input data file). The output report file (Fig. 12.28) is composed of a number of page pairs (iteration). Each page pair has a header on the first page, followed by a page body, with the department sales totals at the end of the second page (sequence). The page body contains sales details, one line for each sale (iteration).

The following correspondences exist between the input and output data structures (Fig. 12.29). The input data file is processed to produce the output

168

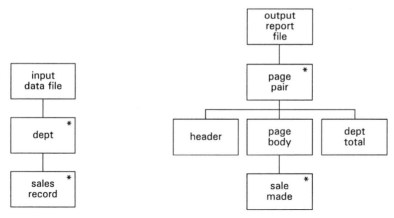

Figure 12.26 Input data structure for the "Good-as-Sold" sales report.

Figure 12.28 Part of a possible output data structure diagram for the "Good-as-Sold" sales report.

```
As Good As Sold - Sept

Gardening           £

Strimmer         75.00
Sprinkler        42.55
:                   :
Glazed Pot       25.99
Weedkiller        3.49
```

```
Hoe              19.75
Shears           12.50
Shredder        399.99
:                   :
Pruning Knife     4.76

Total Sales    1498.92
```

```
As Good As Gold - Sept

Luggage             £

Writing Case     49.75
Music Case       17.99
:                   :
Manicure Case     5.80
```

```
Knitting Bag      4.95
Passport Holder   5.95
PC Travel Case   12.75
:                   :
Overnight Bag    27.50
Total Sales     582.75
```

Figure 12.27 The "Good-as-Sold" sales report.

report file: there is a top level correspondence. Each department on the input data file is represented by a page pair on the output report file, the departments and the page pairs occur the same number of times and in the same order; a correspondence exists between the input and output data structure diagrams at this point. The sales records in the input data file match the sales made in the output report file; these too occur the same number of times and in the same order, and a correspondence can be established at this point.

The relationship between the page pair on the output report file and the

169

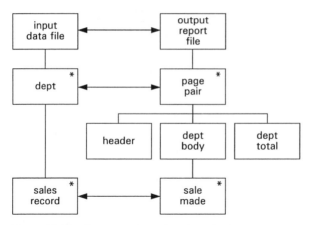

Figure 12.29 Correspondence between the input and output data structures for the "Good-as-Sold" sales report.

department on the input data file is one-to-one; although there are two pages, there is a fixed one-to-one relationship between a page pair and a department. There is no structure clash between these two data structures; the process structure can be created by merging the data structures, and program development can continue in the usual manner from this point.

There is an alternative representation of the output report file (Fig. 12.30); here the department sales total line is considered to be one kind of report line (the other kind being details of a sale). The ability to make alternative repre-

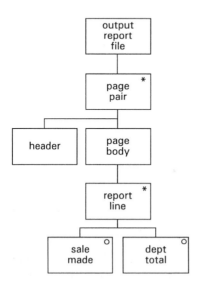

Figure 12.30 An alternative output data structure diagram for the "Good-as-Sold" sales report.

sentations of the same file will be particularly useful later on, in the context of program inversion. The output report file consists of a number of page pairs (iteration). Each page pair has a header on the first page, followed by a page body. The page body is composed of a number of report lines (iteration). Each report line could be either a record of a sale made, or the total sales for the current department (selection).

The following correspondences exist between the input and output data structures (Fig 12.31). The input data file is processed to create the output report file: there is a correspondence at the top level. Each department on the input data file corresponds to a page pair on the output report file, the departments and the page pairs occur the same number of times and in the same order. The sales records in the input data file do not match the report lines in the output report file because the report lines include the department sales total. The sales records on the input file do match the sales made on the report; these arise the same number of times and in the same order, and a correspondence exists between the two.

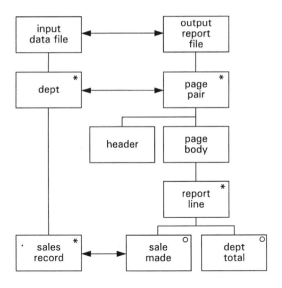

Figure 12.31 Correspondence between the input data structure and the alternative output data structure for the "Good-as-Sold" sales report.

It will be necessary to detect the change from one department to another in order to process the total line for the current department to be printed before beginning to process the next department. This problem does not suffer from a boundary clash because there is a fixed relationship between a department and the number of pages it requires; the relationship is one-to-one because there is one page pair to one department.

12.2.6 Variable page relationship: boundary clash

The "Herb and Spicer" department store requires a weekly report of sales performance in each of its departments. The input file is sorted in date order in each department. A few departments may not require a whole page to show their weekly sales, and there may be more than one department on a page. Some departments will be able to have all transactions recorded on a single page; other departments may require several pages to represent all their activities for the week. Each department will have a total for the value of the sales made that week. Each page will have a heading and be numbered at the bottom of the page.

The records in the input data file will be in department order; as there are many departments, this implies an iteration. There will be many sales made in each department during the course of a week; this implies another level of iteration.

The input data structure would be as shown in Figure 12.32 and the output report would have the appearance of Figure 12.33.

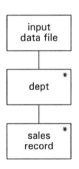

Figure 12.32 Input data structure for the "Herb and Spicer" sales report.

```
* Herb and Spicer Store *

Health Food          £
========================
Lemon Tea          2.99
  :                  :
Vegetarian Pate    3.49

Total Sales:      75.60

Toiletries           £
========================
Shampoo            2.75
  :                  :
Bath Salts         2.50

Total Sales:      36.60

Confectionery        £
========================
Chocolate Drops    1.25
Plain Choc bar      .89

         - 1 -
```

```
* Herb and Spicer Store *

Milk Choc Bar        .76
  :                  :
Chocolate Crunch   1.12

Total Sales:       2.99

Footcare             £
========================
Soothing Cream     1.25
Cushion Insoles    2.25
  :                  :
Foot Spray         2.15
Talcum Powder      2.75
Thermal socks      3.90

Total Sales       154.70

Fine China           £
========================
Zoe 10" Plate     19.75

         - 2 -
```

Figure 12.33 The "Herb and Spicer" sales report.

It can be seen from the sample report shown above that the output report will have many pages (iteration). Each page has a header, followed by the main body of the page, and finally a page number (sequence). The main body of the page might contain details of a single department, of part of a department or of several departments. It is not possible to determine how many departments will be on a page because the number of sales made by each department varies so widely. The implication of this situation is that a page cannot be described in terms of departments, and a department cannot be described in terms of pages; there is a variable relationship between the two. The requirement for a one-to-one relationship in order to identify a correspondence cannot be established. It is, however, possible to describe the main body of the page as consisting of a number of printed lines (iteration). Each line printed on the page could be a department heading, a sales record or a total for the department (selection). This description enables the construction of a valid JSP output data file structure diagram, which would be as shown in Figure 12.34.

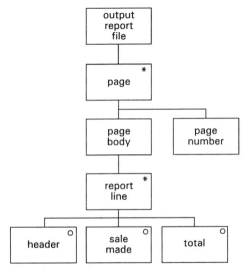

Figure 12.34 The output data structure diagram for the "Herb and Spicer" sales report.

The following correspondences exist between the input and output data structures. The input data file is processed to generate the output report file; there is a correspondence at the top level. Each sales record on the input data file corresponds to exactly one sales line on the output report file; they occur the same number of times and in the same order. The number of departments on the input data file does not match the number of pages on the output report file; this is because there is no regular relationship between the two that can be expressed in terms of a one-to-one mapping. A boundary clash has been detected, preventing the data structures from being merged.

This problem suffers from a boundary clash because the relationship between a page and a department changes throughout the report. Sometimes a single page will hold information for several departments; sometimes one entire department may be represented. At other times, one department may require several pages to record all the transactions that have taken place. In these circumstances, a page may hold information for several departments, for only one department or for part of a department. The structure clash between the input and output data structures is illustrated in Figure 12.35.

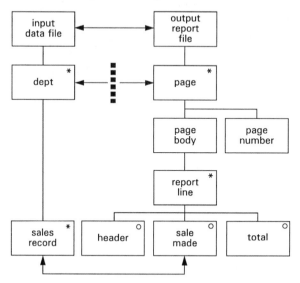

Figure 12.35   The structure clash between the input and output data structures for the "Herb and Spicer" sales report.

Note that the boundary clash would not arise either if the report did not require departmental totals or if page headings and page numbers were not required. These two features mean that the departmental grouping must be recognized as well as the size of a page. This is the reason that this clash is known as a boundary clash: the boundaries of a department and a page do not coincide; rather they are in conflict.

In this situation it will be necessary to design two programs to solve the problem. The first program would read the input data file and produce an intermediate file as output containing all the sales transactions and the calculated departmental totals. The second program would take this intermediate file as its input, and will produce the final report with headers and page numbers as output. This program design would solve the problem, but it would require the first program to run and produce the intermediate data file before the second program can run. A more sophisticated approach would be to use program inversion to resolve the problem.

The solution is to redefine the problem as if we were going to use an intermediate file. As we will see later, the intermediate file will not be physically created, as records will be passed between the main program and a subprogram in the order in which the records would have been written to/read from the intermediate file.

It will be necessary to describe the intermediate file in two ways: one as the intermediate output data structure to merge with the initial input data structure to form the first program, the other as the intermediate input data structure to merge with the final output data structure to produce the second program.

It is important to remember that there is only *one* intermediate file, which can be described in two ways, as appropriate for it being first an output file and then an input file (Fig. 12.36).

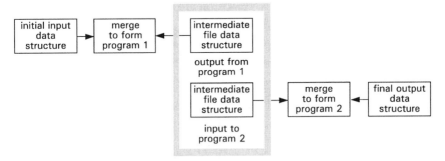

Figure 12.36   The intermediate file as an output *and* an input file.

It can be seen that the records in the intermediate file will be read by the second program in the same order that the first program wrote these records to the intermediate file (Fig. 12.37). The JSP solution to a structure clash takes advantage of this fact and allows us to dispense with the intermediate file altogether.

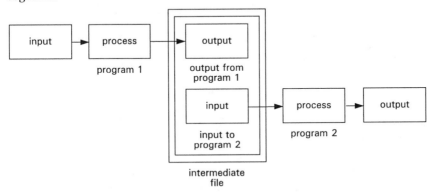

Figure 12.37   Writing to and reading from the intermediate file.

12.2.7 Boundary clash: example with program inversion

A bookshop has a stock file containing details of the books currently in stock. Each record on the file contains the following information:

a subject code
a supplier code
author
book title
publisher
number in stock

The contents of the file are sorted into supplier code within subject code; an example of the file contents is given in Table 12.3.

A report is required so that all books that have fewer than 50 copies in stock are identified. The report will have headings on each page giving the title, page number and date.

The details for each book that is below the reorder level of 50 will be printed one on each line, and a total of the number of different titles that need to be reordered will be printed after each subject code area.

No relationship exists between pages and subject areas; in some cases there may be several subject areas given on a page, and in others a subject area may take up more than one page. This indicates that there will be a boundary clash between the initial input data structure and the final output data structure. The clash between subject group and page can be seen on the input and output data structure diagrams (Fig. 12.38).

As the input and output data structures cannot be merged directly, it will be

Table 12.3 An example of the bookshop stock file.

Subject Code	Supplier Code	Author	Title	Publisher	in stock
01	073	Chadwick	Decipherment	Bloggins	100
01	073	Lucas	Translation	Treen	75
01	192	Jones	Coding	Rivers	12
01	246	Rogers	Linguistics	Castles	16
02	073	Rainbow	Painting	Gravelle	36
02	192	Adams	Drawing	Trimmett	120
02	192	Dawson	Sketching	Trimmett	45
03	055	Sanders	Pot Plants	Shore	84
03	073	Lewis	Rockeries	Bloggins	23
03	246	Harper	Gardening	Terrace	37
03	246	Fletcher	Shrubs	Terrace	65
03	359	Shearsby	Pruning Roses	Fordyce	79
04	022	Eaton	Cookery	Sherriff	66
04	045	Cutler	Cakes and Pies	Castles	84
04	246	Merritt	Baking	Terrace	63
04	359	Dale	Sugarcraft	Fordyce	72

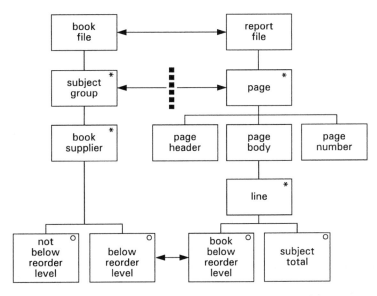

Figure 12.38 The boundary clash between subject group and page.

necessary to develop two programs. The original input data structure will be input to the first program, which will create an intermediate file as output. This intermediate file will provide the input to the second program, which will generate the final required output.

The intermediate file will be described in two different ways:

(a) as the output data structure for creating program 1 by merging with the original input data structure

(b) as the input data structure for creating program 2 by merging with the final output data structure.

If the input data structure (Fig. 12.39) were to be drawn only down to the level of the book supplier, this would give a true representation of the file, but it would omit the details of the number of books in stock. We need to distinguish between the acceptable and unacceptable stock levels by means of a selection.

The intermediate data file produced as output from processing the input file will contain book details in subject group order; only those books where the level of stock is below the reorder level will be held on the intermediate data file, followed by a total for the subject code area. The intermediate file structure is shown in Figure 12.40.

The points of correspondence between the initial input data file structure and the intermediate data file structure (viewed as output) are shown in Figure 12.41. The initial input data file structure and the intermediate data file structure can be merged to form the process structure for program 1, which will produce the intermediate file as output.

177

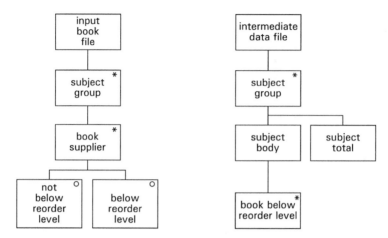

Figure 12.39 The input data structure for the bookshop stock report for program 1.

Figure 12.40 The input data structure for the intermediate file as output for the bookshop stock report for program 1.

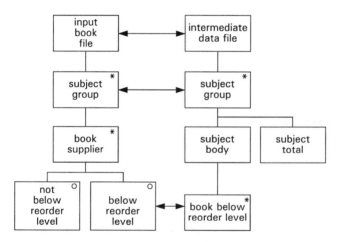

Figure 12.41 Points of correspondence between the input and intermediate data file structures for the bookshop stock report.

Process structure for program 1

The process structure for program 1 is shown in Figure 12.42. To this conditions and operations should now be added. The final process structure for program 1 is shown in Figure 12.43. The conditions for program 1 are:

```
c1: not end of file of the book file
c1: not end of file of the book file
    and same book supplier code
c3: books in stock >= 50
c4: else
```

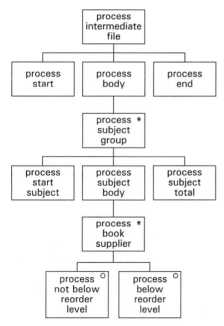

Figure 12.42 The process structure for the bookshop stock report for program 1.

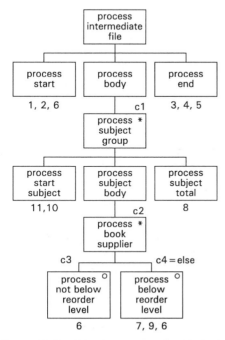

Figure 12.43 The process structure for the bookshop stock report for program 1 with conditions and operations allocated.

The operations list for program 1 is:

1. `Open input book file`
2. `Open output intermediate file`
3. `Close input book file`
4. `Close output intermediate file`
5. `Stop processing`
6. `Read book file record`
7. `Write book record to intermediate file`
8. `Write subject total record to intermediate file`
9. `Add 1 to subject total`
10. `Initialize subject total to 0`
11. `Store book subject code`

Now that program 1 has been designed in order to produce an intermediate file, a second program must be created to produce the output report from the intermediate file. In this case, the intermediate file is being viewed as input. The data structures for input and output for the second program are now drawn. The intermediate file can now be regarded as having many records, each of which may be a book below reorder level or a subject total. This alternative method of description allows correspondences to be established. The intermediate file as input data structure is shown in Figure 12.44, while the output report data structure is shown in Figure 12.45.

The input and output data file structures can be merged on the point of correspondence (Fig. 12.46) to form the process structure for program 2.

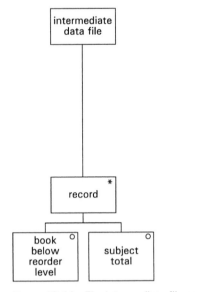

Figure 12.44 The intermediate file as input data structure for the bookshop stock report for program 2.

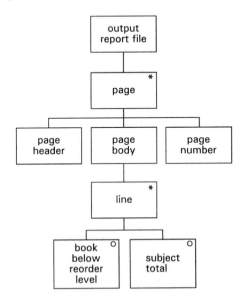

Figure 12.45 The output report data structure for the bookshop stock report for program 2.

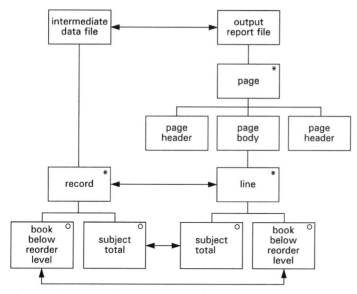

Figure 12.46 The points of correspondence between the intermediate data file and the output report file structures for the bookshop stock report.

Process structure for program 2

The process structure for program 2 is shown in Figure 12.47. To this we now need to add conditions and operations. The final process structure for program 2 is shown in Figure 12.48. The conditions for program 2 are:

c1: not end of intermediate file

c2: not end of intermediate file and not end of page

c3: if supplier change

c4: else

The operations list for program 2 is:

1. **Open intermediate file**
2. **Open report file**
3. **Close intermediate file**
4. **Close report file**
5. **Stop processing**
6. **Read intermediate file record**
7. **Print page headings**
8. **Print book detail line**
9. **Print subject total**
10. **Increment line count by 1**
11. **Increment page number by 1**
12. **Initialize line count to 0**
13. **Initialize page number to 0**
14. **Print page number**
15. **Advance to next page**

181

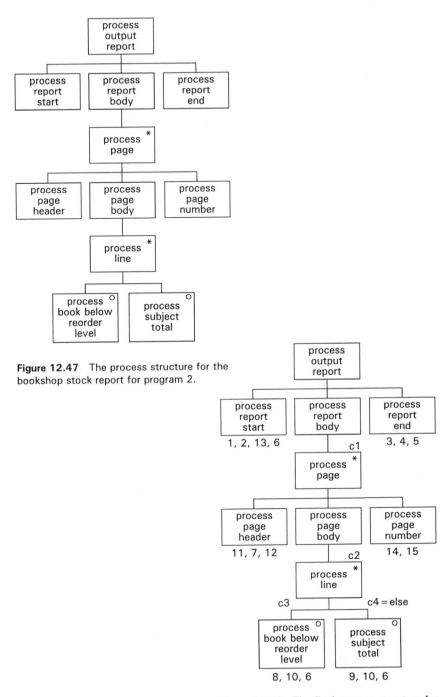

Figure 12.47 The process structure for the bookshop stock report for program 2.

Figure 12.48 The final process structure for the bookshop stock report for program 2.

Program inversion

Now that the design has been completed for each of the two programs assuming the use of an intermediate file, the technique of program inversion can be employed in order to dispense with the intermediate file, but retain the design of each of the individual programs.

The technique of program inversion allows the two programs to communicate with each other by means of individual records rather than by processing the whole of the input file in order to produce an intermediate data file that is then read and processed by the second program to generate the final output.

The design of the two programs means that the intermediate file can be viewed in two ways:

- output from program 1
  merge with input data structure
- input to program 2
  merge with output data structure

It will be necessary to amend the schematic logic in order to deal with records rather than with a file when we do away with the physical creation of an intermediate file by implementing program inversion.

Amending the schematic logic for program inversion

The following changes need to be made to certain operations used in program 1 (the main program) in order that communication with program 2 (the subprogram) can take place record-by-record rather than via an intermediate file.

2. `Open intermediate file` – *deleted*
4. `Close intermediate file` – *deleted*
7. `Write record to intermediate file` – *replace by call to subprogram*
8. `Write group total to intermediate file` – *replace by call to subprogram*

It is necessary to initialize the status variable QS to the value 1 in the main program for the first call to the subprogram. The value for QS will be updated in the subprogram immediately before each return to the main program; this means that control will be transferred to the appropriate point in the subprogram each time it is called from the main program. Control is passed back to the main program from the subprogram every time a record is required for processing; this is why the read and write operations for the intermediate file were deleted as the programs communicate on a record-by-record basis.

The schematic logic for program 1 as main program is:

```
process-intermediate-file seq
   process-start seq
      1. Open input book file
      2. Open output intermediate file
      => move 1 to QS
```

```
      6. Read book file record
   process-start end
   process-body itr while C1
     process-subject-group seq
        process-start-subject seq
           11. Store book subject code
           10. Initialize subject total to 0
        process-start-subject end
        process-subject-body itr while C2
           process-book-supplier sel if C3
              process-not-below-reorder-level seq
                 6. Read book file record
              process-not-below-reorder-level end
           process-book-supplier or C4 (else)
              process-below-reorder-level seq
                 7. Write book record to intermediate file
                 => call subprogram
                 9. Add 1 to subject total
                 6. Read book file record
              process-below-reorder-level end
           process-book-supplier end
        process-subject-body end
        process-subject-total seq
           8. Write subject total record to intermediate file
           => call subprogram
        process-subject-total end
     process-subject-group end
   process-body end
   process-end seq
        3. Close input book file
        4. Close output intermediate file
        5. Stop processing
   process-end end
 process-intermediate-file end
```

If we now consider program 2 as the subprogram, corresponding changes need to be made to certain operations as the intermediate file has been replaced by the transfer of individual records between the programs.

1. Open intermediate file – *deleted*
3. Close intermediate file – *deleted*
5. Stop processing – *return to main program*
6. Read intermediate file – *return to main program*

The return to the main program is necessary in order that the main program can pass the next record to the subprogram for processing. It will be necessary to update the value of the status variable QS in the subprogram, to determine the point at which control should resume. The following code should be included at the start of the subprogram in order to transfer control to the appropriate point of the subprogram each time it is called by the main program:

`GO TO Q1,..., Qn DEPENDING ON QS`

This means that the first call to the subprogram will transfer control to Q1 (at the start of the program). Processing continues until a record is required; the value in QS is then updated to 2 and control is returned to the main program.

When the subprogram is called again, the `GO TO Q1,..., Qn DEPENDING ON` statement will transfer control to Q2 in the subprogram because 2 is the value held in the QS variable. When the iteration is entered for the first time, the first record will be processed. The value 3 will be placed in QS if the record was for a book below reorder level, alternatively the value 4 will be placed in QS if the record represented a subject total. In either case, this updating of QS will take place immediately before control is returned to the main program so that the next record can be transferred for processing, thus ensuring control will be returned to the same place in the program from which it was relinquished. When the final record has been processed, the end-of-file marker will be passed to the subprogram, causing exit from the iteration and the closing of the report file before returning control to the main program for the last time.

The schematic logic for program 2 as subprogram is:

```
process-output-report seq
GO TO Q1, Q2, Q3, Q4 DEPENDING ON QS
Q1
    process-report-start seq
        1. Open intermediate file
        2. Open report file
        13. Initialize page number to 0
        6. Read intermediate file record
    => move 2 to QS
    => return to main program
Q2
    process-report-start end
    process-report-body itr while C1
        process-page-seq
            process-page-header seq
                11. Increment page number by 1
                7. Print page headings
                12. Initialize line count to 0
            process-page-header end
            process-page-body itr while C2
                process-line sel if C3
                    process-book-below-reorder-level seq
                        8. Print book detail line
```

```
                    10. Increment line count by 1
                     6. Read intermediate file record
                    => move 3 to QS
                    => return to main program
Q3
                process-book-below-reorder-level end
            process-line or C4 (else)
                process-subject-total seq
                    9. Print subject total
                    10. Increment line count by 1
                     6. Read intermediate file record
                    => move 4 to QS
                    => return to main program
Q4
                process-subject-total end
            process-line-end
        process-page-body end
        process-page-number seq
            14. Print page number
            15. Advance to next page
        process-page-number end
      process-page-end
    process-report-body end
    process-report-end seq
        3. Close intermediate file
        4. Close report file
        5. Stop processing
        => return to main program
    process-report-end end
process-output-report end
```

12.3 Interleaving clash

An interleaving clash occurs when the entities are not distinct in the data file; the entities overlap each other.

An input file holds clock-on and clock-off times for employees, and start and stop times for the tasks they undertake during the day. A report is required calculating the total amount of time spent on each task and hence the total hours worked during the day for each individual. As individuals will start and finish work at different times, it is not possible to find directly how long any one person has spent on a task: the start and stop times must both be found, but the stop time for a given task may be separated from the start time by the start and stop times of other tasks. One solution would be to sort the file holding the start and stop times, but this would take time. Another option is to use the technique of setting up an intermediate file for each employee, logging the start and stop times as they occur.

It can be seen with the input and output data structures that a correspondence only exists at the top level (Fig. 12.49); the individual tasks in the output file are interspersed with other data in the input file, i.e. they are interleaved.

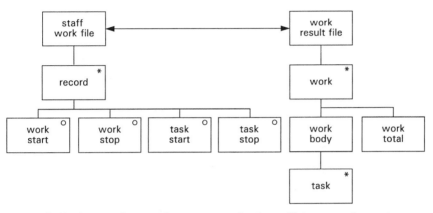

Figure 12.49   Input and output data structures for the staff time-recording system.

When it comes to program inversion in this situation, multiple inversion is required. This means that, for design purposes, every person will be considered as having the data on their working day stored in an intermediate file (there will be as many intermediate files as staff). As usual, when program inversion is implemented, the intermediate file itself is not physically created; rather it is used in order to design the communicating programs. There will be one main program and as many subprograms as there are staff (each subprogram will be activated by a call from the main program involving a work or task record for a specific individual). The work file for a member of staff could be described by the data structure diagram in Figure 12.50.

As there will be many members of staff, each described in this way, a higher level view would be to include the above diagram as part of an iteration. Similarly, the report generated for each member of staff could also be regarded as being part of a higher level iteration. The correspondences between the work file and the output report for an individual are shown diagrammatically in Figure 12.51. Correspondences exist between the person work file and the work result file for each person, as shown.

These data structures for input and output can be merged in the normal manner, producing a process structure diagram.

Each member of staff will have a process structure diagram relating to the work and the tasks they undertake during the day. This means that each mem-

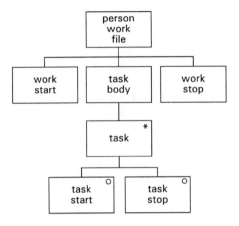

Figure 12.50 An input data structure diagram for an individual member of staff, for the staff time-recording system.

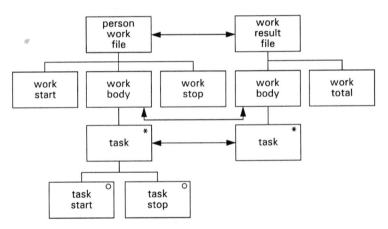

Figure 12.51 Points of correspondence between the person work file and the work result file for an individual member of staff.

ber of staff will trigger a call to the appropriate subprogram every time they start or stop either their work for the day, or a task during the course of the day. As each member of staff has a subprogram, the main program has many subprograms (not just one as in the previous examples); this is referred to as *multiple inversion*.

12.4 Exercises

1. Explain the meaning of the following terms, and how they are related:
   correspondence
   lack of correspondence
   structure clash

2. What are the three types of structure clash? Give an example of each.

3. What is the difference between using an intermediate file and implementing program inversion when dealing with the problem of a structure clash?

4. Why is it necessary to delete references to an intermediate file in the subprogram when program inversion is being used?

5. Demonstration example 7 in Section 4.5 of Chapter 4 illustrated a structure clash when an attempt was made to produce a list of employees by department with titles, totals and page numbers. The example is reproduced below. Identify the type of structure clash that is involved, and complete the solution to the problem by using the technique of program inversion.

   The input file contains employee records grouped by department. The output report file is produced listing employee records, grouped by department. Some departments are small and more than one will fit onto a single page; other departments are large and will need several pages in order to list all members of staff within each one. One record is printed per line and there are 50 lines per page. A department title is printed before the employee records for that department and the total number of staff within each department is printed when all staff records for that department have been printed. The total

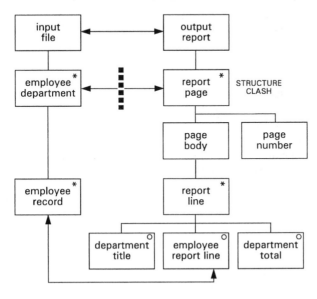

Figure 12.52 Input and output data structures for Exercise 5, showing a boundary clash.

189

number of employees in each department has to be calculated: this information is not stored explicitly on the input file.

It has been recognized that there will be difficulties as the number of departments appearing on a page may vary, and it is not possible to identify where the department titles and totals will appear in relation to the pages. It will be necessary to show that any line on the report can be an employee record, a department total, or a department title.

There is a structure clash between the **employee department** on the input data structure and the **report page** box on the output report structure; there is no relationship between page and department. It is not possible to merge the two data structures to form a single program to solve the problem.

The **employee record** box on the input data structure diagram corresponds to the **employee report line** box on the output data structure diagram: input records occur the same number of times and in the same order as output lines on the report page, and input generates output.

The **department title** box on the output data file structure shows a lack of correspondence with the input data file structure, as the department title is not stored in the input file except as a field within each employee record.

The **department total** box on the output data file structure exhibits a lack of correspondence with the input data file structure; the department total can only be calculated by processing each employee record for that department.

It is not possible to merge these two structures in order to form a basic process structure because of the structure clash between **employee department** on the input data structure and **report page** on the output data structure (Fig. 12.52).

Show how the problem can be solved by using an intermediate data file in order to design two programs. Develop the design to incorporate the technique of program inversion.

12.5 Further reading

Holmes (1991), Sections 13.1–13.7.
King & Pardoe (1992), Chapter 9.
Storer (1991), Chapters 8 and 9.
Thompson (1989), Chapters 18 and 19.

CHAPTER 13

Program dismemberment

When we have a large program, we know that it will be swapped in and out of memory during its period of execution. If we have implemented a program using inversion, we also know that it will not be possible for the whole program to be executed (even if it is granted enough time) because there will be points in the code where control will need to be passed between the main program and the subprogram. Loading the program for it to execute also takes time, and it would therefore be logical only to load that part of the program that we know could be executed at any one time. This has the benefit of loading only that code which is required, as well as reducing the amount of time spent loading, which could be better employed in processing the data.

In order to divide a program into smaller components that can be loaded (rather than load the whole program at any one time) the technique of program dismemberment is employed.

Program dismemberment uses the concept of follow sets, i.e. it is possible to examine the process structure and establish which part or parts of the code may be executed next. Control would be handed back to the calling program at each Q point.

Q1, Q2, Q3, Q4 (Fig. 13.1) are resume/suspend points, showing where control is relinquished and regained when control is passed between the main program and the subprogram. When the subprogram containing the Q points is called for the first time by the main program, control is passed to the beginning of the subprogram. Execution of the subprogram proceeds until a Q point is reached when control must be passed back to the main program by a **return** statement. A value is stored to indicate the Q point at which execution was suspended before the return is performed, so that when the main program calls the subprogram again, control will be routed back to this same Q point in the subprogram.

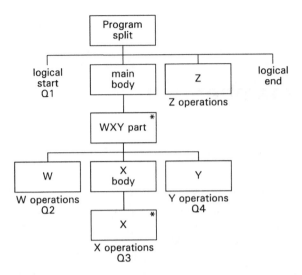

Figure 13.1 A process structure showing resume/suspend points.

13.1 Follow sets

On first entry to program **split**, control can only go to W or Z components; it is not possible for control to pass directly to X or Y. Once control has reached component W, it is then only possible to go to X or Y; control cannot be passed directly to Z. Therefore we can see that only (W or Z) or (X or Y) can occur next from whatever point has been reached in the structure. Thus {W, Z} is the follow set from the logical start of the program at point Q1 and {X, Y} is the follow set from point Q2 in W and also from point Q3 within X itself. It is because X is an iterated component that X may occur again after X itself.

If we write the schematic logic, we can see that only the resume points Q1, Q2, Q3 and Q4 occur in both the WZ and XY modules; all other code is in either the WZ module or the XY module, but not in both these modules.

In some cases the sets of elementary components will not be disjoint; there may be overlap or there may be containment. The technique of program dismemberment will still work but there may be duplications in the modules. It is possible to merge overlapping sets into one module, but this will mean that, on some occasions, more code will be loaded than is required. There is a trade off in this case between the number of modules and the size of modules.

13.2 Graphical dismemberment

Here, we dismember the process structure by inspection. As we know from the follow sets that only {W, Z} can be reached from Q1 and Q4, we can make

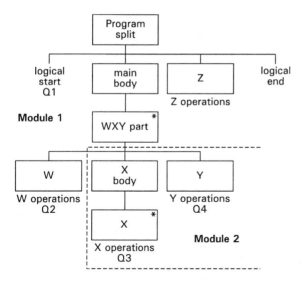

Figure 13.2 Graphic dismemberment of the process structure diagram.

this part of the structure diagram into Module 1. The remainder of the program, {X, Y} (reachable from Q2 and Q3), becomes Module 2. The division between the two modules is shown graphically in Figure 13.2.

The information from Figure 13.2 can be used to construct tables to show the components of the modules and the relationships between them. It is then possible to create individual modules based on the original program. Section 13.4 shows how the schematic logic from the whole program can be partitioned into two modules, which can be loaded and executed as and when required.

13.3 Dismemberment in tabular form

The dismemberment of a program can be described in tabular form, using the resume execution and module link tables. These tables are given for program **split**.

13.3.1 Resume execution table

The resume execution table (Table 13.1) identifies the elementary components that can be reached from each of the Q points. This suggests splitting the program into two modules: one module containing Z and W, the other formed from X and Y.

Table 13.1 Resume execution table.

Resume points	Elementary components
Q1	Z, W
Q2	X, Y
Q3	X, Y
Q4	Z, W

Table 13.2 Module link table.

Module name	Elementary components	Suspend points	Module link
Mod 1	Z	END	NIL
	W	Q2	Mod 2
Mod 2	X	Q3	Mod 2
	Y	Q4	Mod 1

13.3.2 Module link table

The module link table (Table 13.2) gives, for each module that has been identified, the elementary components within each module, the Q point at which execution may be suspended, and the next module that will be loaded following suspension at each Q point. This would result in expanded Query Status pointers, e.g. Mod 1 Q4 (or WZ Q4) to specify the module as well as the Suspend Point.

When the program is divided into modules, it will first be necessary to identify which parts of the schematic logic belong to which module. It will be necessary for all the Q points to appear in all modules, so that the initial control statement (GO TO Q1, ..., Qn DEPENDING ON QS) is able to divert control to the appropriate part of the program within each module. The initial control statement itself will also need to appear in all modules.

13.4 Schematic logic

In the current example, the schematic logic is given below with WZ and XY indicating each specific statement that must appear in either the WZ or XY modules, or in both:

```
XY  WZ        PROGRAM-SPLIT SEQ
XY  WZ        GO TO Q1, Q2, Q3, Q4 DEPENDING ON QS
XY  WZ  Q1    ...
    WZ        /* READ deleted by inversion implementation */
    WZ        MAIN BODY ITR
    WZ        IF Z GO TO MAIN BODY END
XY  WZ            WXY PART SEQ
    WZ                W Operations
    WZ                MOVE 2 TO QS
    WZ                RETURN
XY  WZ  Q2
XY                    X BODY ITR
XY                    IF Y GO TO X BODY END
```

```
XY                      X Operations
XY                      MOVE 3 TO QS
XY                      RETURN
XY  WZ  Q3
XY                      GO TO X BODY ITR
XY                      X BODY END
XY                      Y Operations
XY                      MOVE 4 TO QS
XY                      RETURN
XY  WZ              WXY PART END
XY  WZ  Q4
    WZ          GOTO MAIN BODY ITR
    WZ          MAIN BODY END
    WZ          Z Operations
    WZ          PROGRAM SPLIT END              /* logical end */
```

The schematic logic can now be split into two modules, all statements with
WZ above in module WZ, and all XY statements in module XY. It can be seen
clearly from the two modules that some lines appear in both.

The schematic logic for module WZ alone will be:

```
XY  WZ          PROGRAM SPLIT-WZ SEQ
XY  WZ          GO TO Q1, Q2, Q3, Q4 DEPENDING ON QS
XY  WZ  Q1  ...
    WZ          /* READ */
    WZ          MAIN-BODY ITR
    WZ          IF Z GO TO MAIN-BODY END
XY  WZ              WXY-PART SEQ
    WZ                  W Operations
    WZ                  MOVE 2 TO QS
    WZ                  RETURN
XY  WZ  Q2
XY  WZ  Q3
XY  WZ              WXY-PART END
XY  WZ  Q4
    WZ          GOTO MAIN-BODY ITR
    WZ          MAIN-BODY END
    WZ          Z Operations
    WZ          PROGRAM-SPLIT-WZ END           /* logical end */
```

The schematic logic for module XY alone will be:

```
XY  WZ          PROGRAM SPLIT-XY SEQ
XY  WZ          GO TO Q1, Q2, Q3, Q4 DEPENDING ON QS
XY  WZ  Q1  ...
XY  WZ  Q2
```

```
XY  WZ      WXY PART SEQ
XY              X BODY ITR
XY              IF Y GO TO X BODY END
XY                  X Operations
XY                  MOVE 3 TO QS
XY                  RETURN
XY  WZ  Q3
XY              GO TO X BODY ITR
XY              X BODY END
XY              Y Operations
XY              MOVE 4 TO QS
XY              RETURN
XY  WZ      WXY PART END
XY  WZ  Q4
```

These two modules could now be converted into code using the normal rules for translating schematic logic into a programming language.

13.5 Worked examples using graphical and tabular methods

13.5.1 Simple dismemberment: two modules

Taking the example from the section on using program inversion in Chapter 12 to solve the problem of a boundary clash, we can see how the subprogram lends itself to simple dismemberment.

If the program is entered at the logical start (Q1), the sequence of operations allocated to **process report start** will be executed before control must be returned to the main program; this will therefore form the first module.

When the main program calls the subprogram again, and for each pass in the iteration, the first logical possibility is that there is a line to be printed (either for a book below the reorder level, or for a subject total), after which control will be passed back to the main program in order to obtain the next record to be processed; alternatively, the iteration may terminate. The report file will then be closed and the subprogram will complete execution and return control to the main program for the last time. This gives the second module, as it is not possible to determine whether the iteration will terminate or a book detail or a subject total line will be printed; this is true at Q2, Q3 and Q4.

The resume execution table is given as Table 13.3 and the module link table as Table 13.4. The graphical dismemberment of the subprogram is shown in Figure 13.3. The schematic logic for each of the two modules is also given. As the whole program is fairly small, and the first module in particular has only a few lines of code, it is a valid option to decide against program dismemberment and have the main program call the entire subprogram each time.

Table 13.3 Resume execution table for the book-ordering example.

Resume points	Elementary components
Q1	Process report start
Q2	Process book below reorder level, Process subject total, Process report end
Q3	Process book below reorder level, Process subject total, Process report end
Q4	Process book below reorder level, Process subject total, Process report end

Table 13.4 Module link table for the book-ordering example.

Module name	Elementary components	Suspend points	Module link
Mod 1	Process report start	Q2	Mod 2
Mod 2	Process report end	END	NIL
	Process book below reorder level	Q3	Mod 2
	Process subject total	Q4	Mod 2

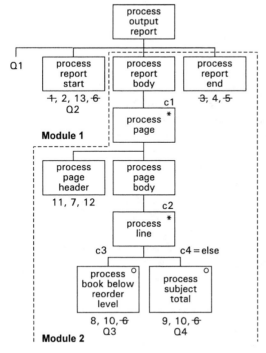

Figure 13.3 Graphic dismemberment of the final process structure for the book-ordering example.

197

The schematic logic for module 1 of the subprogram is as follows:

```
process-output-report seq
GO TO Q1, Q2, Q3, Q4 DEPENDING ON QS
Q1
    process-report-start seq
        1. open intermediate file
        2. open report file
        13. initialize page count to 0
        6. read intermediate file record
        => move 2 to QS
        => return to main program
Q2
    process-report-start end
Q3

Q4
process-output-report end
```

The schematic logic for module 2 of the subprogram is as follows:

```
process-output-report seq
GO TO Q1, Q2, Q3, Q4 DEPENDING ON QS
Q1
Q2
    process-report-start end
    process-report-body itr while C1
        process-page-seq
            process-page-header seq
                11. increment page count by 1
                7. print page headings
                12. initialize line count to 0
            process-page-header end
            process-page-body itr while C2
                process-lines sel if C3
                    process-book-below-reorder-level seq
                        8. print book detail line
                        10. increment line count by 1
                        6. read intermediate file record
                        => move 3 to QS
                        => return to main program
Q3
                    process-book-below-reorder-level end
                process-lines sel or (else)
                    process-subject-total seq
                        9. print subject total
```

198

```
                    10. increment line count by 1
                     6. read intermediate file record
                    => move 4 to QS
                    => return to main program
Q4
                    process-subject-total end
                 process-lines-end
             process-page-body end
         process-page-end
     process-report-body end
     process-report-end seq
         3. close intermediate file
         4. close report file
         5. stop processing
         => return to main program
     process-report-end end
 process-output-report end
```

13.5.2 Disjoint modules: four modules

This process structure diagram (Fig. 13.4) will be dismembered graphically (Fig. 13.5) and in tabular form (Tables 13.5 and 13.6). Note that where a

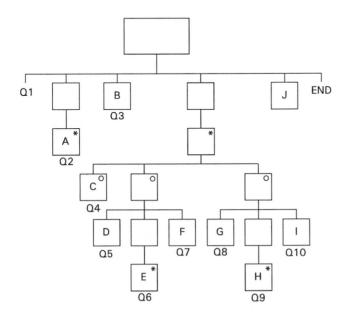

Figure 13.4 A process structure diagram prior to dismemberment.

199

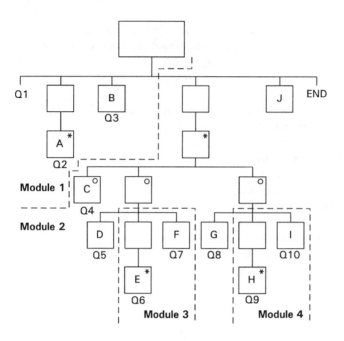

Figure 13.5 Graphic dismemberment of the process structure diagram in Figure 13.4.

selection occurs, all initial selection parts need to appear in the module as it cannot be decided in advance which will be required. In the case of an iteration, the loop may be executed a further time, or it may terminate, so the iteration itself and the subsequent component need to be included in the same module.

Table 13.5 Resume execution table for dismemberment of Figure 13.4.

Resume points	Elementary components
Q1	A, B
Q2	A, B
Q3	C, D, G, J
Q4	C, D, G, J
Q5	E, F
Q6	E, F
Q7	C, D, G, J
Q8	H, I
Q9	H, I
Q10	C, D, G, J

Table 13.6 Module link table for dismemberment of Figure 13.4.

Module name	Elementary components	Suspend points	Module link
Mod 1	A, B	Q2	Mod 1
		Q3	Mod 2
Mod 2	C, D, G, J	Q4	Mod 2
		Q5	Mod 3
		Q8	Mod 4
		END	NIL
Mod 3	E, F	Q6	Mod 3
		Q7	Mod 2
Mod 4	H, I	Q9	Mod 4
		Q10	Mod 2

13.5.3 Disjoint modules: three modules

In a further example demonstrating program dismemberment (Fig. 13.6) it can be seen that in each case an iteration is followed by a selection; this will require both selection parts to be included in the same module as the iteration, because the possibilities are that the iteration may continue or the iteration may terminate and either one of the selection components may be activated. It is not possible to decide in advance which case will apply and so all potentially executable fragments of code will need to be grouped together.

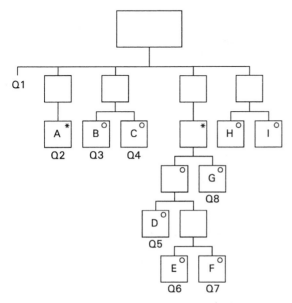

Figure 13.6 A process structure diagram prior to dismemberment.

The process structure can be dismembered both graphically (Fig. 13.7) and in tabular form (Tables 13.7 and 13.8).

13.5.4 Overlapping modules

The examples considered so far have been dismembered into disjoint modules; there have been no areas of the program structure that could be present in more than one module. This has been possible because all terminal nodes contain Q points (except the final nodes, where control is returned to the calling program as the subprogram terminates). This may not always be the case; it is possible that certain parts of a subprogram will not have Q points allocated, as control is not returned to the calling program at such places in the subprogram.

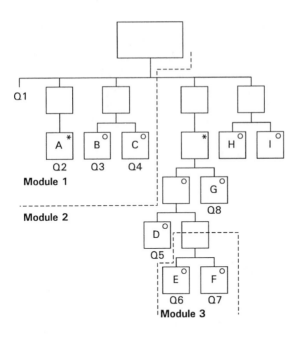

Figure 13.7 Graphic dismemberment of the process structure diagram in Figure 13.6.

Table 13.7 Resume execution table for dismemberment of Figure 13.6.

Resume point	Elementary components
Q1	A, B, C
Q2	A, B, C
Q3	D, G, H, I
Q4	D, G, H, I
Q5	E, F
Q6	D, G, H, I
Q7	D, G, H, I
Q8	D, G, H, I

Table 13.8 Module link table for dismemberment of Figure 13.6.

Module name	Elementary components	Suspend points	Module link
Mod 1	A, B, C	Q2	Mod 1
		Q3	Mod 2
		Q4	Mod 2
Mod 2	D, G, H, I	Q5	Mod 3
		Q8	Mod 2
		END	NIL
		END	NIL
Mod 3	E, F	Q6	Mod 2
		Q7	Mod 2

If we take the last example, consider the effect of there being no suspend point at Q7 in the program (Fig. 13.8, Table 13.9). The possibilities of "what comes next" increase if there is no Q7 suspend point, because processing could continue further until control needs to be returned to the main program.

The absence of a suspend point at Q7 means that more code can be executed from Q5. One set of elementary components is contained within

202

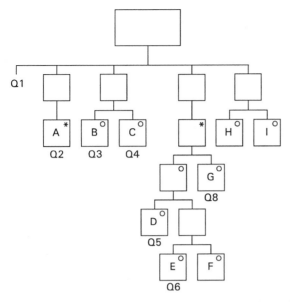

Figure 13.8 A process structure diagram prior to dismemberment.

Table 13.9 Resume execution table for dismemberment of Figure 13.7

Resume point	Elementary components
Q1	A, B, C
Q2	A, B, C
Q3	D, G, H, I
Q4	D, G, H, I
Q5	E, F, D, G, H, I
Q6	D, G, H, I
Q8	D, G, H, I

Table 13.10 Module link table for dismemberment of Figure 13.8

Module name	Elementary components	Suspend points	Module link
Mod 1	A, B, C	Q2	Mod 1
		Q3	Mod 2
		Q4	Mod 2
Mod 2	D, G, H, I	Q5	Mod 3
		Q8	Mod 2
		END	NIL
		END	NIL
Mod 3	E, F, D, G, H, I	Q5	Mod 3
		Q6	Mod 2
		Q8	Mod 2
		END	NIL
		END	NIL

another; therefore we may combine these two modules if we so wish (Table 13.10).

It can be seen that Module 2 is a subset of Module 3; we can use this in order to combine the two modules into one (Table 13.11). The previous Modules 2 and 3 have been combined to produce a single Module 2. This means that when Module 2 is loaded, sometimes more code will be loaded than will actually be required, but, to counterbalance this, there are only two modules rather than three.

Table 13.11 Module link table for three disjoint modules with modules 2 and 3 combined.

Module name	Elementary components	Suspend points	Module link
Mod 1	A, B, C	Q2	Mod 1
		Q3	Mod 2
		Q4	Mod 2
Mod 2	E, F, D, G, H, I	Q5	Mod 2
		Q6	Mod 2
		Q8	Mod 2
		END	NIL
		END	NIL

If the code relating to components E and F were very large, it is unlikely that we would want to combine Modules 2 and 3 in this way. If, however, the code relating to components E and F is relatively small, there would only be a small overhead in combining the modules.

13.6 Exercises

1. Show how you would dismember the process structure diagram shown in Figure 13.9 (a) graphically; and (b) in tabular form.

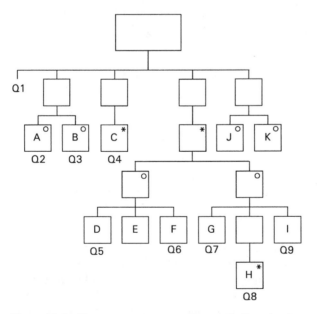

Figure 13.9 The process structure diagram for Exercise 1.

2. Show how you would dismember the process structure diagram shown in Figure 13.10 (a) graphically; and (b) in tabular form.

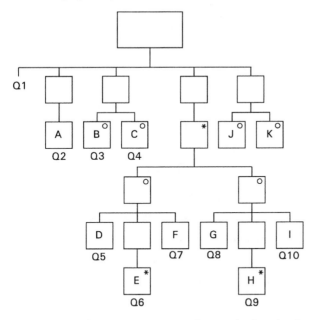

Figure 13.10 The process structure diagram for Exercise 2.

3. Show how you would dismember the process structure diagram shown in Figure 13.11 (a) graphically; and (b) in tabular form.

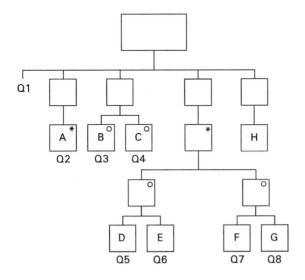

Figure 13.11 The process structure diagram for Exercise 3.

4. Show how you would dismember the process structure diagram shown in Figure 13.12 (a) graphically; and (b) in tabular form.

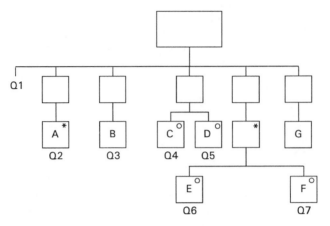

Figure 13.12 The process structure diagram of Exercise 4.

5. Show how you would dismember the process structure diagram shown in Figure 13.13 (a) graphically; and (b) in tabular form.

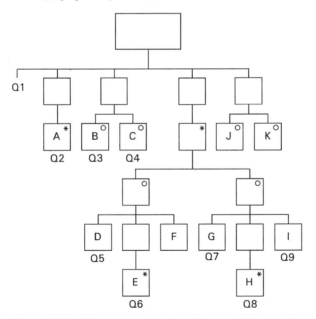

Figure 13.13 The process structure diagram of Exercise 5.

CHAPTER 14

Dealing with multiple input files

All the programs considered so far have employed a single input file and a single output file. On certain occasions we may need to deal with the requirement to process multiple input files (for example, if we are merging two input files to produce a single output file). The JSP approach to program design allows us to deal with this eventuality.

14.1 Describing the input and output files

A common problem that occurs is that of merging two sorted input files in order to produce a single output file. If we assume that each file is sorted into ascending order of the unique key field, we will find that the possibilities shown in Table 14.1 exist.

Table 14.1 is rather like a truth table, demonstrating the four possibilities for each record on the file. We assume that there exists only one record for each key on each file.

We would normally specify each of the two input files as being an iteration of record, but it will be necessary to expand this definition in order to deal with the possibility of a record being present on one file but not on the other. If we do not have compatible data structures we will not be able to combine the data structures.

The file structure for input file 1 is shown in Figure 14.1 and that for input file 2 in Figure 14.2.

Table 14.1 The possibilities for each record with two input files.

	File 1	File 2
record	absent	absent
record	absent	present
record	present	absent
record	present	present

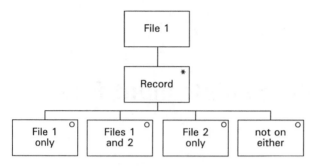

Figure 14.1 Data file structure for input file 1.

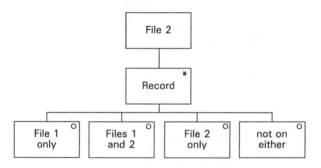

Figure 14.2 Data file structure for input file 2.

It can be seen that in order to create a data structure for each file so that these structures can be successfully combined, it is necessary to represent records that do not actually exist on the specific file. This situation does not cause a contradiction, it is equivalent to a null selection component.

It is now possible for the two input files to be successfully merged on the points of correspondence. The merged input file structure is as shown in Figure 14.3. This is the combined input data structure for the two input data files. If the problem to be solved is to merge the two input files, the output file would be an iteration of record. The output file structure is shown in Figure 14.4.

14.2 Creating the basic process structure

Now that input and output data file structures have been created, they must be merged on the points of correspondence to produce the process structure diagram (Fig. 14.5). This would lead to a process structure of the same appearance (Fig. 14.6) as the input data structure.

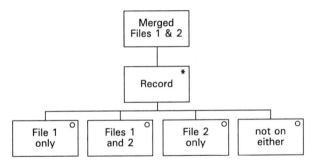

Figure 14.3 The merged input data file structure.

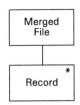

Figure 14.4 The output data file structure.

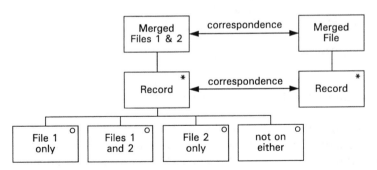

Figure 14.5 Identifying the points of correspondence between the input and output data file structures.

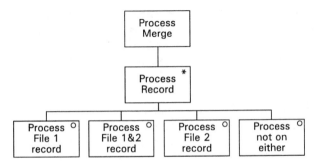

Figure 14.6 The basic process structure diagram.

209

14.3 Creating the final process structure

It is now necessary to add sequence components to the structure of Figure 14.6 to deal with opening and closing files, and other "housekeeping" activities. The final process structure will have the appearance of Figure 14.7; conditions and operations can be added to create the schematic logic, which can then be converted into code.

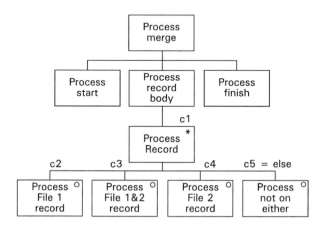

Figure 14.7 The final process structure diagram.

14.4 Allocating conditions

The merging of the two files will continue until all records in both input files have been read and processed. The condition on the iteration must therefore test for the end-of-file condition on both input files. If all records in one file have been read, processing must continue in order that the remaining records on the other file are transferred to the output file.

Condition $c1$: **while (not end of file 1) or (not end of file 2)**
Since records are sorted in order on their key fields, it is possible to detect if a record present on one file is absent from the other, as the key field value will be greater on the latter file if the record is not present. The tests for a record being present on each file will therefore relate to the relative values of the key field.
  • If the keys are both the same, the records match.
  • If one key value is higher than the other, the records do not match and the record with the lower key value does not appear on the other file.
It will be necessary to continue processing until all records have been copied

from file 1 as well as from file 2. Therefore the condition here must test for end of file on both input files, terminating only when there are no further records in either file, indicating that all records from both files have been processed. An equivalent form is: **while not (end of file 1 and end of file 2).**

Condition c2: `if record on file 1 only`
In file 1, the key of the current record is less than the key value of the current record in file 2, showing that the same record is not present in the latter file. The record from file 1 needs to be written to the output file and a new record read from file 1.

Condition c3: `if record on file 1 and file 2`
In file 1, the key of the current record has the same value as the key value of the current record in file 2, showing that the same record is present in both files. One copy of the record (either from file 1 or from file 2, as the records match) needs to be written to the output file and a new record read from both file 1 and file 2.

Condition c4: `if record on file 2 only`
In file 1, the key of the current record is greater than the key value of the current record in file 2, showing that the same record is not present in the first file. The record from file 2 needs to be written to the output file and a new record read from file 2.

Condition c5: `else`
In this case there is no action to be taken. The last selection box shows the theoretical possibility of a record not being present on either file; this can be catered for by the **else** condition on the last part of a selection, as usual. There will be no explicit action associated with this branch; it is essentially a "do nothing" operation, as we can only merge records from files where there is a record in existence on at least one of the files.

The full list of conditions for the final process structure is now:
```
c1: while not end of input file 1 or not end of input file 2
c2: if record on file 1 only
c3: if record on file 1 and file 2
c4: if record on file 2 only
c5: else
```

14.5 Allocating operations

The operations list must be created and each operation allocated to the relevant process box in the diagram. Operations are required to open and close both the input files and also the output file. Records must be written to the output file in the correct order, taking care not to create duplicate records in the output file where a record exists in both input files. No calculations are involved in this problem; the only other operations required are those to read from the input files.

The operations list is:

1. Stop processing
2. Open input file 1
3. Open input file 2
4. Open output file
5. Read record from file 1
6. Read record from file 2
7. Write file 1 record to output file
8. Write file 2 record to output file
9. Close input file 1
10. Close input file 2
11. Close output file

The final process structure with operations and conditions is shown in Figure 14.8.

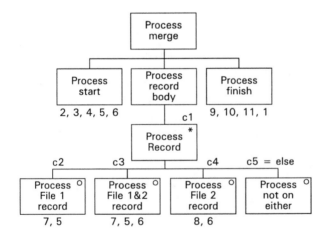

Figure 14.8 The final process structure diagram with operations and conditions.

14.6 Generating the schematic logic

The schematic logic for the process structure is:

```
Process Merge seq
   Process Start seq
         2. Open input file 1
         3. Open input file 2
         4. Open output file
         5. Read record from file 1
         6. Read record from file 2
   Process Start end
   Process Body itr while (not end of File1) or
                          (not eof File 2)
         (* continue processing while records present
         on either file *)
      Process Record sel if File 1 record < File 2 record
         (* if record on File 1 only *)
         Process File 1 record seq
               7. Write file 1 record to output file
               5. Read record from file 1
         Process File 1 record end
      Process Record or if File 1 record = File 2 record
         (* if record on File 1 and record on File 2 *)
         Process File1&2 record seq
               7. Write file 1 record to output file
               5. Read record from file 1
               6. Read record from file 2
         Process File1&2 record end
      Process Record or if File 1 record > File 2 record
         (* if record on File 2 only *)
         Process File 2 record seq
               8. Write file 2 record to output file
               6. Read record from file 2
         Process File 2 record end
      Process Record or else
         Process not on either seq
               (* do nothing *)
         Process not on either end
      Process Record end
   Process Body end
   Process End seq
         8. Close input file 1
         9. Close input file 2
         10. Close output file
```

```
        1. Stop processing
    Process End end
  Process Merge end
```

14.7 Optimization

Michael Jackson suggested two rules for optimization:
- **Rule 1** Do not do it.
- **Rule 2** (for experts only) Do not do it yet.

Programs can be optimized, for example by extracting statements from loops where such statements could be placed before or after the loop in the code (this should not be necessary if the JSP approach has been followed during the design of the program). Another approach to optimization includes deleting areas of code that appear to have no effect. This may be contrary to the expectations and requirements of the programmer, for example an optimizing compiler might delete the following code as having no effect:

```
new_number := (number/number) * number;
if new_number <> number then
    . . .
```

whereas the intention of the programmer is to test the accuracy of number representation.

A further possibility is to delete portions of code that should never be activated. In our current example, it should never be possible to activate the final selection component of the process structure as a record must be present on one, or other, or both of the files being merged. Consider the problems that might arise given the following code:

```
if number < minimum then
    (* calculation statements *);
if number > minimum then
    (* calculation statements *);
```

What should the result be if the value of **number** is equal to the value of **minimum**? It may be that equality should be included in the comparison with **minimum**, or it may be the case that a different set of calculations should be associated with the circumstances where equality exists. The following code will not remedy the situation; rather there is the problem of the "dangling else". Pascal will take the **else** to refer to the nearest **if** statement, but this in turn could create problems; did the programmer intend the **else** part of the second **if** statement to be activated when **number** is less than **minimum**? If not, the second **if** statement should be enclosed within the **else** part of the first **if** statement:

```
if number < minimum then
    (* calculation statements *);
if number > minimum then
    (* calculation statements *)
else
    (* calculation statements *)
```

The following code will deal with all possibilities for value comparisons between the variables **number** and **minimum**:

```
if number < minimum then
    (* calculation statements *);
else
    if number > minimum then
        (* calculation statements *)
    else
        (* calculation statements *)
```

It can be the case that a well designed program can be damaged by optimization. Alternatively, the design may become difficult to maintain if changes are required to the original design. However, trade offs may need to be made and often take the form of processing (frequently calculation) versus storage. One example is the swapping of values between variables. A typical approach would be to copy one value into a dummy variable, making use of storage:

```
value-1 copied into dummy
value-2 copied into value-1
dummy copied into value-2
```

This would achieve the swapping of values held in **value-1** and **value-2**, but at the price of another variable. An alternative approach would be to use calculation to achieve the same result:

```
value-1 added to value-2 and stored in value-2
value-1 subtracted from value-2 and stored in value-1
value-1 subtracted from value-2 and stored in value-2
```

The values in the two variables have again been swapped, but without the use of an additional variable; calculation has removed the need for another variable. So it is possible to use different methods to achieve the same effect *in principle*, but there may be hidden problems, for example, rounding errors in calculations, resulting in unexpected results if one method is used rather than another.

In the not-too-distant past, optimization was often necessary to improve the efficiency of a program, or even to ensure that it could be loaded into a restricted amount of memory space so that it could run. Now that hardware is cheaper and major costs of software development are associated with the time spent developing, debugging and maintaining code, the construction of correct and reliable programs has assumed greater importance.

In the context of the file merging example, the final selection part can never be activated and thus may be safely removed. It will then be necessary to change the conditions on the selection; the final condition will be deleted and one of the remaining conditions will need to be redefined as **else**.

14.7.1 Optimizing the process structure

The optimized final process structure with operations and conditions is shown in Figure 14.9. Here, the additional selection component, which had no active operations associated with it, has been removed. This has implications for the schematic logic in that the final selection component has been removed, and with it the **else** condition. The solution is to convert one of the other selection conditions to **else**.

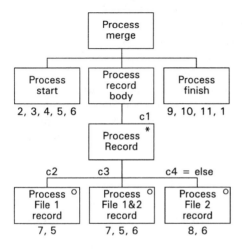

Figure 14.9 The optimized final process structure diagram with operations and conditions.

14.7.2 Generating schematic logic from the optimized process structure

The changes made to the process structure can now be reflected in the schematic logic. It is important, if any changes are made, to change the design first and this will automatically filter through to the schematic logic. If the schematic logic alone is altered, the design and the program no longer match, a recipe for trouble.

The schematic logic for the process structure now becomes:

```
Process Merge seq
    Process Start seq
        2. Open input file 1
        3. Open input file 2
```

```
        4. Open output file
        5. Read record from file 1
        6. Read record from file 2
    Process Start end
    Process Body itr while c1
        Process Record sel if c2
            Process File 1 record seq
                7. Write file 1 record to output file
                5. Read record from file 1
            Process File 1 record end
        Process Record or if c3
            Process File1&2 record seq
                7. Write file 1 record to output file
                5. Read record from file 1
                6. Read record from file 2
            Process File1&2 record end
        Process Record or if c4 (else)
            Process File 2 record seq
                8. Write file 2 record to output file
                6. Read record from file 2
            Process File 2 record end
        Process Record end
    Process Body end
    Process End seq
        8. Close input file 1
        9. Close input file 2
        10. Close output file
        1. Stop processing
    Process End end
Process Merge end
```

14.8 Exercises

1. Consider how you would deal with the case study example in Chapter 10 if the updates were to be made from a file rather than from an interactive user.

2. How would you deal with more than two input files? What effect would this have on the final program structure?

14.9 Further reading

Holmes (1991), Chapter 10.
King & Pardoe (1992), Chapter 8.
Storer (1991), Chapters 5 and 8.
Thompson (1989), Chapter 12.

CHAPTER 15

Getting started with JSP-Tool

This chapter will guide you through the stages of using JSP-Tool to enable you to enter a process structure, allocate conditions and operations, generate the schematic logic and finally produce executable code that the structure represents. It will usually be necessary to develop the process structure manually from the input and output data structures in the normal way, but for demonstration purposes in this tutorial session an example has been prepared. JSP-Tool does not support the creation of process structures from data structures; rather it allows the automatic production of code from a process structure that has been manually prepared.

15.1 The tutorial example

The purpose of this tutorial session is to enter the JSP process structure shown in Figure 15.1 (a solution to the problem of counting the number of male and female records on a student file), to generate the schematic logic and produce

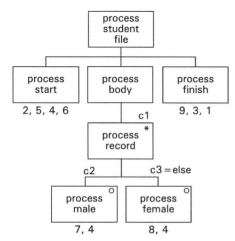

Figure 15.1 The process structure for the tutorial example.

executable code (for example, in COBOL, C or Pascal) using JSP-Tool. Note that the process structure has been simplified so that the printing of totals is included under **process finish**, which closes the files and terminates the program.

The conditions are:

C1: while not end of file
C2: if male student
C3: else

The operations list is:

1. **Stop run**
2. **Open input student file, output report file**
3. **Close student file, report file**
4. **Read record from student file, at end move "Y" to EOF**
5. **Move "N" to EOF**
6. **Move zero to male total, female total**
7. **Add 1 to male total**
8. **Add 1 to female total**
9. **Print male total, female total to report file**

15.2 Starting JSP-Tool

You may use JSP-Tool from Windows or from DOS. If you elect to use DOS, you should change directory to JT as your working directory in order to proceed

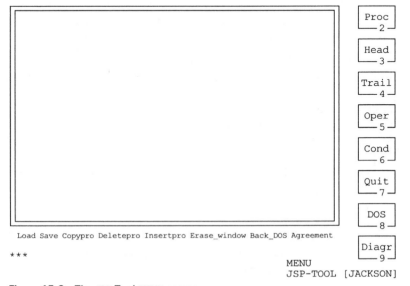

Load Save Copypro Deletepro Insertpro Erase_window Back_DOS Agreement

***

MENU
JSP-TOOL [JACKSON]

Figure 15.2 The JSP-Tool MENU screen.

(i.e. **cd\jt**). In DOS, start by typing **jt** at the prompt. In Windows, double click on the JSP-Tool icon. In either case, JSP-Tool will wait for you to enter the file name of a JSP process structure diagram. On this occasion press return as a new diagram will be created. Later you may wish to specify an existing file that contains a process structure.

JSP-Tool will clear the screen and give a display as shown in Figure 15.2. Note that the boxes down the right-hand margin of the screen can be activated either by clicking the left button on the mouse when the mouse cursor is over the chosen option, or by pressing the appropriate function key number.

Items from the menu bar across the lower part of the screen can be selected either by clicking the left mouse button when the mouse cursor is over the item required, or by entering the lower menu by pressing the escape key; the required item can be chosen either by typing the initial character of the option or by jumping from one option to the next by pressing the space bar; pressing the return key will then select the option identified.

15.2.1 Leaving JSP-Tool

Quit on the right-hand menu bar does *not* allow you to exit from JSP-Tool; it represents the JSP **QUIT** operation.

To leave JSP-Tool pick **Back_DOS** from the lower menu.

REMEMBER TO SAVE YOUR WORK BEFORE LEAVING JSP-TOOL.

Using the mouse
Click the left mouse button over **Back_DOS**.

Using the function keys
There are two methods when using the function keys.
1. Press **escape** to enter lower menu, then space bar across to **Back_DOS**; press **return**.
2. Press **escape B**.

REMEMBER TO SAVE YOUR WORK BEFORE LEAVING JSP-TOOL.

If you have entered a process structure which you have not saved, JSP-Tool will prompt:

    Q to Quit? C

leaving **c** (for continue) as the default option.

    Press **return** to remain in JSP-Tool.

    Press **Q** then **return** to exit from JSP-Tool, without saving your work.

The MENU screen options are described in Section 15.11.

15.3 Creating a process module

In order to sketch a JSP process structure diagram, it is first necessary to create a module box for that diagram at the main menu screen in JSP-Tool. It is possible to enter more than one module on this screen, but at this stage we are only interested in producing one.

Using the mouse
Select process by clicking the left mouse button on **Proc** on the right-hand menu bar; move the mouse cursor back into the main window and press the left mouse button again. You will find a white box appears at the lower left-hand corner of the screen waiting for you to enter the name of the module. Here the name **program** was entered, followed by pressing the left mouse button (or hitting the **return** key), and the module is now represented by a double edged box in the main window (Fig. 15.3)

Using the function keys
Select **Proc** by pressing **F2** followed by **return**. You will find a white box appears at the lower left-hand corner of the screen waiting for you to enter the name of the module. Here the name **program** was entered, followed by hitting the **return** key, and the module is now represented by a double-edged box in the main window (Fig. 15.3).

The next stage is to draw the process structure diagram itself, at the SKETCH screen in JSP-Tool.

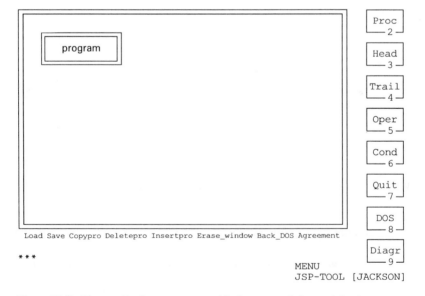

Figure 15.3 The JSP-Tool MENU screen with the name of the module shown.

15.4 Entering the process structure diagram

The SKETCH screen in JSP-Tool allows the JSP process structure diagram to be drawn on the screen. The **Diagr** option needs to be chosen from the right hand menu bar.

Using the mouse
Move the mouse cursor onto **Diagr** at the lower right-hand corner of the screen and press the left mouse button; the SKETCH screen and menus will be displayed (Fig. 15.4).

Using the function keys
Select **Diagr** by pressing the **F9** function key; the SKETCH screen and menus will be displayed (Fig. 15.4).
The SKETCH screen options are described in Section 15.12.

Cpy Era Dbox Insrt Mov Bdy P_A Lft Rght Attr Sma Gre Ope* Nam* Find Tidy

★ ★ ★

SKETCH
JSP-TOOL [JACKSON]

Figure 15.4 The JSP-Tool SKETCH screen.

15.4.1 Entering the root process box

Using the mouse
Move the mouse cursor over the top box on the right-hand menu bar and click the left mouse button; this indicates a sequence box. Move the mouse cursor back onto the main screen and click the left mouse button again; a solid white process box will be displayed on the screen.

Using the function keys

Select a sequence box by pressing the function key **F2**; this indicates a sequence box. Press **return**; a solid white process box will be displayed on the screen.

15.4.2 Displaying outline process boxes

The solid white box display can be changed to an orange outline, which is easier to read (Fig. 15.5). This is achieved by changing the attribute associated with the process structure diagram display screen.

Using the mouse

Move the mouse cursor over **Attr** on the lower menu; click the left mouse button and the display will change to give an orange outline to the box. Click the left mouse button again and the white box display returns; click again and the orange outline format reappears.

Using the function keys

There are two methods when using the function keys.
1. Press the **escape** key and then move to the **Attr** option by pressing the space bar; press the **return** key.
2. Press the **escape** key followed by the **A** key.

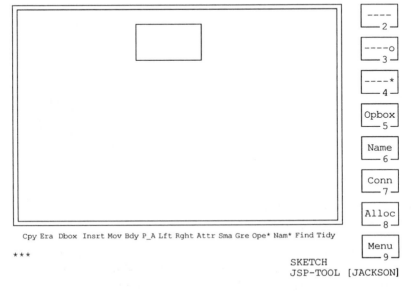

Figure 15.5 The JSP-Tool SKETCH screen with the root process box displayed.

15.4.3 Entering the three sequence components

Using the mouse
The sequence box has already been chosen from the right-hand menu bar. Move the mouse cursor below and to the left of the original box and click the left mouse button; a new box appears. Move the mouse cursor directly under the original box and click the left mouse button again; a further process box appears. Move the mouse cursor to the right, click the left mouse button again; a third sequence component box appears (Fig. 15.6).

Using the function keys
The sequence box from the right-hand menu bar has already been chosen. Move the cursor (using the cursor keys) below and to the left of the original box and press return; a process box appears. Move the cursor directly underneath the original process box and press return again; a further process box appears. Move the cursor to the right and press return again; a third sequence component appears (Fig. 15.6).

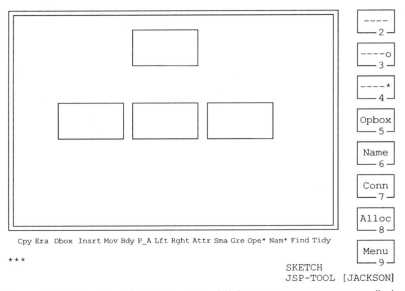

Figure 15.6 The JSP-Tool SKETCH screen with three sequence components displayed.

15.4.4 Connecting the sequence components to the root

In order to connect the components of a structure to the parent process box it is necessary to identify the parent process box as the current (or active) node and then indicate the child nodes in turn.

Using the mouse

Move the mouse cursor onto the root process box and press the right mouse button. This process box is now the current box, and this is indicated by the **n** in the top left-hand corner of the process box. Move the mouse cursor onto **Conn** on the right-hand menu bar and click the left mouse button; this selects the **Connect** option. Move the mouse cursor across to the main window and onto the first of the sequence components; click the left mouse button. The first box is connected to the root (Fig. 15.7).

Using the function keys

Move the cursor (using the cursor keys) onto the root process box and press the **F10** function key. This process box is now the current box, and this is indicated by the **n** in the top left-hand corner of the process box. Choose the **Connect** option by pressing the **F7** function key. Move the cursor onto the first of the sequence component boxes and press return; the box is connected to the root (Fig. 15.7).

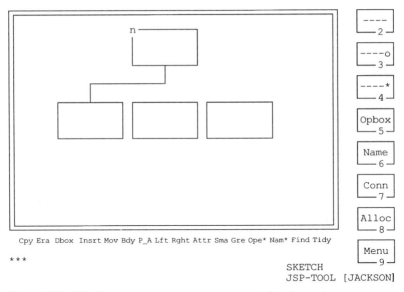

Figure 15.7 The first sequence component connected to the root.

Using the mouse

Move the mouse cursor across to the second sequence component and click the left mouse button; the second box is also connected to the root (Fig. 15.8).

226

Using the function keys
Move the cursor to the next box and press **return**; the second box is connected to the root (Fig. 15.8).

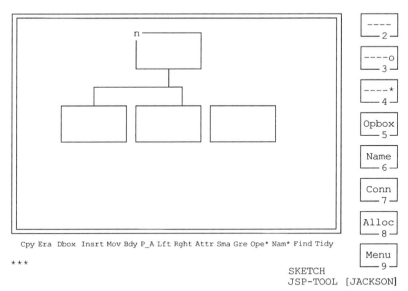

```
n ───
```

```
 ----
  └─ 2 ─┘

 ----o
  └─ 3 ─┘

 ----*
  └─ 4 ─┘

 Opbox
  └─ 5 ─┘

 Name
  └─ 6 ─┘

 Conn
  └─ 7 ─┘

 Alloc
  └─ 8 ─┘

 Menu
  └─ 9 ─┘
```

```
Cpy Era Dbox Insrt Mov Bdy P_A Lft Rght Attr Sma Gre Ope* Nam* Find Tidy

* * *
                                            SKETCH
                                            JSP-TOOL [JACKSON]
```

Figure 15.8   The second sequence component connected to the root.

Using the mouse
Move the mouse cursor across to the third sequence component and click the left mouse button; all three sequence component boxes are now connected to the root (Fig. 15.9).

Using the function keys
Move the cursor to the third sequence component box and press **return**; all three sequence component boxes are now connected to the root (Fig. 15.9).

15.4.5 Entering the iterated component

Using the mouse
Move the mouse cursor onto the second of the three sequence components and then click the right mouse button; this will make this process box the current box, designated by **n** in the top left-hand corner of the box (Fig. 15.10).

Using the function keys
Move the cursor onto the second of the three sequence components and then press the **F10** function key; this will make this process box the current box, designated by **n** in the top left-hand corner of the box (Fig. 15.10).

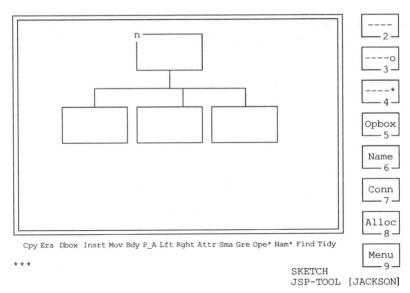

Figure 15.9 All three sequence components connected to the root.

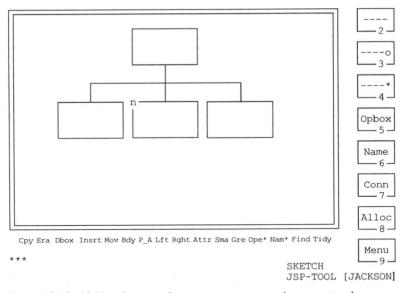

Figure 15.10 Making the second sequence component the current node.

Using the mouse
Move the mouse cursor onto the third box in the right-hand menu and click the left mouse button; this indicates an iterated component box. Move the mouse cursor below the second sequence component box (the current box)

and press the left mouse button; an iterated component box will appear (Fig. 15.11). The iterated component will be connected to the current box automatically because the parent node was already identified as the current (active) node.

Using the function keys

Press the **F4** function key; this indicates an iterated component box. Move the cursor below the second sequence component box (the current box) and press **return**; an iterated component box will appear (Fig. 15.11). The iterated component will be connected to the current box automatically because the parent node was already identified as the current (active) node.

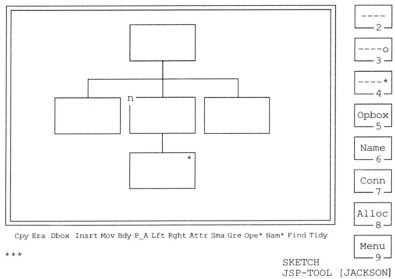

Figure 15.11   The iterated component entered.

15.4.6 Entering the selection components

Using the mouse

To make the iterated component the current box, move the mouse cursor onto the iterated component and press the right mouse button. The **n** sign will appear in the top left-hand corner of the box, indicating that this is now the current (active) box.

Move the mouse cursor onto the second box on the right-hand menu bar and click the left mouse button; this indicates a selection component box. Move the mouse cursor below the iterated component and click the left mouse button; a selection component will appear. Move the mouse cursor to the right and click the left mouse button again; a further selection component

229

will appear (Fig. 15.12). The selection components will be connected auto-matically as the parent node is the current node.

Using the function keys

To make the iterated component the current box, move the cursor onto the iterated component and press the **F10** function key. The **n** sign will appear in the top left-hand corner of the box indicating that this is now the current (active) box.

Press the **F3** function key; this indicates a selection component. Move the cursor below the iterated component and press **return**; a selection compo-nent appears on the process structure. Move the cursor to one side and press **return** again; a further selection component appears (Fig. 15.12). The selec-tion components will be connected automatically as the parent node is the current node.

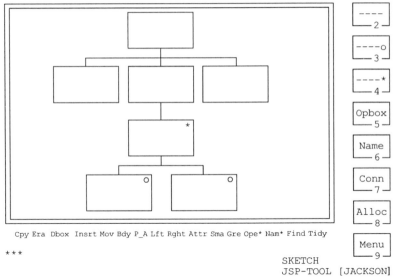

```
Cpy Era Dbox  Insrt Mov Bdy P_A Lft Rght Attr Sma Gre Ope* Nam* Find Tidy

* * *
                                              SKETCH
                                              JSP-TOOL  [JACKSON]
```

Figure 15.12   The selection components entered.

15.5 Viewing the process structure diagram

It is possible to change the mode of display of the process structure diagram on the screen.

15.5.1 Moving about the diagram

If the process structure diagram becomes too large to be viewed as a whole on the display screen, it is possible to move from top to bottom and left to right by means of the cursor keys. See Section 15.5.4. for details of viewing the process structure diagram as a whole by reducing it in size.

15.5.2 Changing the display

Process boxes will initially appear as white on a black background. It is usually easier to read the process structure if the boxes are made to appear as outlines, rather than solids. This is achieved by selecting **Attr** from the lower menu; this toggles between the two options.

Using the mouse
Click mouse button over **Attr**; the display will switch between a solid white box display and an orange outline display each time the option is selected.

Using the function keys
Either:
    1. **escape** to enter lower menu, space bar across to **Attr**; press **return**.
or:
    2. Press **escape A**.
The display will switch between a solid white box display and an orange outline display each time the option is selected.

15.5.3 Tidying the process structure diagram

It is possible to make the process structure diagram appear more neatly on the screen.

Using the mouse
Move the mouse cursor across to **Tidy** on the lower menu bar; press the left mouse button. The process structure diagram will be redrawn on the screen.

Using the function keys

Select the **Tidy** option from the lower menu bar (either by entering **escape T**, or by entering escape and then moving to **Tidy** by hitting the space bar, followed by **return**). The process structure diagram will be redrawn on the screen.

15.5.4 Reducing the display

Using the mouse

Click the left mouse button over **Sma** on the lower menu bar. The process structure diagram will now appear reduced in size on the screen (Fig. 15.13). Note that when the names of the process boxes have been entered, they may be truncated when the display is reduced in size.

Using the function keys

Either:

    1. **escape** to enter lower menu, space bar across to **Sma**; press **return**.

or:

    2. Press **escape S**.

The process structure diagram will now appear reduced in size on the screen (Fig. 15.13). Note that when the names of the process boxes have been entered, they may be truncated when the display is reduced in size.

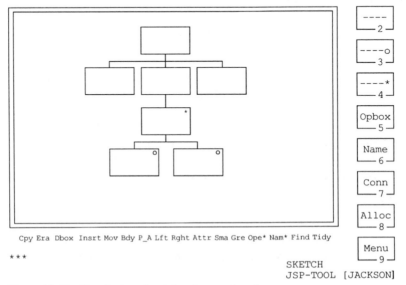

Cpy Era Dbox Insrt Mov Bdy P_A Lft Rght Attr Sma Gre Ope* Nam* Find Tidy

* * *

SKETCH
JSP-TOOL [JACKSON]

Figure 15.13   The display after it has been reduced.

It is possible to reduced the size of the display more than once. At the limit of reduction, the process structure diagram appears with small solid orange boxes representing sequence components, the "o" symbol representing selection components and the "*" symbol representing iterated components.

15.5.5 Enlarging the display

Using the mouse
Click the left mouse button over **Gre** on the lower menu bar. The process structure diagram will now appear enlarged in size on the screen (Fig. 15.14).

Using the function keys
Either:
1. **escape** to enter lower menu, space bar across to **Gre**; press **return**.
or:
2. Press **escape G.**
The process structure diagram will now appear enlarged in size on the screen (Fig. 15.14).

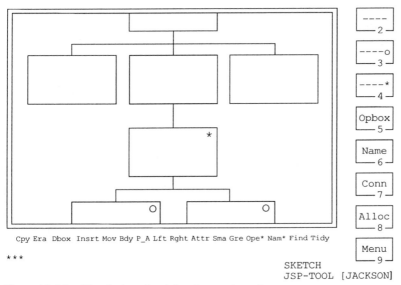

Cpy Era Dbox Insrt Mov Bdy P_A Lft Rght Attr Sma Gre Ope* Nam* Find Tidy

* * *

SKETCH
JSP-TOOL [JACKSON]

Figure 15.14   The display after it has been enlarged.

When the process structure has been enlarged, it is likely that not all the process structure will be visible on the screen.

15.6 Naming the processes

The name associated with each process box can now be given. It is possible to insert the names in the process boxes in two ways: stepping through all process boxes automatically or choosing each box to be named individually.

15.6.1 Stepping through automatically

Using the mouse
Move the mouse cursor onto the root node of the process structure diagram; press the right mouse button to make this process box the current (active) node.

Move the mouse cursor onto the **Nam*** option on the lower menu bar and click the left mouse button. A white box will appear at the bottom of the screen waiting for the name for the root node to be entered (return or the left mouse button should be pressed after the name has been typed). JSP-Tool will then move to the next box and wait for the name to be entered in the same way. This continues until a name has been allocated to each box in the process structure diagram (Fig. 15.15).

Using the function keys
Move the cursor onto the root node of the process structure diagram; press **F10** to make this process box the current (active) node.

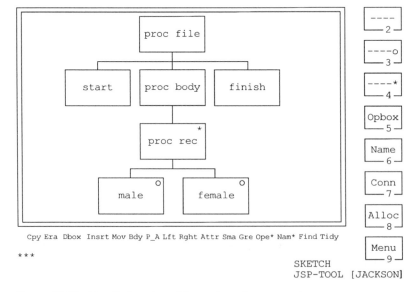

Figure 15.15   The display after all boxes have been named.

Select **Nam*** from the lower menu panel (either by entering **escape** and **N**, or **escape** and hop to the **Nam*** option by presssing the space bar, followed by pressing **return**). A white box will appear at the bottom of the screen waiting for the name for the root node to be entered (**return** should be pressed after the name has been typed). JSP-Tool will then move to the next box and wait for the name to be entered in the same way. This continues until a name has been allocated to each box in the process structure diagram (Fig.15.15).

15.6.2 Naming individual boxes

Using the mouse
Move the mouse cursor onto **Name** on the right-hand menu bar and click the left mouse button. Move the mouse cursor onto one of the boxes in the process structure diagram and click the left mouse button. A white box will appear at the bottom of the screen waiting for the name of the process for that box to be entered. When the name of the process has been typed in, either press **return** or press the left mouse button again. When all the boxes have been named in this way the screen will again appear as in Figure 15.15.

Using the function keys
Press the **F6** function key to select **Name** from the right-hand menu bar. Move the cursor onto one of the boxes in the process structure diagram and press **return**. A white box will appear at the bottom of the screen, waiting for the name of the process for that box to be entered. When the name of the process has been typed in press **return**. When all the boxes have been named in this way the screen will again appear as in Figure 15.15.

15.7 Adding operations

Before any operations can be allocated, special "open" boxes must be added to the process structure diagram to hold the operation numbers. It is not possible to allocate operations to ordinary sequence process boxes in JSP-Tool.

15.7.1 Adding the operations boxes

Rather than writing operations below the process boxes, JSP-Tool has a special open-ended box that must be placed under a process box; the identification numbers of the operations allocated to a particular process box will be placed in these operations boxes.

Although it is possible to add operations boxes automatically at all legal positions in the process structure diagram, it is *strongly recommended* that you do not take this approach. The preferred method is to add each individual operations box directly under the terminal (or leaf) process box to which it refers. This ensures that all operations boxes are associated with a named process.

Using the mouse

Move the mouse cursor onto a **leaf** node on the process structure diagram; make this node current by pressing the right mouse button. The **n** sign will appear. Move the mouse cursor across to **Opbox** on the right-hand menu and select this option by clicking the left mouse button. Move the mouse cursor under the leaf node where the operations box is to appear and click the left mouse button; an open-ended operations box will appear on the diagram under the chosen process box.

Move the mouse cursor to the next **leaf** node and make it the current node by pressing the right mouse button; the **n** sign will now appear in the top left-hand corner of this process box. Move the mouse cursor below this box and then click the left mouse button and an open-ended operations box will appear below the process box.

Figure 15.16 shows that all operations boxes have been added, the last one to be inserted being under **finish**.

Using the function keys

Move the cursor onto a **leaf** node on the process structure diagram; make this node current by pressing the **F10** function key. The **n** sign will appear. Select

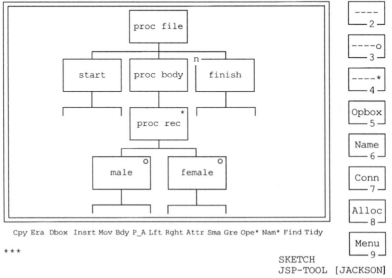

Cpy Era Dbox Insrt Mov Bdy P_A Lft Rght Attr Sma Gre Ope* Nam* Find Tidy

***

SKETCH
JSP-TOOL [JACKSON]

Figure 15.16 The display after all operations boxes have been added.

the **Opbox** option by pressing the **F5** function key. Move the cursor under the leaf node where the operations box is to appear and press **return**. An open-ended operations box will appear on the diagram under the chosen process box.

Move the cursor to the next **leaf** node and make it the current node by pressing the **F10** function key; the **n** sign will now appear in the top left-hand corner of this process box. Press **return** and an open-ended operations box will appear below the process box.

Figure 15.16 shows that all operations boxes have been added, the last one to be inserted being under finish.

15.7.2 Entering the operations list

The list of operations must be entered before they can be allocated to the process structure diagram. The easiest way to do this is to return to the main menu screen of JSP-Tool.

Using the mouse
Move the mouse cursor over **Menu** and click the left mouse button; the MENU screen reappears (Fig. 15.17).

Using the function keys
Press the **F9** function key; the MENU screen reappears (Fig. 15.17).

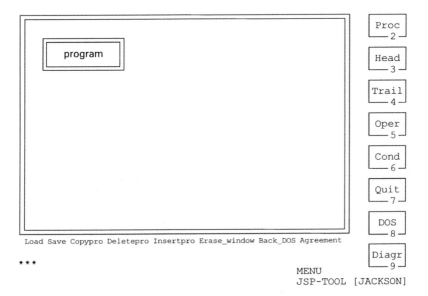

Figure 15.17 Return to the MENU screen.

From the main menu in JSP-Tool, the **Oper** option must be selected from the right-hand menu bar to enable the operations list to be entered.

Using the mouse
Move the mouse cursor over **Oper** and click the left mouse button; the **Operlist ALLOC** screen appears (Fig. 15.18).

Using the function keys
Press the **F5** function key; the **Operlist ALLOC** screen appears (Fig. 15.18).

```
                                                            ┌────────┐
                                                            │ Edlst  │
                                                            └── 6 ──┘
                                                            ┌────────┐
                                                            │ Newid  │
                                                            └── 7 ──┘
                                                            ┌────────┐
                                                            │ Edtxt  │
                                                            └── 8 ──┘
   Copy  Append  Insert  Delete  Operlist  Condlist  Quitlist
                                                            ┌────────┐
 ***                                                        │ Exit   │
                                                            └── 9 ──┘
                                            ALLOC
        Ins   program            Operlist   JSP-TOOL  [JACKSON]
```

Figure 15.18 The **Operlist ALLOC** screen.

JSP-Tool is now ready for each operation to be entered, each with its unique number.

Using the mouse
Move the mouse cursor onto **Newid** and click the left mouse button. A small white box will appear in the lower left-hand corner of the screen; enter the operation number and press return or the left mouse button. A "smiley" cursor appears in the top left-hand corner of the screen. Enter the text of the operation associated with the number and then click the left mouse button over **Exit** on the right-hand menu bar.

The operation you have just entered will be displayed on the screen as shown in Figure 15.19. At the same time, another small white box is displayed in the bottom left-hand corner of the screen waiting for the next operation to be dealt with in the same way.

238

As each operation is entered, it will appear at the top of the screen. The number in square brackets shows how many times that particular operation has been allocated; at this stage it will be zero for each operation as no allocations have taken place. When all the operations have been entered, press **return** at the white box prompt. This leaves you at the **Operlist ALLOC** screen.

Using the function keys

Select the **Newid** option by pressing the **F7** function key. A small white box will appear in the lower left-hand corner of the screen; enter the operation number followed by **return**. A "smiley" cursor appears in the top left-hand corner of the screen. Enter the text of the operation associated with the number and then press the **F9** function key to select **Exit**.

The operation you have just entered will be displayed on the screen as shown in Figure 15.19. At the same time, another small white box is displayed in the bottom left-hand corner of the screen waiting for the next operation to be dealt with in the same way.

As each operation is entered, it will appear at the top of the screen. The number in square brackets shows how many times that particular operation has been allocated; at this stage it will be zero for each operation as no allocations have taken place. When all the operations have been entered, press **return** at the white box prompt. This leaves you at the **Operlist ALLOC** screen.

As shown in Figure 15.19, only the operation most recently entered is displayed at the top of the screen.

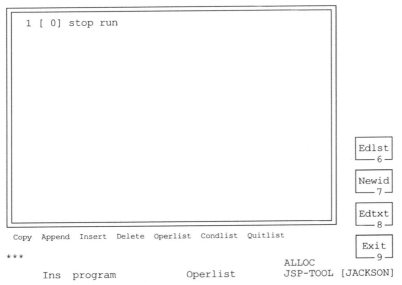

Figure 15.19 The **Operlist ALLOC** screen with the first operation entered.

239

15.7.3 Inspecting the operations list

In order to inspect the operations list in full, the **Edlst** option should be selected from the right-hand menu bar. Notice the format of the operations: each operation number is on a separate line, preceded by **%%** and terminated by a full stop. Further operations could be added at this point, or amendments made to existing operations, providing this format is maintained.

Using the mouse
Move the mouse cursor onto the **Edlst** option on the right-hand menu bar and click the left mouse button. The full operations list appears (Fig. 15.20). Changes to the operations can be made at this stage providing the format of the operation numbers is retained.

Using the function keys
Press the **F6** function key to select the **Edlst** option from the right-hand menu bar. The full operations list appears (Fig. 15.20). Changes to the operations can be made at this stage providing the format of the operation numbers is retained.

```
%%    1.
stop run
%%    2.
open input student file, output report file
%%    3.
close student file, report file
%%    4.
read record from student file, at end Y to EOF
%%    5.
move N to EOF
%%    6.
move zero to male total, female total
%%    7.
add 1 to male total
%%    8.
add 1 to female total
%%    9.
print male total, female total to report file

>>...5.>>.10.15...20...25...30...35>>..40...45...50.>>.55...60...65...70>>.75...
    Copy Append Delete Insert Load Write Find Replace *All_Sel Sel_write    Exit
***                         Operlist                    TEXTED          ─9─
{................} Ins  program                  JSP-TOOL [JACKSON]
```

Figure 15.20   The full operations list.

If you are satisfied with the operations you have entered, leave the text editor screen shown above and return to the previous screen display.

Using the mouse

Move the mouse cursor to the **Exit** option on the right-hand menu bar and click the left mouse button. The original **Operlist** screen appears.

Using the function keys

Select the **Exit** option from the right-hand menu bar by pressing the **F9** function key. The original **Operlist** screen appears.

15.7.4 Allocating the operations

Now that the operations have been entered, it will be necessary to allocate each operation to its appropriate place in the operations boxes in the process structure diagram. The next step is to return to the process structure diagram and enter the allocation phase.

Using the mouse

Return to the main menu by clicking left mouse button on the **Exit** option on the right-hand menu bar.

Return to the process structure diagram display by clicking the left mouse button over the **Diagr** option on the right-hand menu bar at the main menu screen.

Click the left mouse button over the operations box to which you wish to allocate operations, and then enter the allocation phase by clicking the left mouse button over the **Alloc** option on the right-hand menu bar. Begin by allocating operations to the operations box under **process start**.

If not all the operations are visible on the screen, select **Edlst** from the right-hand menu bar, and then return immediately to the allocation menu by selecting **Exit** from the **Operlist** screen. The full range of operations should now appear on the screen. Move the mouse cursor over the operation you wish to allocate and click the left mouse button.

Move the mouse cursor over the first box in the line of boxes and click the left mouse button; the operation chosen has now been allocated. The operation will be allocated to whichever box is selected. Repeat this procedure until all relevant operations have been allocated.

If you make a mistake and allocate the wrong operation, select the **Deall** option with the left mouse button to de-allocate the operation that is in error by clicking the left mouse button over it.

Using the function keys

Return to the main menu by pressing the **F9** function key for the **Exit** option on the right-hand menu bar. Return to the process structure diagram display by pressing the **F9** function key to select the **Diagr** option on the right-hand menu bar at the main menu screen.

Begin by allocating operations to the operations box under **process start**. Move the cursor over this operations box and then enter the allocation phase by pressing the **F8** function key to select the **Alloc** option on the right-hand menu bar. The **F2** function key toggles the **Alloc** option on and off at the **Operlist** screen..

If not all the operations are visible on the screen, select **Edlst** from the right-hand menu bar, and then return immediately to the allocation menu by selecting **Exit** from the **Operlist** screen. The full range of operations should now appear on the screen. Move the cursor against the operation number required and press **return** to select that operation (the operation number will now be highlighted in white).

Move the cursor up to the line of boxes and press **return**. The operation number will appear in the box, and the number in square brackets will show that the operation you have just allocated has been allocated once. Repeat this procedure until all relevant operations have been allocated.

If you make a mistake and allocate the wrong operation, use the function key **F3** to choose the **Deall** option to de-allocate the operation that is in error.

Figure 15.21 shows the allocation of the first operation to the process start operations box. Figure 15.22 shows the completion of the allocation of all relevant operations for that operations box.

Note: it is also possible to allocate operations to operations boxes using the **Name** function, and entering the operation numbers rather than a name at the prompt.

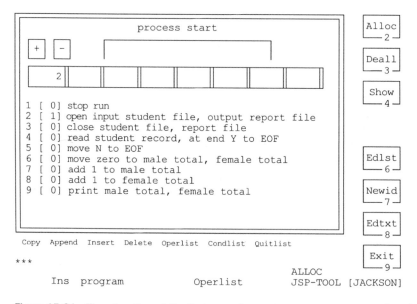

Figure 15.21 The allocation of the first operation to the process start operations box.

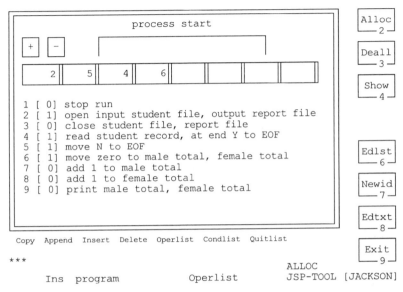

```
                    process start                          Alloc
                                                           └─ 2 ┘
  ┌─┐ ┌─┐   ┌─────────────────────────────────┐           Deall
  │+│ │-│   │                                 │            └─ 3 ┘
  └─┘ └─┘                                                   
  ┌───┐┌───┐┌───┐┌───┐┌───┐┌───┐┌───┐┌───┐                Show
  │ 2 ││ 5 ││ 4 ││ 6 ││   ││   ││   ││   │                 └─ 4 ┘
  └───┘└───┘└───┘└───┘└───┘└───┘└───┘└───┘

  1 [ 0]  stop run
  2 [ 1]  open input student file, output report file
  3 [ 0]  close student file, report file
  4 [ 1]  read student record, at end Y to EOF
  5 [ 1]  move N to EOF                                    Edlst
  6 [ 1]  move zero to male total, female total            └─ 6 ┘
  7 [ 0]  add 1 to male total
  8 [ 0]  add 1 to female total                           Newid
  9 [ 0]  print male total, female total                   └─ 7 ┘

                                                          Edtxt
                                                           └─ 8 ┘
  Copy  Append  Insert  Delete  Operlist  Condlist  Quitlist
                                                          Exit
  ***                                                      └─ 9 ┘
                                          ALLOC
        Ins   program           Operlist  JSP-TOOL [JACKSON]
```

Figure 15.22 The completion of the allocation of all relevant operations for the process start operations box.

Now return to the process structure diagram. The operation numbers will be shown in the operations box under process start.

Using the mouse
Select the **Exit** option from the right-hand menu bar by clicking the left mouse button over it. The process structure diagram will now appear on the screen, showing the operations allocated to the operations box under process start (Fig. 15.23).

Using the function keys
Select the **Exit** option by pressing the **F9** function key. The process structure diagram will now appear on the screen, showing the operations allocated to the operations box under process start (Fig. 15.23).

When all the operations have been allocated to the process structure, the process structure diagram will appear as shown in Figure 15.24.

15.8 Adding conditions

Conditions are allocated on the iterations and selections in the process structure. In order to enter the conditions list it is necessary to be at the main menu screen.

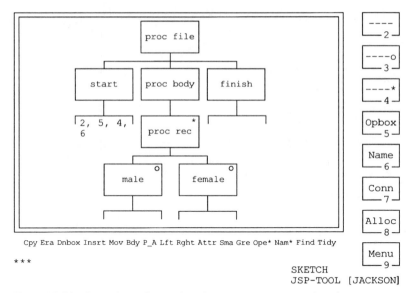

Figure 15.23 Operations allocated to the process start operations box.

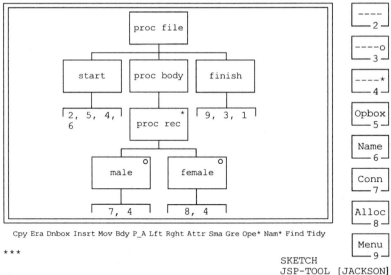

Figure 15.24 Operations allocated to all boxes.

15.8.1 Entering the conditions list

Using the mouse

Move the mouse cursor over **Cond** and click the left mouse button; the **Condlist ALLOC** screen appears (Fig. 15.25).

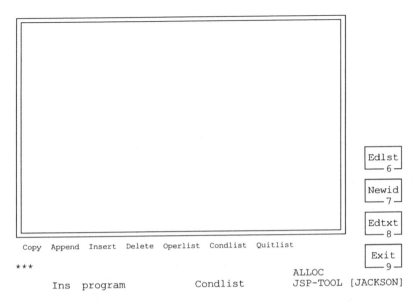

<pre>
                                                        ┌──────┐
                                                        │Edlst │
                                                        └─ 6 ─┘
                                                        ┌──────┐
                                                        │Newid │
                                                        └─ 7 ─┘
                                                        ┌──────┐
                                                        │Edtxt │
                                                        └─ 8 ─┘
  Copy Append Insert Delete Operlist Condlist Quitlist
                                                        ┌──────┐
                                                        │Exit │
  ***   ALLOC   └─ 9 ─┘
      Ins   program   Condlist   JSP-TOOL [JACKSON]
</pre>

Figure 15.25 The Condlist ALLOC screen.

Using the function keys
Press the **F6** function key; the **Condlist ALLOC** screen appears (Fig. 15.25).

Conditions may be entered in a similar manner to the operations.

Using the mouse
Move the mouse cursor onto **Newid** and click the left mouse button. A small white box containing **C** will appear in the lower left-hand corner of the screen; enter the condition number and press **return** or the left mouse button. A "smiley" cursor appears in the top left-hand corner of the screen. Enter the text of the condition associated with the number and then click the left mouse button over **Exit** on the right-hand menu bar.

The condition you have just entered will be displayed on the screen as shown in Figure 15.26. At the same time, another small white box is displayed in the bottom left-hand corner of the screen waiting for the next condition to be dealt with in the same way.

As each condition is entered, it will appear at the top of the screen. The number in square brackets shows how many times that particular condition has been allocated; at this stage it will be zero for each condition as no allocations have taken place.

When all the conditions have been entered, press **return** at the white box prompt. This leaves you at the **Condlist ALLOC** screen. Return to the main menu screen by selecting **Exit**, and then back to the process structure diagram by selecting **Diagr**.

245

Using the function keys

Select the **Newid** option by pressing the **F7** function key. A small white box containing **C** will appear in the lower left-hand corner of the screen; enter the condition number followed by **return**. A "smiley" cursor appears in the top left-hand corner of the screen. Enter the text of the condition associated with the number and then press the **F9** function key to select **Exit**.

The condition you have just entered will be displayed on the screen as shown in Figure 15.26. At the same time, another small white box is displayed in the bottom left-hand corner of the screen waiting for the next condition to be dealt with in the same way.

As each condition is entered, it will appear at the top of the screen. The number in square brackets shows how many times that particular condition has been allocated; at this stage it will be zero for each condition as no allocations have taken place.

When all the conditions have been entered, press **return** at the white box prompt. This leaves you at the **Condlist ALLOC** screen. Return to the main menu screen by selecting **Exit**, and then back to the process structure diagram by selecting **Diagr**.

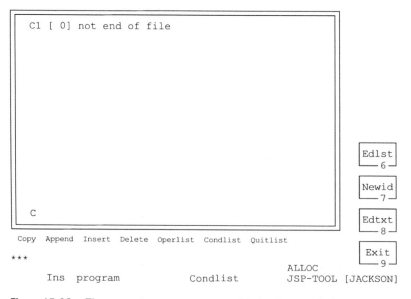

Figure 15.26 The **Condlist ALLOC** screen with the first condition entered.

15.8.2 Allocating a condition to an iteration

Using the mouse
Click the left mouse button on the iterated component and then select **Alloc** from the right-hand menu bar. Select the condition you wish to allocate and click the left mouse button in the **process record** box shown on the screen. Click over the **w** box to indicate that this is a **while** condition (Fig. 15.27).

When the condition has been allocated, click the left mouse button on **Exit** to return to the process structure diagram.

Using the function keys
Move the cursor onto the iterated component and select **Alloc** from the right-hand menu bar. Select the condition you wish to allocate by moving the cursor keys up and down until the required condition number is highlighted, and press **return**. Move the cursor into the **process record** box and press return to allocate the condition. To indicate that this is a **while** condition, move the cursor over the **w** box and press **return** (Fig. 15.27). The **F2** function key toggles the **Alloc** option on and off at the **Condlist** screen.

When the condition has been allocated, press function key **F9 (Exit)** to return to the process structure.

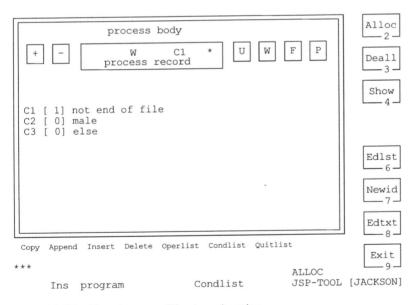

Figure 15.27 Allocating a condition to an iteration.

15.8.3 Allocating a condition to a selection

Using the mouse
Click the left mouse button on the selection component and then select **Alloc** from the right-hand menu bar. Select the condition you wish to allocate and click the left mouse button in the **process male** box shown on the screen (Fig. 15.28).

When the condition has been allocated, click the left mouse button on **Exit** to return to the process structure diagram.

Using the function keys
Move the cursor onto the first selection component and select **Alloc** from the right-hand menu bar. Select the condition you wish to allocate by moving the cursor keys up and down until the required condition is highlighted, and press **return**. Move the cursor into the **process male** box and press **return** to allocate the condition (Fig. 15.28). The **F2** function key toggles the **Alloc** option on and off at the **Condlist** screen.

When the condition has been allocated, press function key **F9 (Exit)** to return to the process structure.

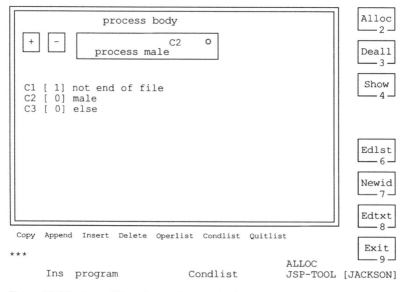

Figure 15.28   A condition allocated to a selection.

In a similar way, allocate the **else** condition to the other selection part.

When the conditions have been added to the iteration and to the selection components, the process structure diagram will appear on the screen as shown in Figure 15.29.

248

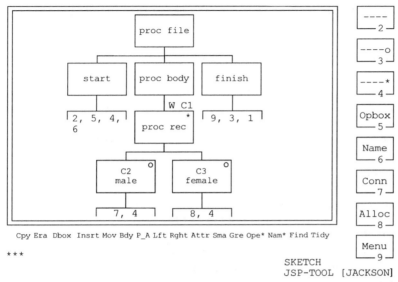

Figure 15.29 The process structure diagram with conditions allocated.

15.9 Generating schematic logic (pseudocode)

In order to generate the schematic logic (also known as structure text or pseudocode) it is necessary to leave JSP-Tool and work from DOS. To do this it is necessary to exit from JSP-Tool by choosing the **Back_DOS** option from the lower menu.

REMEMBER TO SAVE YOUR WORK BEFORE LEAVING JSP-TOOL.

To exit from JSP-Tool:

Using the mouse
Click the left mouse button over **Back_DOS**.

Using the function keys
 1. Press **escape** to enter lower menu, then space bar across to **Back_DOS**;
 press **return**.
 2. Press **escape B**.

REMEMBER TO SAVE YOUR WORK BEFORE LEAVING JSP-TOOL.

If you have not saved your work, JSP-Tool will prompt:
   Q to Quit? C
leaving **C** (for continue) as the default option.
  Press **return** to remain in JSP-Tool.
  Press **Q** then **return** to exit from JSP-Tool, without saving your work.

REMEMBER TO SAVE YOUR WORK BEFORE LEAVING JSP-TOOL.

At the system prompt, enter **jtdoc file1 * file2**, where **file1** is the name of the JSP-Tool file that has just been created and saved, and **file2** is the name of the output file to hold the schematic logic (including operations list, conditions list and process structure diagram).

The contents of the file produced by JSP-Tool for the tutorial example is as follows:

```
JTDOC  FILE1  program    1995-05-20    11:25:02
                                       PAGE 1
```

Operation List:

    1. [1] Stop run
    2. [1] Open input student file, output report file
    3. [1] Close student file, output report file
    4. [3] Read record from student file
    5. [1] Move N to eof
    6. [1] Move 0 to male total, female total
    7. [1] Add 1 to male total
    8. [1] Add 1 to female total
    9. [1] Print male total, female total

```
JTDOC  FILE1  program    1995-05-20    11:25:02
                                       PAGE 2
```

Condition List:

```
C1.  [ 1] not end of file
C2.  [ 1] male
C3.  [ 1] else
```

```
JTDOC  FILE1  program    1995-05-20    11:25:02
                                       PAGE 3
```

Diagram:

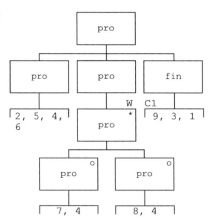

250

JTDOC FILE1 program   1995-05-20   11:25:02   PAGE 4

Structure Text:
```
proc file      SEQ
   process start    SEQ
            DO 2   : open input student file, output⏎
                     report file
            DO 5   : move N to eof
            DO 4   : read record from student file
            DO 6   : move 0 to male total, female total
   process start    END
   process body    ITR W ( C1): not end of file
      process record      SEL  ( C2): male
         process male     SEQ
               DO 7   : add 1 to male total
               DO 4   : read record from student file
         process male     END
      process record      ALT  ( C3): else
         process female    SEQ
               DO 8   : add 1 to female total
               DO 4   : read record from student file
         process female    END
      process record      END
   process body    END
   finish    SEQ
            DO 9   : print male total, female total
            DO 3   : close student file, output⏎
                     report file
            DO 1   : stop run
   finish    END
proc file    END
```

JTDOC FILE1 program   1992-11-20   11:25:02
                                      PAGE 5

15.10 Generating code

If the schematic logic does not appear to do what is required, it will be necessary to re-examine the following and make amendments where necessary in order to remove any errors:

process structure diagram
operations list
allocation of operations
conditions list
allocation of conditions

When the schematic logic is considered correct, the next step is to expand the operations to include a syntactically correct statement (or statements) equivalent to each operation in whatever language has been chosen to implement the program design, e.g. in C, COBOL or Pascal. The operations themselves can be converted to comments using the correct format for the language concerned.

This will produce code directly equivalent to the schematic logic previously created. In order to create a complete program it will also be necessary to generate header text to contain, for example, declarations of the variables that are to be used within the program. This is done at the main menu within JSP-Tool.

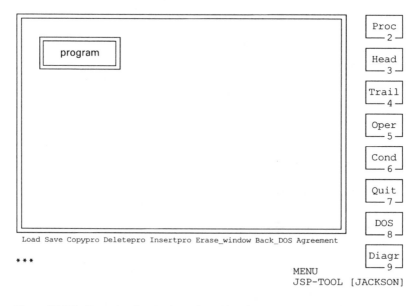

Figure 15.30 Preparing for the insertion of header text.

15.10.1 Header text: declaring the variables

Using the mouse
Move the mouse cursor to the **program** module box and click the left mouse button; this indicates that the text to be entered will be associated with this module (Fig. 15.30).

Move the mouse cursor to the **Head** option in the right-hand menu bar and click the left mouse button; this indicates that header text is to be inserted. The header text will appear before the program instructions when the code is generated.

Using the function keys
Move the cursor to the **program** module box and press **return**; this indicates that the text to be entered will be associated with this module (Fig. 15.30).

Press the **F3** function key; this indicates that header text is to be inserted. The header text will appear before the program instructions when the code is generated.

15.10.2 Invoking the code generator

It is necessary to leave JSP-Tool in order to generate the program code.

REMEMBER TO SAVE YOUR WORK BEFORE LEAVING JSP-TOOL.

When at the system level, the code generator can be invoked; for COBOL the code generator is JTCOBA, which will produce in-line, i.e. nest-free code, from a module file created using JSP-Tool. The COBOL code generated will retain the structure of the process design and will indicate the start and end of sequence, selection and iteration constructs, and also the operation numbers associated with each program statement.

At the system prompt, type **jtcoba file1 * file3** where **file1** is the JSP-Tool file that you have created, and **file3** is the output file to contain the COBOL program. A similar action is required for generating code in other languages.

REMEMBER TO SAVE YOUR WORK BEFORE LEAVING JSP-TOOL.

The contents of the final program using the above example are given below. Note that the operations have not been expanded into full COBOL statements in this example; this means that the program would not run as it stands (for example, no full stops at end of statements, no variables declared).

```
PROC FILE-0010-SEQ.                                    SEQ
PROCESS START-0020-SEQ.                                SEQ
    OPEN INPUT STUDENT FILE, OUTPUT REPORT FILE     DO 2
    MOVE N TO EOF                                   DO 5
    READ RECORD FROM STUDENT FILE                   DO 4
    MOVE 0 TO MALE TOTAL, FEMALE TOTAL              DO 6
PROCESS START-0020-END.                                END
PROCESS BODY-0030-ITR.                                 ITR W
IF                                                     C1
    NOT END OF FILE
NEXT SENTENCE ELSE GO TO PROCESS BODY-0030-END.
PROCESS RECORD-0040-SEL.                               SEL
    IF                                                 C2
        MALE
    NEXT SENTENCE ELSE GO TO PROCESS RECORDS-0040-ALT1.
    PROCESS MALE-0050-SEQ.                             SEQ
        ADD 1 TO MALE TOTAL                         DO 7
        READ RECORD FROM STUDENT FILE               DO 4
    PROCESS MALE-0050-END.                             END
        GO TO PROCESS RECORD-0040-END.
    PROCESS RECORD-0040-ALT1.                          ALT
*   ELSE                                               C3
    PROCESS FEMALE-0060-SEQ.                           SEQ
        ADD 1 TO FEMALE TOTAL                       DO 8
        READ RECORD FROM STUDENT FILE               DO 4
    PROCESS FEMALE-0060-END.                           END
    PROCESS RECORD-0040-END.                           END
        GO TO PROCESS BODY-0030-ITR.
PROCESS BODY-0030-END.                                 END
FINISH-0070-SEQ.                                       SEQ
    PRINT MALE TOTAL, FEMALE TOTAL                  DO 9
    CLOSE STUDENT FILE, OUTPUT REPORT FILE          DO 3
    STOP RUN                                        DO 1
FINISH-0070-END.                                       END
PROC FILE-0010-END.                                    END
```

15.11 MENU screen options

The lower screen menu options have meaning as follows:

Load load a process structure from another file
Save save the process structure to a file
Copypro copy a process structure

Deletepro	delete a process structure
Insertpro	insert a process structure
Erase_window	erase contents of window
Back_DOS	leave JSP-Tool, return to DOS
Agreement	prints licence agreement details

The right-hand menu bar options have meanings as described below:

Proc — 2 — Allows a module to be given a name at the top level. If there is more than one module, they will be executed in left to right, top down order.

Head — 3 — Allows the entry of any header text. This may be associated with a module name or with the whole window. Used for variable declarations, etc.

Trail — 4 — Allows the entry of any text to appear after the program text.

Oper — 5 — Enables the list of operations to be entered and edited. Operations can then be allocated to specific operation boxes on the process structure.

Cond — 6 — Enables the list of conditions to be entered and edited. Conditions can then be allocated to the iterations and selections on the process structure diagram.

Quit — 7 — Allows a quit to be entered for backtracking.

DOS — 8 — Produces the list of files in the directory in the main window; these can be displayed as a tree structure.

Diagr — 9 — Displays a new screen allowing the process structure to be entered.

15.12 SKETCH screen options

The meaning of each entry on the lower menu bar is as follows:

Cpy	copies a process structure
Era	erases the process structure from below the cursor
Dbox	deletes a process box from the process diagram
Insrt	insert
Mov	move
Bdy	allows a body box to be entered in the process structure diagram
P_A	allows a condition to be expressed as posit or admit for backtracking

255

Lft allows process box to be moved to the left

Rght allows process box to be moved to the right

Attr toggles between solid white box and orange outlines for displaying process structure diagram

Sma allows process structure diagram to be displayed on screen in a reduced format

Gre allows process structure diagram to be displayed on screen in an enlarged format

Ope* adds open-ended operations boxes to the process structure diagram at each leaf node and also before and after every group of sequence components

Nam* allows names to be added to each process box in turn starting with the root node

Find enables a process box containing a string of characters to be found on the process structure diagram

Tidy redisplays the process structure diagram on the screen ensuring process boxes appear evenly spaced

The meaning of each option on the right-hand menu bar is given below.

Places an unmarked box on the screen, either for the top level of a construct or for a sequence component.

Adds a selection component to the process structure being built on the screen.

Adds an interated component to the process structure being built on the screen.

Places an open box under a terminal node to hold details of the operations to be allocated.

Allows a name to be given to a process box on the process structure being sketched.

Enables a connection to be made between a box at a higher level and its component boxes.

Allows operations to be allocated to an operations box.

Returns to the menu screen (module level).

CHAPTER 16

Getting started with PDF

This chapter will guide you through the stages of using the Program Development Facility (PDF) to enable you to enter a process structure, allocate conditions and operations, generate the schematic logic and finally produce executable code that the structure represents. It will usually be necessary to develop the process structure manually from the input and output data structures in the normal way, but for demonstration purposes in this tutorial session an example has been prepared. PDF does not support the creation of process structures from data structures; rather it allows the automatic production of code from a process structure that has been manually prepared.

16.1 The tutorial example

The purpose of this tutorial session is to enter the JSP process structure shown in Figure 16.1 (a solution to the problem of counting the number of male and female records on a student file), to generate the schematic logic and produce

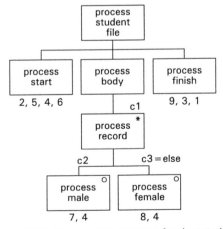

Figure 16.1 The process structure for the tutorial example.

257

executable code (for example, in COBOL, C or Pascal) using PDF. Note that the process structure has been simplified so that the printing of totals is included under **process finish**, which closes the files and terminates the program.

The conditions are:

    C1: not end of file
    C2: male student
    C3: else

The operations list is:

1. **Stop run**
2. **Open input student file, output report file**
3. **Close student file, report file**
4. **Read record from student file, at end move "Y" to EOF**
5. **Move "N" to EOF**
6. **Move zero to male total, female total**
7. **Add 1 to male total**
8. **Add 1 to female total**
9. **Print male total, female total to report file**

16.2 Starting PDF

You may use PDF from Windows or from DOS. If the PDF directory does not appear in your PATH, you will need to change to PDF as your working directory (**cd\pdf**) in order to proceed. Start PDF by typing **pdf** at the prompt. In Windows, double click on the PDF icon. In either case, PDF will wait for you to enter the filename of a JSP process structure diagram. On this occasion it will be a new file, but later you may wish to specify an existing file that contains a

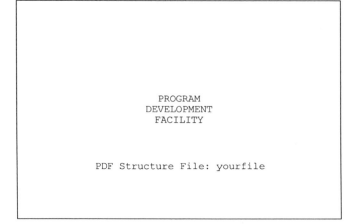

```
                        PROGRAM
                      DEVELOPMENT
                        FACILITY


            PDF Structure File: yourfile
```

Figure 16.2 Starting PDF with a new structure file.

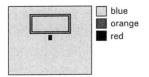

Figure 16.3 The initial PDF display.

process structure. Type in the filename for your new structure in response to
PDF (Fig. 16.2).

PDF will clear the screen and give a display with the following characteris-
tics, shown diagrammatically in Figure 16.3:

- blue background
- orange box at centre top of screen
- blue box within the orange box
- red cursor below the orange box

The orange box is the root node, under which child nodes will be added to
form a process structure. When further nodes are created, they will also
appear as orange boxes and will be connected by a red line to the parent node.
The central blue box is the current node indicator; the root node is the only
node that exists and is the current node at present. The red cursor can be
moved using the cursor keys; it is used to indicate the point on the screen
where a new node will appear.

It will be useful to remember that the current node is represented by a blue
box, and the position of a new node is indicated by the red cursor.

16.3 Adding nodes

PDF will not allow an illegal JSP structure to be created; a warning beep and an
error message will be produced at any stage if an attempt at building an illegal
construct has been made.

In order to create a new node, the **INSERT** key on the numeric keypad is
pressed. The screen will show the new node (Fig. 16.4):

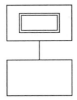

Figure 16.4 Adding a new node.

Three nodes at the level of the new node are required. If the **INSERT** key is
pressed twice more, the screen display will not change, but two additional
nodes will have been created; the two new nodes are invisible because they

259

overlap with the first new node. In order to see the structure clearly, it is necessary to **TIDY** the structure by pressing **Alt-F8**. The screen will now display the full structure that has been entered so far, as shown in Figure 16.5.

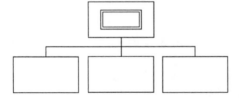

Figure 16.5   Three new nodes added.

To prevent the new nodes from overlapping when they are created, it is possible to move the cursor to another position on the screen before pressing **INSERT**, so that the new node is created at the cursor position. Sometimes the connecting lines between nodes added in this way are crooked; the display can be corrected in this case too by using **TIDY** (**Alt-F8**).

16.4 Moving around the structure diagram

There are now three boxes below the root node, as required for the desired process structure. In order to add further nodes to the different parts of the structure diagram, it is necessary to move the current node indicator to the node to which a child node is to be added. The function keys **F7**, **F8**, **F9** and **F10** move the current node indicator up, down, left and right respectively.

The movement of the current node indicator is with respect to the structure diagram (rather than to the screen). In order to make the central child node the new current node, moving down (**F8**) will make the first child node current; it is then necessary to move right (**F10**) onto the second node. Moving down from the current node (by using **F8**) will not necessarily make the box immediately below into the new current node; rather, the first box at the next level down becomes the current node.

PDF will beep and print an error message if an attempt is made to move to a new current node, up, down, left or right, where no such node exists, e.g. it is not possible to move up from the root node.

Move the current node to the middle node at the second level of the process structure diagram on the screen by typing **F8** and then **F10**. The screen will now show the structure with the new current node (Fig. 16.6). The current node indicator is now in the correct position for a new node to be added at the lower level. The cursor should be moved below the existing structure to a position where the new node is required; if the cursor is too high, PDF will beep and print a message. The new node is added by pressing **INSERT** (Fig. 16.7).

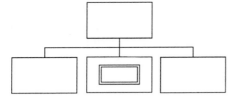

Figure 16.6 The middle node at the second level designated as the current node.

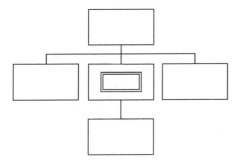

Figure 16.7 A new node added below the current node.

There are two further boxes to be added to the process structure diagram; those representing the selection components below the node which has just been added. In order to add these two further nodes, it is necessary to move the current node indicator down again so that the new node is made the current node; press **F8**. Move the cursor down and left to a suitable position for the first selection component, then press **INSERT**. Move the cursor to the right at the same level and add the second selection component by pressing **INSERT**. Use **Alt-F8** to **TIDY** the display if necessary. The result is shown in Figure 16.8.

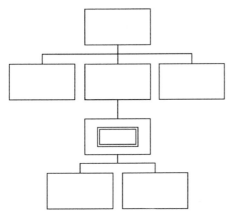

Figure 16.8 Two further components added to the process structure.

261

It can be seen that at this stage all the components are sequences; iteration and selection components will be identified and marked later (iteration in Section 16.7., selection in Section 16.8.). It is also possible to insert new nodes in the structure other than as terminal nodes. This is achieved by pressing **SHIFT INSERT**; the new node is then inserted below the current node.

16.5 Deleting nodes and subtrees

It sometimes happens that one or more unnecessary nodes have been added. In order to delete nodes which are not required, the decimal point key "**.**" (**DELETE**) on the numeric keypad is used. To delete a single *node*, make that node the current node and press **SHIFT** "**.**" (**SHIFT DELETE**); to recover the deleted node, press **SHIFT** "**.**" (**SHIFT DELETE**) again and the deleted node will reappear.

To delete a *subtree* under the current node, press "**.**" (**DELETE**); to recover a deleted subtree, press "**.**" (**DELETE**) again and the deleted subtree will reappear.

16.6 Naming nodes

The process structure does not have any text associated with its components; the next stage is to place a name inside each node.

To start with the root node, press **HOME** to make the root node the current node. The root node can be given a name by pressing "**-**" (the minus sign key on the numeric keypad) and entering a name, such as **process student**

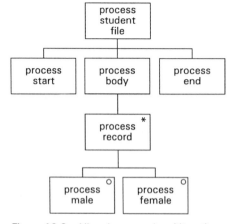

Figure 16.9 All nodes named and iteration and selection components identified.

file at the prompt. When **return** is pressed, the name entered will appear in the box.

Give a name to each box on the process structure by making each node the current node (using **F7**, **F8**, **F9** and **F10**), pressing "-" (minus sign), and typing in the name for that node. The result is shown in Figure 16.9.

16.7 Identifying an iteration

There is one iteration in this process structure; the iterated component is the single box at the third level of the process structure diagram. Make this box the current node. An iteration is marked by placing an asterisk in the iterated component (the box below). **SHIFT F10** will mark a node with an asterisk "*", thus identifying it as an iterated component (Figure 16.9).

If a current node is wrongly marked as an iterated component, it can be made into a sequence component again by typing **SHIFT F8**.

16.8 Identifying a selection

There is one selection with two component parts in this process structure; the selection components are at the lowest level of the process structure diagram. Make the first selection component the current node. A selection is marked by placing a circle in the selection components (the boxes below). **SHIFT F9** will mark a node with a circle "o", thus identifying it, and its sibling nodes, as selection components (Figure 16.9).

If a current node is wrongly marked as a selection component, it can be made into a sequence component again by typing **SHIFT F8**.

16.9 Assigning conditions to iterations and selections

Conditions must be allocated where there are iterations and selections on a process structure. In PDF, the conditions are assigned to the component parts of iterations and selections.

Make the iterated component (marked with "*") the current node. Press **SHIFT F3** to enter the condition on the iteration, which will be **not end of file**. Terminate the entry of conditions by "+" (the plus sign key on the numeric keypad). PDF supplies the **while** when it generates the schematic logic. **While** is used rather than **repeat** as an iteration can be executed zero or more times, whereas a repetition can be carried out one or more times, i.e. at least once.

The contents of the condition on this node can be inspected by using **F2**; exit by pressing **F2** again, or "+" on the numeric keypad. **SHIFT F1** can be used to edit the conditions on a node.

Now make the first selection component the current node. Press **SHIFT F3** to enter the condition on the selection, which will be **student = male**. The second selection component does not require an explicit condition; it should be entered as **else**.

The contents of the condition on this node can be inspected by using **F2**; exit by pressing **F2** again, or "+" on the numeric keypad. **SHIFT F1** can be used to edit the conditions on a node.

16.10 Entering the operations list

In order to enter the operations list, press **SHIFT F2**. This will invoke an editor to enable the operations to be entered. PDF may be set up to invoke a variety of editors, depending on what is available on the system; a line editor may be used, or a word processor. The choice of editing software is specified within one of the PDF files and may be changed to suit the user.

The screen will clear with a first line as follows:

```
--------T----------------------------------------------------
```

Do not delete this first line or enter anything above it.

The **T** in the first line indicates the position where the text of each operation should appear; the operation number should be entered to the left, thus:

```
--------T----------------------------------------------------
     1  Stop run
```

If any characters in the text of the operation (other than the operation number) appear to the left of the **T** they will be ignored when the schematic logic is generated.

Enter the operations (as given in Section 16.1.). The operations list should look like this:

```
--------T----------------------------------------------------
     1  Stop run
     2  Open input student file, output report file
     3  Close student file, report file
     4  Read record from student file, at end move "Y" to EOF
     5  Move "N" to EOF
     6  Move zero to male total, female total
     7  Add 1 to male total
     8  Add 1 to female total
     9  Print male total, female total
```

To save the operations list and return to the process structure, use the normal save and exit command for the editor or word processor you are using.

To abandon editing the operations list, exit without saving. (It is good practice to save the operations list from time to time during editing to prevent loss of work from a power failure.)

The process structure diagram screen of PDF will now reappear.

16.11 Allocating the operations to the process structure

In order to allocate operations to the process structure, PDF requires that a further node is added below each terminal node in the existing process structure, and that the operation numbers are entered in these new nodes in the same way that names were entered in process box nodes.

Move the current node indicator to each terminal node on the process structure in turn (using **F7**, **F8**, **F9** and **F10**), and add a new node below each one by moving the cursor underneath and pressing **INSERT**. Make the new node the current node, then allocate the operations by pressing "**-**" (minus sign on the numeric keypad) to name the new node and enter the operation numbers in the correct order as if they were the node name, then **return** or "**+**" on the numeric keypad.

The process structure diagram should now appear as shown in Figure 16.10. Note that the conditions are not seen on the process structure diagram on the screen.

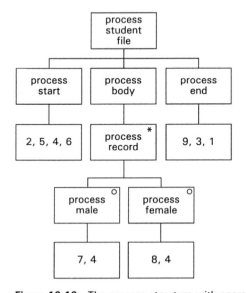

Figure 16.10 The process structure with operations allocated.

The process structure has been entered, the iterations and selections identified and conditions added, and the operations have been entered and allocated. It remains to instruct PDF to generate the schematic logic for this process structure.

16.12 Generating schematic logic (pseudocode)

Once the process structure has been entered and the conditions and operations have been allocated, PDF will automatically generate the schematic logic.

Enter command mode by **Alt-F9**, then type **TEXT** at the prompt. PDF will confirm that the schematic logic has been written to a file with extension **.TXT** and will report whether any errors were found.

If there are errors in the schematic logic, examine the operations allocated to the structure to locate the error(s). If the error cannot be found easily, obtain a printout of the files containing the schematic logic, operations list, conditions and the process structure itself.

It is useful to note that PDF marks operations with an asterisk ("*") in the operations list if they have not been allocated to any part of the process structure diagram. PDF cannot detect whether operations have been allocated to appropriate parts of the structure, or whether they have been allocated in the correct sequence.

16.13 Leaving PDF

To leave PDF and save the process structure, enter command mode by typing **Alt-F9** and then **EXIT** at the prompt.

To leave PDF without saving the process structure, enter command mode by typing **Alt-F9** and then **QUIT** at the prompt. This will abandon the structure that has been entered, or any changes since the last **SAVE**.

To save the process structure without leaving PDF, enter command mode by typing **Alt-F9** and then **SAVE** at the prompt.

16.14 Files produced by PDF

PDF will create files with the same name as you entered when starting PDF, but with different extensions as follows:

yourfile.pdf process structure screen file for PDF use
yourfile.PRT process structure print file
yourfile.TXT schematic logic text file

The `.PRT` file is created by entering command mode and typing **PRINT** at the prompt. The `.PRT` and `.TXT` files can only be printed after leaving PDF.

The schematic logic can be manually translated into the language of your choice. Alternatively, if a code generator module is available, the code can be generated automatically, providing the operations are expressed in the correct syntactic format of the particular language. It will also be necessary to add the data declarations at the beginning of the code.

16.15 Keyboard layout for PDF

The function keys have specified actions associated with them for PDF; these are illustrated in Figure 16.11; the actions associated with the numeric keypad are shown in Figure 16.12.

	F1	F2	F3	F4
	help	list	tab up	tab down
SHIFT:	EDIT CONDITIONS	EDIT OPERATIONS	ENTER CONDITION	JOIN

	F5	F6	F7	F8
	tab left	tab right	current up	current down
SHIFT:	PAGE	VIEW	ATTRIBUTE	SEQUENCE COMPONENT
Alt:				TIDY

	F9	F10	F11	F12
	current left	current right	not used	not used
SHIFT:	SELECTION COMPONENT	ITERATION COMPONENT		
Alt:	Command mode	Size		

Figure 16.11 The actions associated with the function keys in PDF.

267

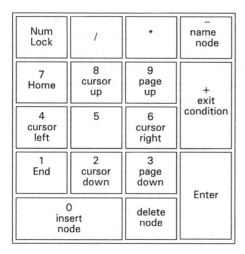

Figure 16.12 The actions associated with the numeric keypad in PDF.

16.16 Quick reference guide to PDF

ADD node	press **INSERT** adds a terminal node
ALLOCATE condition	**SHIFT F1** in current node
ALLOCATE operation	add node (**INSERT**) then name node ("-" minus sign)
COMMAND MODE	**Alt-F9** then enter command in window
COMMANDS	exit, print, quit, save, text
CONDITION	**SHIFT F3** in current node enters condition
CONDITIONS	**F2** shows current node conditions; "+" exits
CURRENT node	**SHIFT page up** makes nearest box current
CURSOR	cursor keys or **F3**, **F4**, **F5**, **F6**
DELETE node	**SHIFT** "." (**SHIFT DELETE**) on numeric keypad
DELETE subtree	"." (**DELETE**) on numeric keypad
DOWN current node	**F8**
DOWN cursor	cursor key or **F4**
EDIT conditions	**SHIFT F1** in current node
EDIT node operations	"-" (minus sign) then enter new operations
EDIT operations list	**SHIFT F2** then use editor/word processor
ENTER conditions	**SHIFT F3** in current node enters condition
ENTER operations list	**SHIFT F2** then use editor/word processor
EXIT PDF	**Alt-F9** then type **EXIT** to save structure and exit
EXIT edit operations	save in the editor/word processor
HELP	**F1** shows keyboard layout

INSERT node	**SHIFT INSERT** inserts new node in structure
INSPECT condition	**F2** on current node; "**+**" (plus sign) to exit
INSPECT operation	**F2** on current node; "**+**" (plus sign) to exit
ITERATION	**SHIFT F10** marks "*****" (asterisk) in current node
LEFT current node	**F9**
LEFT cursor	cursor key or **F5**
NAME node	"**-**" (minus sign) on numeric keypad then type name
OPERATIONS	**F2** shows current node operations; "**+**" (plus sign) to exit
OPERATIONS list	**SHIFT F2** then enter operations using editor/word processor
PRINT structure	**Alt-F9** then type **PRINT**
PRINT schematic logic	**EXIT pdf** then print **.TXT** file
PRINT structure file	**EXIT** PDF then print **.PRT** file
QUIT PDF	**Alt-F9** then **QUIT** abandons structure diagram and leaves PDF
QUIT edit operations	quit without saving from editor/word processor
RIGHT current node	**F10**
RIGHT cursor	cursor key or **F6**
ROOT node	**HOME** returns indicator to root node
SAVE	**Alt-F9** then type **SAVE**
SCHEMATIC LOGIC	**Alt-F9** then type **TEXT**
SCROLL	**SHIFT** together with cursor keys
SELECTION	**SHIFT F9** marks "o" in current node
SEQUENCE	**SHIFT F8** removes "*****" or "o" from current node
TEXT	**Alt-F9** then type **TEXT** for schematic logic
TIDY	**Alt-F8**
UNDELETE node	**SHIFT** "**.**" (**SHIFT DELETE**) again on numeric keypad (toggles with DELETE node)
UNDELETE subtree	"**.**" (**DELETE**) again on numeric keypad (toggles with DELETE subtree)
UP current node	**F7**
UP cursor	cursor key or **F3**

This tutorial has covered the basic elements of PDF, and you should now be able to use the software to generate the schematic logic from a process structure diagram. There are more advanced features that are available (as shown by the function keys in Section 16.14.) but these are not discussed here. Consult your manual for further details of these features.

APPENDIX

Solutions to selected exercises

2.3 Exercises

1. Draw a JSP structure diagram of a student record, using only those elements specified in the following description: A student record consists of the name of the student, the student registration number, date of birth, course attended, year of course.

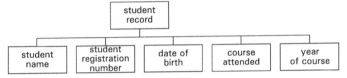

Figure A.1 Solution to Exercise 1.

2. Draw simple JSP structure diagrams for the following elements of the student record specified in Exercise 1:
(a) each student name is represented as last name followed by first name;
(b) student registration number is year of entry combined with a unique application number;
(c) date of birth is held as year, month and day (to facilitate sorting into age order).

Figure A.2 Solution to Exercise 2(a).　　　**Figure A.3** Solution to Exercise 2(b).

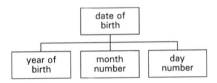

Figure A.4 Solution to Exercise 2(c).

3. Draw the full JSP structure diagram for the student record described in Exercise 1, incorporating the elements from Exercise 2.

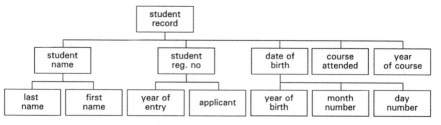

Figure A.5 Solution to Exercise 3.

4. Draw the JSP structure diagram for which the description is as follows. The academic year is a sequence of three terms: term 1, term 2 and term 3. Term 3 is a sequence of revision followed by an examination.

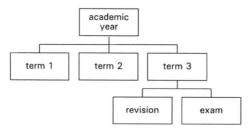

Figure A.6 Solution to Exercise 4.

5. Describe in words what the JSP structure diagram shown in Figure 2.10 (repeated as Figure A.7) represents.

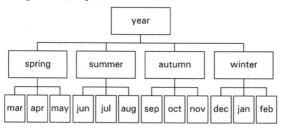

Figure A.7 Structure diagram for Exercise 5 (repeat of Fig.2.10).

A year is a sequence of the seasons Spring, Summer, Autumn and Winter. Spring is a sequence of the months March, April and May; Summer is a sequence of June, July and August. The season of Autumn is a sequence of September, October and November and Winter is a sequence of December, January and February.

The boxes Spring, Summer, Autumn and Winter are sequence components of the sequence structure year; each season is also a sequence structure with sequence components comprising the months of the season.

2.5 Exercises

1. A company employee may be either a technical specialist or an administrator. Express this as a JSP structure diagram.

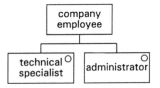

Figure A.8 Solution to Exercise 1.

2. A technical specialist within an organization may be a lawyer, an accountant, a systems analyst, an architect or a chemist. A company employee who is a chemist may work in the field of organic or inorganic chemistry. Express this as a JSP structure diagram.

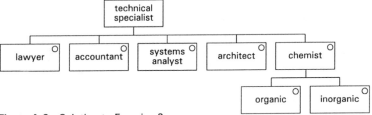

Figure A.9 Solution to Exercise 2.

Figure A.10 also represents the situation described above. Note that as the structure is a selection, the order of the selection components is not important.

See Figure A.10 (p. 274).

3. A company administrator could work in one of the following departments: personnel, payroll and pensions, registry and records, sales, marketing, or purchasing. Use a JSP structure diagram to describe this.

See Figure A.11 (p. 274).

4. Combine the details described in Exercises 1 to 3 to produce a single JSP diagram.

See Figure A.12 (p. 274).

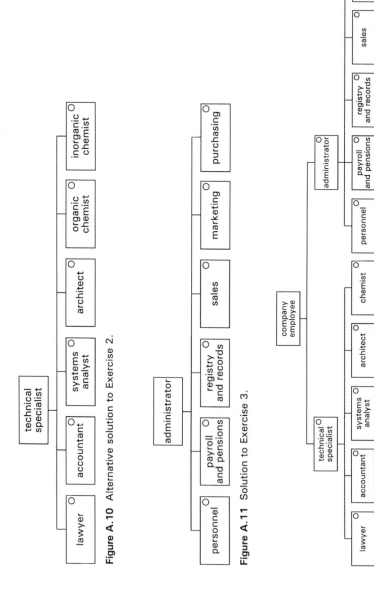

Figure A.10 Alternative solution to Exercise 2.

Figure A.11 Solution to Exercise 3.

Figure A.12 Solution to Exercise 4.

5. An athlete may be tall (5 feet 10 inches or above), or below this height; each individual will be male or female. Show how this can be expressed in a JSP structure diagram in different ways.

The first possible solution (Fig. A.13) distinguishes between those who are tall and those who are not, and then differentiates between male and female in each case.

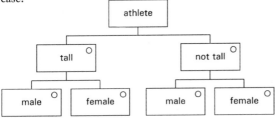

Figure A.13 First possible solution to Exercise 5.

The second possible solution (Figure A.14) differentiates between male and female athletes, and then distinguishes between those who are tall and those who are not in each case.

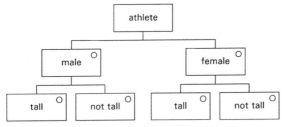

Figure A.14 Second possible solution to Exercise 5.

A third possible solution (Figure A.15) differentiates between each classification of male, female, tall and not tall at the same level.

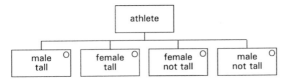

Figure A.15 Third possible solution to Exercise 5.

If we were only interested in the tall female athletes, the simple diagram in Figure A.16 would be sufficient for our purposes.

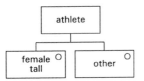

Figure A.16 Solution to Exercise 5 for tall female athletes only.

275

2.7 Exercises

1. A century consists of 100 years. Each year lasts 365 days (ignoring leap years for this exercise). A century could also be considered to consist of 10 decades. Show different ways in which a century can be represented using JSP structure diagrams.

   A century is an iteration of decade (10 decades to a century) (Fig. A.17).
   A century is an iteration of decade (10 decades to a century). A decade is an iteration of year (10 years to each decade) (Fig. A.18).
   A century is an iteration of year (100 years to each century) (Fig. A.19).
   A century is an iteration of day (36500 days to each century) (Fig. A.20).
   A century is an iteration of decade (10 decades to a century). A decade is an iteration of year (10 years to each decade). A year is an iteration of day (365 days to each year) (Fig. A.21).

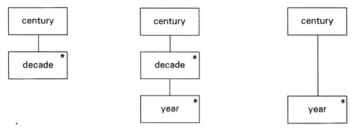

Figure A.17 Century is an iteration of decade.

Figure A.18 Century is an iterations of decade; decade is an iteration of year.

Figure A.19 Century is an iteration of year.

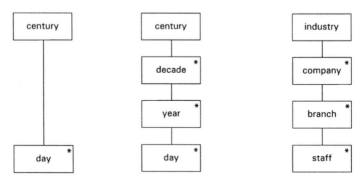

Figure A.20 Century is an iteration of day.

Figure A.21 Century is an iteration of decade; decade is an iteration of year; year is an iteration of day.

Figure A.22 Solution to Exercise 2.

2. A particular industry, e.g. travel, consists of a number of individual companies (such as travel agents). An individual company may have several branches in different locations. Each branch employs a number of staff. Illustrate the structure of the industry using a JSP diagram.

   A solution is given in Figure A.22 (above).

2.11 Exercises

1. A vending machine dispenses a bar of chocolate when the correct money is inserted (there is only one type of chocolate bar available in the machine). Use a structure diagram to illustrate the activity of inserting money and taking a bar of chocolate. *Hint: sequence* – the order of activities is important.

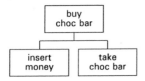

Figure A.23 Solution to Exercise 1.

2. A more sophisticated vending machine dispenses a variety of bars of chocolate: plain chocolate, milk chocolate, fruit and nut, white chocolate (all at the same price). Draw a structure diagram to illustrate the action of choosing which bar of chocolate is to be dispensed (ignoring all other activities, such as inserting money, for the present). *Hint: selection* – a bar of chocolate can only be **one** of those available, so the order is not important.

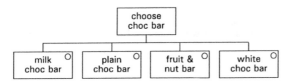

Figure A.24 Solution to Exercise 2.

3. Consider the purchase of several chocolate bars from the machine described in Exercise 2. Draw the structure diagram. *Hints: selection* – a bar of chocolate can only be **one** of those available, so the order is unimportant; *iteration* – there may be many purchases.

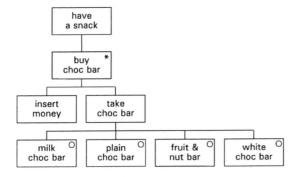

Figure A.25 Solution to Exercise 3.

4. A book consists of a number of pages. On each page there are many lines, and on each line there are many words. Draw the structure diagram. *Hint: iteration* – a book has many pages, etc.

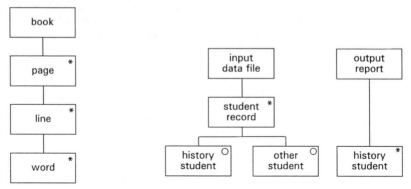

Figure A.26 Solution to Exercise 4.

Figure A.27 Solution to Exercise 1.

3.3 Exercises

Draw the input and output data file structures for the following:

1. From a file of student records, you wish to list all students who are taking a course in history.

   See Figure A.27 (above).

2. From the same student file you wish to list all the female students who are taking a mathematics module.

   Three approaches are shown as a solution to this problem: (a) Figure A.28; (b) Figure A.29; (c) Figure A.30.

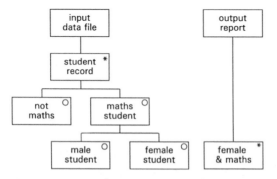

Figure A.28 One possible solution to Exercise 2.

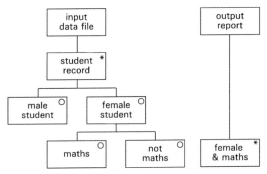

Figure A.29   A second possible solution to Exercise 2.

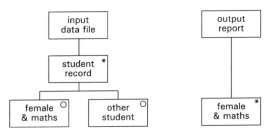

Figure A.30   A third possible solution to Exercise 2.

4. From the same student file you wish to list all the environmental science students who are female, and print the total number of these students and the grand total of all students on the file.

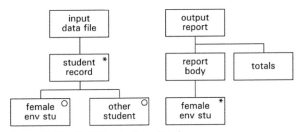

Figure A.31   Solution to Exercise 4.

5. From the same student file you wish to find the total number of all philosophy students who are over 25 years old.

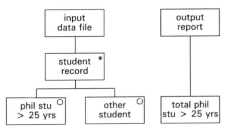

Figure A.32   Solution to Exercise 5.

279

6. From an employee file you wish to list all the employees earning over £30,000 who speak Italian.

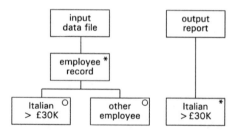

Figure A.33 Solution to Exercise 6.

7. From the same employee file you wish to print out details of all employees who are not qualified in accountancy.

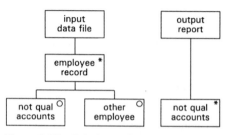

Figure A.34 Solution to Exercise 7.

12. The data structure shown in Figure 3.5 (repeated as Figure A.35) represents a file that may contain records A, B, C, D and E. These are the leaves of the tree. Is the file structure compatible with each of the following record sequences:

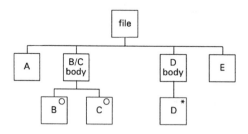

Figure A.35 Data structure for Exercise 12 (repeat of Fig. 3.5).

(a) A B C D E   No, cannot have both B and C
(b) A C E   Yes
(c) A D E   No, must have B or C (but not both)
(d) A B C E   No, cannot have both B and C
(e) A B E E   Yes
(f) A B E   Yes

(g) B D E   No, A is absent
(h) A B C   No, must have E present
(i) A B D D D E   Yes
(j) A C D D E   Yes
(k) A C B E   No, cannot have both B and C
(l) A C C D E   Yes

4.7 Exercises

Consider the following problems, draw the input and output data file structures, identify the points of correspondence and merge to form the basic process structure in each case.

1. From a file of student records, you wish to list all students who are taking a course in history.

   The input and ouput structures, together with their points of correspondence are shown in Figure A.36. Input and output data structures merged on the points of correspondence to form basic process structure are shown in Figure A.37.

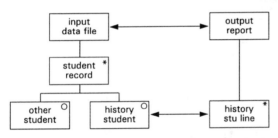

Figure A.36 Points of correspondence for Exercise 1.

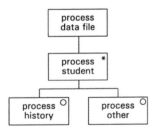

Figure A.37 The basic process structure for Exercise 1.

2. From the same student file you wish to list all the female students who are taking a mathematics module.

   Taking the three approaches shown earlier (Exercises 3.3) as a solution to this problem: (a) Figure A.38; (b) Figure A.39; (c) Figure A.40.

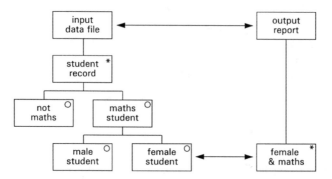

Figure A.38 Points of correspondences for first possible solution to Exercise 2.

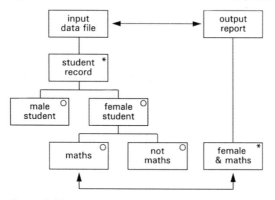

Figure A.39 Points of correspondence for second possible solution to Exercise 2.

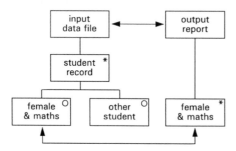

Figure A.40 Points of correspondence for third possible solution to Exercise 2.

5.4 Exercises

From the input and output file structures for the following exercises, identify the "housekeeping" activities that need to be performed and add process boxes to the process structure diagram to allow these actions to be made.

1. From a file of student records you wish to list all students who are taking a course in history.

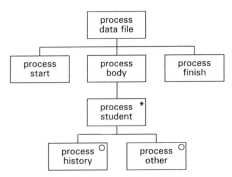

Figure A.41 Solution to Exercise 1.

6.6 Exercises

From the input and output file structures for the following exercises, introduced in the previous exercises, establish the points of correspondence, merge the data structures to form a process structure, specify the conditions and operations and allocate these to the process structure.

1. From a file of student records you wish to list all students who are taking a course in history.

<table>
<tr><td>The conditions are:</td><td>The operations list is:</td></tr>
</table>

The conditions are:

c1 not end of file

c2 if history student

c3 else

The operations list is:

1. Read student record from input file
2. Open input file for input
3. Open report file for output
4. Write student record to output report file
5. Stop processing
6. Close input file
7. Close output file

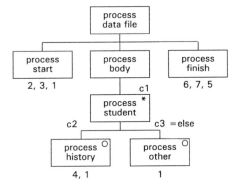

Figure A.42 The process structure for Exercise 1.

7.5 Exercises

1. Write the schematic logic for the structures shown in (a) Figure 7.13 (repeated as Figure A.43), (b) Figure 7.14 (repeated as Figure A.44), (c) Figure 7.15 (repeated as Figure A.45) and (d) Figure 7.16 (repeated as Figure A.46).

The logic for (a) is:

```
A seq
    B seq
        B operations
    B end
    C itr while c1
        D seq
            D operations
        D end
    C end
A end
```

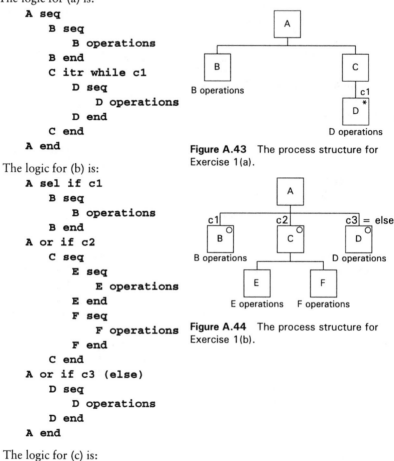

Figure A.43 The process structure for Exercise 1(a).

The logic for (b) is:

```
A sel if c1
    B seq
        B operations
    B end
A or if c2
    C seq
        E seq
            E operations
        E end
        F seq
            F operations
        F end
    C end
A or if c3 (else)
    D seq
        D operations
    D end
A end
```

Figure A.44 The process structure for Exercise 1(b).

The logic for (c) is:

```
A sel if c1
    B seq
        B operations
    B end
A or c2 (else)
    C itr while c3
        D seq
            D operations
        D end
    C end
A end
```

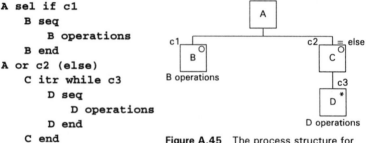

Figure A.45 The process structure for Exercise 1(c).

284

The logic for (d) is:

```
A seq
    B seq
        B operations
    B end
    C sel if c1
        E seq
            E operations
        E end
    C or if c2 (else)
        F seq
            F operations
        F end
    C end
    D seq
        D operations
    D end
A end
```

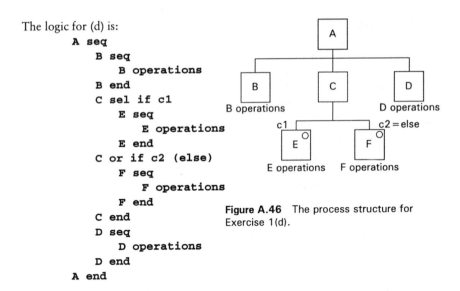

Figure A.46 The process structure for Exercise 1(d).

2. Reconstruct the process structures from the schematic logic:

(a)
```
A seq
    B seq
        C seq
            do C operations
        C end
        D seq
            do D operations
        D end
    B end
    E sel if c1
        F seq
            do F operations
        F end
    E or c2 (else)
        G seq
            do G operations
        G end
    E end
    H itr while c3
        J seq
            do J operations
        J end
    H end
A end
```

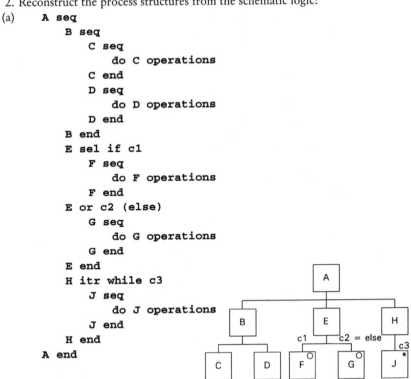

Figure A.47 The process structure for Exercise 2(a).

285

(b)
```
A itr while c1
   B sel if c2
      C itr while c5
         D seq
            do D operations
         D end
      C end
   B or if c3
      L seq
         E seq
            do E operations
         E end
         F sel c6
            P seq
               G seq
                  do G operations
               G end
               H seq
                  do H operations
               H end
            P end
         F or c7 (else)
            J seq
               do J operations
            J end
         F end
      L end
   B or c4 (else)
      K seq
         do K operations
      K end
   B end
A end
```

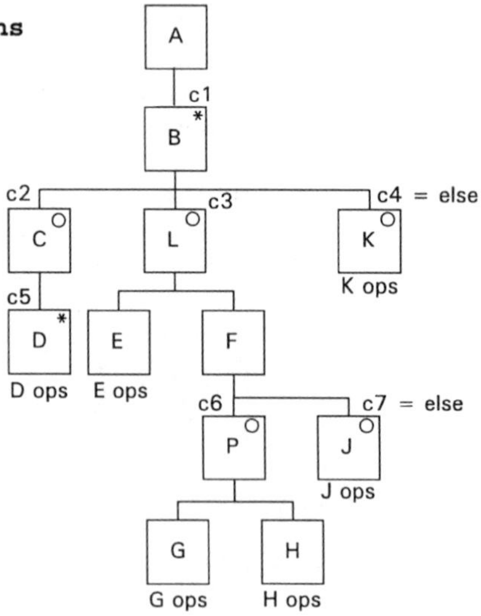

Figure A.48 The process structure for Exercise 2(b).

Consider the following problems. Generate the schematic logic for each process structure.

i. From a file of student records, you wish to list all students who are taking a course in history.

The schematic logic is as follows:

```
process data file seq

  process start seq
    2. open input file for input
    3. open report file for output
    1. read student record from input file
  process start end

  process body itr while not end of file

    process student sel if history student
      4. write student record to output report file
      1. read student record from input file
    process student or (else)
      1. read student record from input file
    process student end

  process body end

  process finish seq
    6. close input file
    7. close output file
    5. stop processing
  process finish end

process data file end
```

8.5 Exercises

1. Convert the following schematic logic into the programming language of your choice.

(a) In the following translation of the schematic logic into Pascal the schematic logic is given as comments, e.g. **(* process total staff seq *)**:

```
begin
(* process total staff seq *)
  (* process start seq *)
    assign(staffile, 'staffile');
    reset(staffile);    (* open staff file for input *)
    assign(report, 'report');
    rewrite(report);    (* open report file for output *)
    staff_tot := 0;     (* set staff total to zero *)
    readln(staffile, name, job_title);
              (* read staff record from
                 input staff file *)
  (* process start end *)
```

```
    (* process staff body itr while not end of staff file *)
    while not eof(staffile) do
    begin
       (* process record seq *)
         staff_tot := staff_tot + 1;
                (* add 1 to staff total *)
         readln(staffile, name, job_title);
                (* read staff record from
                   input staff file *)
       (* process record end *)
    end;
    (* process staff body end *)
    (* process total seq *)
      writeln(report, 'Starlight Staff');
        (* write company title to output report file *)
      writeln(report, 'staff total: ', staff_tot:8)
        (* write staff total to output report file *)
      writeln(report, 'October 1996');
        (* write date to output report file *)
    process total end
    (* process finish seq *)
      close(staffile);        (* close staff file *)
      close(report);          (* close report file *)
      end.                    (* stop processing *)
    (* process finish end *)
  (*process total staff end*)
```

Consider the following problems. Produce the code for each process structure, using the programming language of your choice.

3. From a file of student records, you wish to list all students who are taking a course in history.
   In the following translation of the schematic logic into Pascal the schematic logic is given as comments, e.g. **(* process data file seq *)**:

```
begin
(* process data file seq *)
  (* process start seq *)
    assign(stufile, 'stufile');
    reset(stufile);
    assign(report, 'report');
    rewrite(report);
    readln(stufile, name, course);
  (* process start end *)
  (* process body itr while not end of file *)
  while not eof(stufile) do
    (* process student sel if history student *)
    if course = 'history' then
```

```
begin
  (writeln(report, name:20, course:10);
   readln(stufile, name, course);
  (* process student or (else) *)
  end
  else
     readln(stufile, name, course);
  (* process student end *)
(* process body end *)
(* process finish seq *)
  close(stufile);
  close(report);
  end.
(* process finish end *)
(* process data file end *)
```

Note that it will be necessary to add the appropriate data declarations, etc., in order to achieve a program that runs.

9.5 Exercises

The following structures represent files; valid record types are A, B, C, D and E. Records in error are of type **X**, and may be inserted at any point and in any number. The original records retain their order. Elaborate the structures below for errors of
(a) insertion
(b) substitution
(c) omission
and then elaborate for further errors in each case.

1. A simple input file, contains only two records, A followed by B (Fig. 9.13; repeated as Fig. A.49).

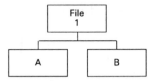

Figure A.49 The input file for Exercise 1 (repeat of Fig. 9.13).

Figures A.50, A.51 and A.52 show the structure elaborated for errors of (a) insertion; (b) substitution and (c) omission respectively.

289

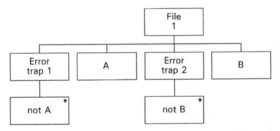

Figure A.50 Elaboration for errors of insertion: exercise 1.

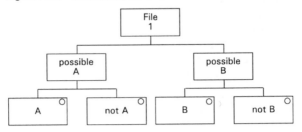

Figure A.51 Elaboration for errors of substitution: exercise 1.

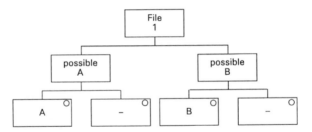

Figure A.52 Elaboration for errors of omission: exercise 1.

2. An input file contains an initial record A, followed by several B records (Fig. 9.14, repeated as Fig. A.53).

Figures A.54, A.55 and A.56 show the structure elaborated for errors of (a) insertion; (b) substitution and (c) omission respectively.

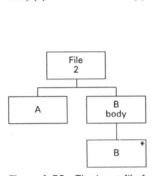

Figure A.53 The input file for Exercise 2 (repeat of Fig. 9.14).

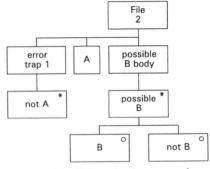

Figure A.54 Elaboration for errors of insertion: exercise 2.

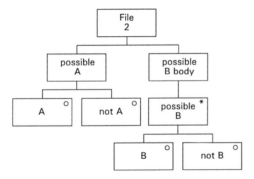

Figure A.55 Elaboration for errors of susbstitution: exercise 2.

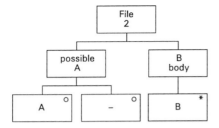

Figure A.56 Elaboration for errors of omission: exercise 2.

3. An input file contains an initial A record, followed by several B records, and then a single terminating record that may be of type C, D or E (Fig. 9.15, repeated as Fig. A.57).

Figures A.58, A.59 and A.60 show the structure elaborated for errors of (a) insertion; (b) substitution and (c) omission respectively.

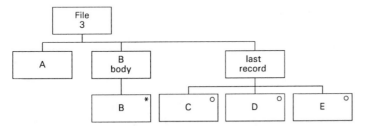

Figure A.57 The input file for Exercise 3 (repeat of Fig. 9.15).

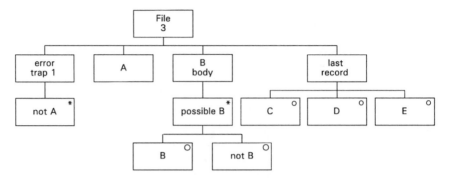

Figure A.58 Elaboration for errors of insertion: exercise 3.

10.7 Exercises

1. How could the process structure diagram for the case study be developed to allow for additional functions? Such functions could be, for example, to inspect a customer record without changing it, or to print a customer record.

   The process structure diagram is designed in order to allow such flexibility of approach. It would be possible to add another function as another selection part within the function iterated component. It would also be possible to remove a function, for example, to prevent records from being deleted from the customer database. The process structure diagram would have the appearance of Figure A.61 if inspect and print options were to be added. (The cancel option has been omitted for clarity).

   Note that the new functions inspect and print have been added including the ability to deal with errors of insertion.

2. Do you consider that elaborating for errors of insertion would be the best choice if the customer database system were to run in batch rather than interactive mode? Explain your reasoning.

   Elaborating for errors of insertion is a suitable choice for dealing with data entered interactively by a user; if the user makes an error, it is likely that further attempt(s) will be made until a correct entry is made (or the user terminates the session).

   In the context of a batch system, it will not be possible for the user to respond to errors in the same way as with an interactive system; it is therefore necessary to consider which type of error is most likely to be made if the updating of the customer database is performed by reference to an input file. If errors arise in the records stored for processing against the main database, this could be regarded as an error of substitution because each erroneous record can be regarded as occurring in substitution for a correct record. It would be difficult to determine if errors of omission had occurred, as, if there is no update record for a particular record on the database, this may simply mean that the record concerned does not need to be updated on this occasion.

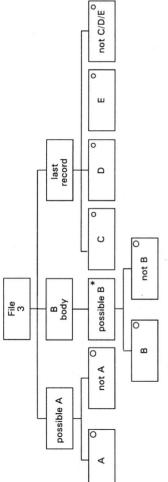

Figure A.59 Elaboration for errors of substitution: exercise 3.

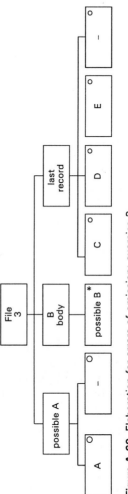

Figure A.60 Elaboration for errors of omission: exercise 3.

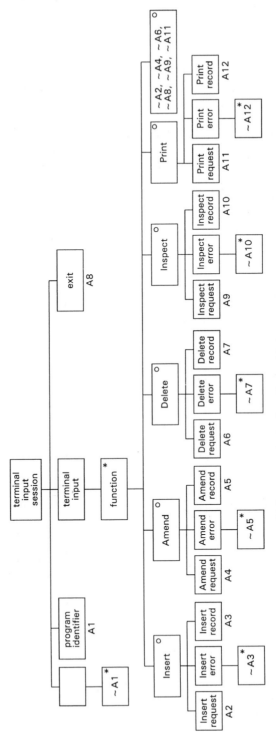

Figure A.61 Customer database system with inspect and print functions added.

11.5 Exercises

1. Describe the role of **posit**, **admit** and **quit** in backtracking.

   Posit and **admit** are used to replace **if . . . then . . . else . . .** when the information needed to test the condition on a selection is not available, and therefore it is not possible to decide with absolute certainty which selection branch should be taken. **Posit** replaces the **if . . . then . . .** part of the selection; the result of this is that one branch of the selection is entered without first testing the condition. It is possible, using this approach, that the wrong branch is taken. When sufficient information is available to establish whether or not the right path has been chosen, a test can be carried out; if the chosen path is the correct one, processing can continue as if the test had been performed at the usual point at the start of the selection. However, if it is found that the wrong branch has been selected, control must be transferred to the other branch, labelled by **admit** (replacing the **else** branch). The transfer of control to the **admit** part is executed by means of a **quit**, which is normally implemented as a **go to** statement. It is important that any intolerable side effects are avoided or reversed if control needs to be transferred from the **posit** branch to the **admit** branch.

12.4 Exercises

1. Explain the meaning of the following terms, and how they are related
   correspondence
   lack of correspondence
   structure clash.

   A *correspondence* is said to occur between an input and an output data structure, where input is processed to generate output, if the elements in each are related by the following rules:
   • the elements are found in the same order
   • the elements appear the same number of times
   • the elements occur in the same context
   If these rules are satisfied at all appropriate points in the two data structures, the structures can be merged to form the basic process structure. If there is a point in the data structures where the rules are broken, e.g. because the elements do not occur in the same order, there is a structure clash; this will prevent the data structures from being merged to form a process structure. If there are boxes in one data structure that do not occur in the other, e.g. a title on an output report, this is a lack of correspondence which does not prevent the structures from being merged. All boxes in either data structure diagram must be represented by a box in the process structure diagram.

   A *lack of correspondence* means that an element on either the input file or the output file does not occur in the other file. Examples include: a total will be calculated during processing, a heading will be at the top of a page, and a page number will be at the bottom of a report page; these will therefore appear on the output file but not on the input file.

A *structure clash* indicates that there is conflict between some part of the input data structure and the output data structure because one or more of the rules for establishing a correspondence has been broken. This means that the input and output data structures cannot be merged and another solution method must be adopted. It may be possible to redesign the data structures in order to avoid the structure clash, or it may be necessary to redesign as if using an intermediate data file by creating two process structures; this latter approach can be converted to program inversion (the intermediate file is not physically created; the two programs communicate record-by-record).

2. What are the three types of structure clash? Give an example of each.

An *ordering clash* occurs when the records do not appear in the same order in the input file and the output file; sorting the input file into the required order will resolve the clash.

A *boundary clash* occurs when the boundaries (e.g. departments) on the input file do not match up with the boundaries (e.g. pages) on the output file. In this case, two programs need to be designed; an intermediate file is used as the output file from the first process and as the input file to the second process. Implementing program inversion does away with the need to create the intermediate file – the two programs communicate by passing each record between the main program and the subprogram as and when required.

An *interleaving clash* can be regarded as a combination of a boundary clash and an ordering clash; the records in the input file relating to a specific entity are interspersed with other records, i.e. they are interleaved. One solution would be to sort the input file (as with an ordering clash). Another option would be to design several different programs (one for each distinct entity) and implement these using multiple program inversion.

3. What is the difference between using an intermediate file and implementing program inversion when dealing with the problem of a structure clash?

There is no difference in the *structure* of the two programs if an intermediate file is created or if program inversion is implemented. The difference that does occur is that the intermediate data file is not physically created if program inversion is implemented, as each record that would have been written to the intermediate data file as output is instead passed to the other program for processing; this removes the need for the second program to read the intermediate data file explicitly because the records are passed across as and when they require processing.

4. Why is it necessary to delete references to an intermediate file in the subprogram when program inversion is being used?

References to the intermediate file are no longer required as the main program will call the subprogram passing the record that would have been read from the intermediate file. The records are passed between the main program and the subprogram in the same order as they would have been written to the intermediate file (and read from the intermediate file). Therefore there is no need for the intermediate file to be created in a physical sense, it is only used as an aid to the design of the two communicating programs.

13.6 Exercises

1. Show how you would dismember the process structure diagram shown in Figure 13.9 (repeated as Fig. A.62) (a) graphically; and (b) in tabular form.

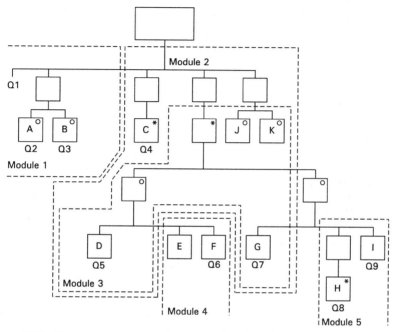

Figure A.62 The process structure diagram for Exercise 13.6.1 (repeat of Fig. 13.9).

Note that module 3 is completely contained within module 2; it would be possible to merge these into a single module if required.

The resume execution table is shown as Table A.1, the module link table as Table A.2 and the module link table produced by merging modules 2 and 3 as Table A.3.

Table A.1 Resume execution table: exercise 1.

Resume points	Elementary components
Q1	A, B
Q2	C, D, G, J, K
Q3	C, D, G, J, K
Q4	C, D, G, J, K
Q5	E, F
Q6	D, G, J, K
Q7	H, I
Q8	H, I
Q9	D, G, J, K

Table A.2 Module link table: exercise 1.

Module name	Elementary components	Suspend points	Module link
Mod 1	A, B	Q2	Mod 2
		Q3	Mod 2
Mod 2	C, D, G, J, K	Q4	Mod 2
		Q5	Mod 4
		Q7	Mod 5
		END	NIL
Mod 3	D, G, J, K	Q5	Mod 4
		Q7	Mod 5
		END	NIL
Mod 4	E, F	Q6	Mod 3
Mod 5	H, I	Q8	Mod 5
		Q9	Mod 3

APPENDIX

Table A.3 Module link table: exercise 1, merged modules.

Module name	Elementary components	Suspend points	Module link
Mod 1	A, B	Q2	Mod 2
		Q3	Mod 2
Mod 2	C, D, G, F, J, K	Q4	Mod 2
		Q5	Mod 3
		Q7	Mod 4
		END	NIL
Mod 3	E, F	Q6	Mod 2
Mod 4	H, I	Q8	Mod 4
		Q9	Mod 2

Table A.3 shows that the two modules, where module 3 was contained within module 2, can be merged into a single module. The overhead for doing this is that there will be some cases where the elementary component **C** will be loaded when it is not required, i.e. module 2 will be loaded where the "old" module 3 would have been loaded.

If a large amount of code is involved with elementary component **C** it might be considered wasteful to load the entire module if it is known that **C** will not be required; in these circumstances, the previous dismemberment would be employed.

2. Show how you would dismember the process structure diagram shown in Figure 13.10 (repeated as Fig. A.63) (a) graphically; and (b) in tabular form.

The resume execution table is shown as Table A.4 and the module link table as Table A.5.

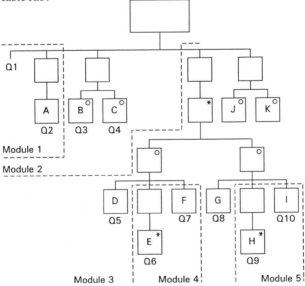

Figure A.63 The process structure diagram for Exercise 2 (repeat of Fig. 13.10) with graphic dismemberment.

298

Table A.4 Resume
execution table: exercise 2.

Resume points	Elementary components
Q1	A
Q2	B, C
Q3	D, G, J, K
Q4	D, G, J, K
Q5	E, F
Q6	E, F
Q7	D, G, J, K
Q8	H, I
Q9	H, I
Q10	D, G, J, K

Table A.5 Module link table: exercise 2.

Module name	Elementary components	Suspend points	Module link
Mod 1	A	Q2	Mod 2
Mod 2	B, C	Q3	Mod 3
		Q4	Mod 3
Mod 3	D, G, J, K	Q5	Mod 4
		Q8	Mod 5
		END	NIL
Mod 4	E, F	Q6	Mod 4
		Q7	Mod 3
Mod 5	H, I	Q9	Mod 5
		Q10	Mod 3

3. Show how you would dismember the process structure diagram shown in Figure 13.11 (repeated as Fig. A.64) (a) graphically; and (b) in tabular form.

The resume execution table is shown as Table A.6 and the module link table as Table A.7.

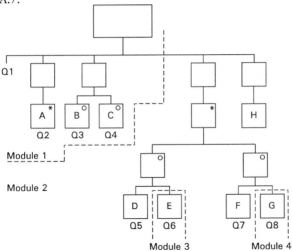

Figure A.64 The process structure diagram for Exercise 3 (repeat of Fig. 13.11) with graphic dismemberment.

Table A.6 Resume
execution table: exercise 3.

Resume points	Elementary components
Q1	A, B, C
Q2	A, B, C
Q3	D, F, H
Q4	D, F, H
Q5	E
Q6	D, F, H
Q7	G
Q8	D, F, H

Table A.7 Module linke table: exercise 3

Module name	Elementary components	Suspend points	Module link
Mod 1	A, B, C	Q2	Mod 1
		Q3	Mod 2
		Q4	Mod 2
Mod 2	D, F, H	Q5	Mod 3
		Q7	Mod 4
		END	NIL
Mod 3	E	Q6	Mod 2
Mod 4	G	Q8	Mod 2

4. Show how you would dismember the process structure diagram shown in Figure 13.12 (repeated as Fig. A.65) (a) graphically; and (b) in tabular form.

The resume execution table is shown as Table A.8 and the module link table as Table A.9.

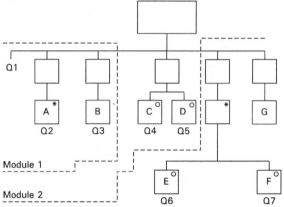

Figure A.65 The process structure diagram for Exercise 4 (repeat of Fig. 13.12) with graphic dismemberment.

Table A.8 Resume execution table: exercise 4.

Resume points	Elementary components
Q1	A, B
Q2	A, B
Q3	C, D
Q4	E, F, G
Q5	E, F, G
Q6	E, F, G
Q7	E, F, G

Table A.9 Module link table: exercise 4.

Module name	Elementary components	Suspend points	Module link
Mod 1	A, B	Q2	Mod 1
		Q3	Mod 2
Mod 2	C, D	Q4	Mod 3
		Q5	Mod 3
Mod 3	E, F, G	Q6	Mod 3
		Q7	Mod 3
		END	NIL

References

Delannoy, C. 1989. *Turbo Pascal programming*. Basingstoke: Macmillan.

Farmer, M. 1989. *The intensive Pascal course*. 2nd edn. Kent: Chartwell-Bratt.

Findlay, W. & D. A. Watt 1990. *Pascal: an introduction to methodical programming*. 3rd edn. London: Pitman.

Gottfried, B. S. 1990. *Theory and problems of programming in C*. Schaum's Outline Series in Computers. New York: McGraw-Hill.

Haiduk, H. P. 1990. *Object oriented Turbo Pascal. Problem solving and programming*. New York: McGraw-Hill.

Holmes, B. J. 1991. *Structured programming in COBOL*, 2nd edn. London: DP Publications.

Jackson, M. A. 1975. *Principles of program design*. New York: Academic Press

King, M. J. & J. P. Pardoe 1992, *Program design using JSP: a practical introduction*. 2nd edn. Basingstoke: Macmillan.

Konvalina, J. & S. Wileman 1987. *Programming with Pascal*. Singapore: McGraw-Hill.

Perry, P. J. 1993. *Crash course in C*. Indianapolis, IN: Que Corp.

Robson, D. J. 1990. *Programming for change with Pascal*. Kent: Chartwell-Bratt.

Storer, R. 1991. *Practical program development using JSP*. Oxford: Blackwell Scientific Publications.

Thompson, J. B. 1989. *Structured programming with COBOL and JSP*. Kent: Chartwell-Bratt.

Index